BEYOND MY GRASP

A TRUE STORY OF THE GREAT WAR

Sergeant Jacob Miller, M.S.M.

(As told to Albert Litzenberger)

20170425 Edition

Contact: Trevor Miller (trevor@miller-time.ca) for comments or feedback

This is written also in remembrance of me, for my four sons – Norman Jacob John; Harold Philip; Laurence Frederick and Albert Raymond Miller"

- Jacob Miller

TO THE BELOVED MEMORY

OF

MY DEAR MOTHER

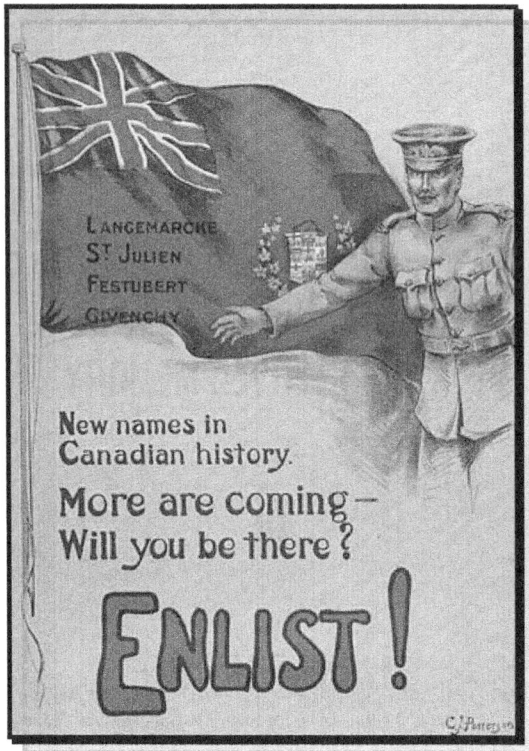

"We must not forget that days may come when our patience, our endurance and our fortitude will be tried to the utmost. In those days, let us see to it that no heart grows faint and that no courage be found wanting. . ."

Sir Robert Borden, Canadian Prime Minister, 1911-1920

Contents

Preface

We were many when we went over there.

Not many of us returned.

And some have since passed over the rapids to join our old comrades in the peaceful waters beyond.

It is hard for the younger generation to realize that the Great War was a war; a struggle against Death, for it has been glorified so that many think of it as a Great Adventure, and fortunate for those who were able to take part.

In writing this historical account of my experiences overseas, I have tried to describe truly, in simple language, everything as I saw it, taking into consideration the reader, for although many things can now be told, many things are better left untold. I have tried to be fair in every way to those whose names are mentioned. To my close mates, most loyal comrades and truest friends that they were, I have attached fictitious names for reasons which will be obvious to the reader.

If this story does not gain the approval of those who look for romance and beauty, may it not be criticized too severely: I have not tried to be romantic; and war is not beautiful. To know that my efforts have given anyone a truer conception of the war will be my great reward.

- Jacob Miller

Chapter 1

Jacob Miller (left) and the RMS Lapland (right)

It is easy to recall the memorable morning in March 1916, on which we waved farewell to Canada on our way overseas. The troopship "Lapland" had gained momentum and was swiftly drawing away from Halifax Harbor, leaving in its wake a diverging stream of white water churned up by the submerged propeller. The deck was crowded with soldiers. Those who had been able to jostle their way to the side stood closely wedged together, mildly fascinated by the greenly-transparent, mysterious depths; others, less fortunate in securing an advantageous position, lounged idly about, inquisitively admiring the overhead structures.

To us, youths reared on the rolling prairies, the scene was quite new and thrilling. Everyone was visibly impressed: smiles played on the happy young faces, and laughter floated lightly about. It was a sensation of pleasure and wonder. But yet there was another feeling present, always predominant amongst us. In the eyes of my khaki-clad comrades a peculiar eagerness was discernible, an intensity of desire that was not excited by the prospects of the voyage. Obviously, though without reason, this feeling was engendered by the knowledge that we were on the threshold of a greater adventure – we were going to war!

Our training had seemed so very monotonous, month after month of severe drill at Brandon, Camp Sewell, and lastly Winnipeg. At first we had been patient, eager to learn; but soon we had grown discontented in the belief that war would terminate before we were ready to take an active part. However, we were not entirely ungrateful: the enforced discipline had instilled in us a respect for our superiors, which was equaled only by our faith in their judgment. We were well trained in the art of modern warfare and could carry out every maneuver with clock-like precision: we believed ourselves to be thorough in everything, efficient to the highest degree. Is it any wonder that we were eager to get into action?

With every turn of the fast-revolving propeller, the gulf, which separated us from our country, was growing wider. Beyond that limitless stretch of savage blue-black waves, which lashed out their defiance at the March wind, our dear Canada was sinking lower and lower, gradually becoming a thin, dark line, straining our eyes, in the endeavor to retain as long as possible the fading vision of the land which embodies all our hopes and dreams. In that brief moment, while lingering at the taffrail, we lived again our glorious past.

The majority of us were still quite young, many, like myself, scarcely being able to boast of twenty years. We were part of that generation which has since been called the War Generation. And such it was. Under pressure of the war, we developed into sudden maturity: with the call to arms, the tenderness of our youth was cast aside; obsessed with the burning desire to fight for our King and Country, we cared not about the possibilities of death – perhaps, should it be known the secret of our undaunted courage was that should we die in the venture, we were resolved to feel that we had lived well and done our duty. Our patriotic seal stamped us as heroes. School day companionship ripened into deep, passionate love – for what girl was not enamored of the wearer of the King's uniform? Those who had previously ignored us in our insignificant station of life treated us with marked deference – we were loved and honored by all. Our imaginations knew no bounds; over the rapture of the present, the future glowed with glorious possibilities. We pictured ourselves returning from war, loaded down with spoils of glory and honor. Perhaps we were arrogant. Life was too easy and gay – it was this very ease and gaiety of life, which later rendered the stern realities of war the more horrible and repulsive.

The final parting from our loved ones was indeed trying. As we watched one another say good-bye, the knowledge of our common danger served to knit us closer in the bonds of mutual sympathy and understanding. There were wives, tearful yet brave, clinging to their beloved husbands; sweethearts pledging themselves to their lovers; mothers, between sobs bestowing the last blessings on their soldier boys; and fathers, anxious yet proud, giving a last word of encouragement. It was not easy. With an outward composure that was far from what we were feeling, we forced ourselves to smile, in order to convey the assurance that it was easy. It was the closing of an act of drama taken from real life. For many it was the last act!

With the passing of that faint line from the horizon, the last natural feature that bound us to our past disappeared. Eager to know what Fortune held in store, we turned our faces to the broad expanse of ocean, beyond which our future lay.

The morning sun was bright, the salt breeze crisp and refreshing. Huge billows of smoke poured from the large funnels, and the wide deck vibrated with the incessant throbbing of the engines below, as the gallant ship ploughed majestically on, ever toward the shimmering path of brightness which stretched far ahead over the ruffled surface of the Atlantic.[1]

* * * * *

On arriving in England, we suffered a keen disappointment. Instead of leaving shortly for France, as we had expected, we were taken by train to Folkestone, Kent, and placed in camp at the foot of Caesar's Hill. Here we underwent daily route marches and rifle practices on the Dover Ranges.

Life had suddenly grown dull. It seemed to me that no excitement would come our way for some time. But it was not long until I had an exciting experience, which threatened to end my adventure before it had even begun.

[1] Jacob departed for England Mar 13, 1916, and arrived in England Mar 25.

I was sitting alone in our tent, writing a letter home to Canada, when "Ted" Davies, my closest pal, brought the news –

"Miller, I heard that there is a German spy in our outfit." This information seemed too absurd to be true.

"Impossible!" I stated. "How could a spy get around in our camp without being spotted?"

"According to the rumor, he is supposed to be a German who enlisted in Canada and came over with us. Furthermore, he is one of our Company."

I was electrified by a sudden fear. To the best of my knowledge, I was the only soldier of German descent in the company. I recalled the warning I had received at my enlistment: "Miller, you must be careful, or you may be suspected as a spy."

"Have you any idea whom they suspect?" I asked Ted, watching him closely to see if he might betray any sign that would justify my fears.

"None", he answered, quite unconcerned, "and I don't suppose they would advertise it anyway."

I felt slightly relieved, yet a persistent shadow of doubt pursued me. The circumstances surrounding my enlistment had been quite singular compared to those of my comrades, because, being of German descent, I had enlisted against the wisdom of my father. He had objected strenuously to my volunteering to fight against his Fatherland. When this had failed, he had pitifully entreated me, but in vain. I had been adamant, determined to risk my life for Canada, the country that was dear to my heart. Now, however, I wondered if he had not been right, and doubted whether I had acted wisely, because, if I should be the one suspected as a spy, there was a chance that I should not see France after all.

My fears were confirmed when, on the following day, the battalion orderly sergeant appeared and advised the four of us who shared one tent that we were under quarantine. He ordered us to move our tent to the northwest corner of the campground, where two other tents already stood in isolation. After we had carried out his instructions, he calls me aside, and asked me a number of questions similar to those I had been asked at the time of my enlistment.

"What is your full name?"

"Jacob Miller", I answered promptly.

"Where were you born?"

"In Austria"

"When did you immigrate to Canada?"

"When I was six years old."

"Can you speak German?"

"Yes, quite well. I can also read and write it."

"Where were your father and mother born?"

"Both in Germany."

"Now, Miller, tell me why you enlisted to fight against the country of your parents?"

I was painfully aware that it was the same questions my father had asked me a year ago.

"I enlisted because I feel like all other Canadians. I want to fight for my King and country."

"That will be all, Miller", he said amiably, as he wrote down the last of the information, and walked away, leaving me quite bewildered.

As none of us four were suffering from any physical ailments, it was evident that our confinement was in some way connected with the rumor of a German spy being in our camp. I felt certain, after having been cross-questioned by the orderly sergeant, that I was the unfortunate victim of suspicion and was filled with gloom apprehension. Ted tried to enlighten me by saying that if was all a mistake which would soon be rectified – in the meantime we were fortunate in escaping the monotony of drill. The other two fellows did not show the same faith in me, but positively believed me to be a spy. Their suspicions were plainly evidenced by their hostile attitudes for they hardly spoke to me and shunned me at every opportunity. I did not blame them, however, because when the battalion would leave for France, my unfortunate predicament might cause them to be left behind.

The companionship of Ted compensated for any unfriendliness on the part of the others. Although he was considerably older than I, he treated me as his equal. He was a big, overgrown chap, with simplicity of good nature that was quite in accordance with his size. Though it gave him not end of trouble in getting a uniform to fit properly, his great stature presented a very striking figure. He was quite humorous, entertaining anyone with his hearty laugh; the combination of a receding chin and sandy moustache produced on his face an expression which, when he smiled, was very comical. But then he also had his serious moments. Sometime, as if from painful memory, his big, blue eyes became wistful and sad, and there was something plaintive about him that bespoke loneliness. I believe that was the reason I had been attracted to him from the beginning.

We had orders from the guard to stay within bounds, being restricted to the area that extended from his beat, in front of our tent, to the fence along the Folkestone-Dover Road, and our privileges were further limited by being forbidden to keep company with any passing soldiers or civilians.

One Sunday afternoon Ted and I stood beside the fence, idly watching the civilians passing by. The day was warm and many people were out enjoying the balmy spring air. Two girls came along the road from Folkestone, one of them wheeling a baby carriage. Our guard was nowhere in sight at the time, so, when they came opposite us, Ted call to them –

"Hello Kiddo."

They smiled a greeting in return and stopped for a few minutes conversation. On learning that we were in quarantine, they expressed sympathy and promised to bring us some books to read the next time they would pass by. Before they went on, they gave us their names and addresses and asked us to call on them as soon as we got out of quarantine.

"How did you like the blondie?" Ted asked me after they had gone.

"She is very pretty", I remarked. Ted grinned happily. "You know Miller, it was a plumb case of love at first sight for this kid. I fell for her like a comet."

"Quit your kidding" I laughed. "You are just imagining things. How about the school marm back home that you were telling me about?"

"I don't think she loves me. I had a letter from a friend the other day, telling me that she's been stepping out with someone since I left. She is much older than I, anyway; and besides, this one is far better looking."

"Maybe so, but she doesn't love you," I pointed out. "Not yet anyway."

"Oh, I don't know about that. She gave me the glad eye, didn't she? I bet it's a case of love at first sight with her too."

"I wouldn't be surprised, Ted. You are *quite* a handsome fellow, you know."

"None of your sarcasm!" he retorted. "Just because they handed me a funny-looking uniform doesn't say I can't step with the best of them."

One night in the latter part of May, as we were preparing for sleep, the guard stuck his head through the opening of our tent and ordered us to put out the lights. Information had been received that there was an air raid on over Dover.

We rushed outside, hoping to get a glimpse of the zeppelin, but all we could see were the rays of the powerful searchlights criss-crossing in the sky, probing the darkness in an effort to locate the hidden enemy.

On June 2nd, 1916, a faint rumble came to us from across the channel; it sounded like distant thunder[2]. We were told that a heavy bombardment was taking place at Ypres, Belgium. I felt a queer sensation as the reverberations of the heavy guns continued – how I longed to be at the front and in action!

Next morning, the battalion orderly sergeant appeared and freed us from quarantine. We learned that the Canadians had been terribly cut up by one of the worst barrages put on since the beginning of the war. On reporting back to our company, we were told to be ready at a moment's notice to leave for France!

---

[2] On June 2nd, 1916 the Battle of Mont Sorrel began with a devastating artillery barrage against the 3rd Canadian division. The battle would have taken place across the channel, over 80km from Dover.

Chapter 2

Canadians moving up to the Front Line

It was dusk when the train stopped at Goddervelde, Belgium. Our company was ordered to detrain, and we were glad to have an opportunity to exercise our cramped bodies after the tiresome journey from Le Havre in the overcrowded boxcars.

A strange captain came up and spoke briefly to the officer in charge, meanwhile looking us over in an appraising manner. We were then numbered off, placed in fours, and ordered to follow him through the street of the small village. We passed a few civilians; but intent only on their own business, whatever it might have been, they paid little attention to us. The houses were for the most part in darkness. Here and there a window showed a dull glow that came from a shaded light inside, but in all, the place was silent, gloomy – guarded.

On leaving the village, we marched east along a well-paved road until we came to a farmyard. He we halted. Two platoons of us were ordered to occupy a large barn for the night. The rest of the company went on.

The barn was already occupied by a number of old soldiers, who lay about in the corners on hay. They were some of the survivors of the battle of June 2nd. We were surprised at their appearances and demeanors; their uniforms were ragged and soiled, and their faces bore traces of terrible suffering and were lined with fatigue and anxiety. They were not lively like our fellows, but seemed cheerless and glum. I detected a faint flicker of compassion in their weary eyes, as they looked us over.

We soon settled ourselves in the uncomfortable quarters and started a conversation. Occasionally there was a loud boom in the east. The sound was thrilling, making us realize the immediate proximity of the war zone. We urge the old veterans to tell us of their adventures, but they were reticent, and acted as if they had no desire to discuss them with us inexperienced recruits. Throughout the evening they remained silent and reserved – all we were able to learn was that we were within eight kilometers of the front line.

The next day being Sunday, we were off duty. Ted and I decided to take a stroll. East of us there was a lone hill which rose to a lofty elevation above the level country surroundings, and on top of which there was a large windmill. It was to this solitary landmark, from which we hoped to get a glimpse of the front line that we proceeded, following a narrow road which led us through green fields of grain and across pastures. Everything seemed beautiful, bathed in the warm June sunshine. On our left ran the Poperinghe-Ypres Road, flanked on both sides with tall, green trees. Beyond the road, aeroplanes were taking off and landing, and we concluded that there must be a landing field. We soon came to the foot of the hill where several trails converged into a wide road leading to the top. At the side was a signpost, which read – "MONT-DES-CATS".

"Mont-des-Cats", said Ted slowly, "that must mean Cat Mountain."

"I believe you are right" I offered. "Likely there are quite a few cats around here to give it that name."

"Well I don't mind the cats, so long as they are not black ones. You know, I am a bit superstitious about those things."

We started up the steep slope. The road showed signs of very little recent travel, and small patches of grass had sprung up in places.

At the side, and all over the face of the hill was an abundant growth of shrubs and bushes. On the highest point of the hill stood the windmill which we had seen from the distance, and a short distance away was erected a crucifix, about thirty feet high, with stones piled around the base.

From our position we commanded a wide view of the landscape. The surrounding country was speckled with small villages and farm buildings, adorned by orchards and rows of hedges. The fields of grain and the gardens lay in neat squares, divided by rows of tall trees. Here and there a few cows were peacefully grazing in the pastures. Some of the scenes reminded me of the farming districts we had seen on our way through eastern Canada.

But there the likeness ended. Looking east, we saw the tops of the high buildings and the broken spires of Ypres. Beyond lay the Ypres-Menin Road, with its trees on both sides stripped of branches, looking bare and lifeless; in places there were gaps of trees missing, with only a few broken stumps remaining. Farther on – we judged beyond the enemy line – the road was again visible, but without any signs of mutilation, stretching like a green ribbon over the country until it disappeared in the southeast. In the distance, small puffs of smoke began to open up in the sky. A moment later the sharp staccato reports of field guns came to us. On looking closely, we saw an aeroplane in the midst of the small puffs, which were miraculously opening up on all sides. Anti-aircraft guns were evidently trying to bring down the plane. But they were unsuccessful; the plane escaped, leaving the sky spotted with white as if some monstrous creature had walked indiscriminately about, leaving its footprints. The little clouds drifted together, forming thin, white streaks, and gradually disappeared. A loud, ripping boom drew our attention to the right in time to see a cloud of dust settle on a distant ridge. The slope of the ridge seemed ragged and torn, disfigured by many broken trees and patches of yellow earth; parallel, dark line, from which we caught glints of light as the sun was reflected from moving metal objects, would their way along the top; a faint haze hung over the entire strip of fighting line. A dark column of earth shot suddenly up in the air, followed by a loud 'kerr-r-rupp' as the roar of an explosion reached our ears. It was very thrilling.

I turned to Ted. "By the looks of things, there seems to be a little war on over there."

"Yes, I shouldn't be surprised," he grinned. "It sounds a lot different than a Mills bomb – just as if someone were ripping a piece of canvas."

"Well, I hope we get into the line soon. So far, all we've been doing is forming fours. It's high time we had some excitement."

Ted was silent for a while, and then he said, "Maybe after we get there, we'll be sorry and wish we could get out of it. Look at the way the old veterans acted last night; it seemed to pain them every time we mentioned the front line."

On the way back to our billet, we met a Belgian drawing a two-wheeled cart. Underneath the cart, hitched to the axle between the wheels was a dog in harness. It was a very comical, as well as unusual sight.

"I'll be darned, it that isn't the funniest contraption I ever saw!" Ted burst out.

We both started to laugh. The Belgian, however, did not seem to share our mirth; feeling somewhat abashed, he looked away as he passed by. Ted and I felt sorry afterwards for having hurt his feelings by our lack of courtesy.

On arriving at our billet, we related what we had seen from Mont-des-Cats. That evening several parties made the trip.

More reinforcements arrived to strengthen the battalion, which had recently suffered such heavy losses. We were lined up to be placed in the ranks with the old soldiers. Ted and I stayed close together and were fortunate in being placed in the same section. We were now in No. 11 platoon, "C" company of the 1st C.M.R. Battalion.[3]

The leader of our section, Corporal Ribbons, was an old veteran of the trenches. Unlike most of the others, he mixed freely. He willingly told us about the conditions at the front. He warned us to be careful when German snipers would be around; and, should an enemy plane be sighted, to stay under cover so as not to give away our position because it would direct the shelling on us. From him we learned the various sounds of approaching shells and how to flop away from them before they burst, to lessen the chances of being

[3] According to government documents, he was taken on strength to join the 1st Canadian Mounted Rifles (C.M.R.) on June 8, 1916. (See Appendix C)

wounded. It was at his suggestion that we bought a Primus gas stove to take to the front.

Our section consisted of six men – Ted, myself, and four others. These were jovial fellows, and we soon became quite intimate. They were James Thomson, and elderly man, whom we referred to as "Dad" on account of his seniority; his son "Skinny" a quiet lad who stayed close to his father's side; J.C. Brown, who would not be called anything but J.C.; and a Swedish chap, Jensen, nicknamed "Sneezigs" by J.C. because- "He doesn't use his tongue when he speaks, but sneezes out the words".

Every day we were given drill; physical exercise, bayonet practice, bomb throwing, grenade firing. Some days we received instructions in first aid – how to bandage wounds, use rifles as splints, and carry wounded on stretchers.

One afternoon, about the middle of June, we were ordered on parade. General Byng inspected us and gave us a short address on courage. We were now passed as fit for the front. A wave of excitement came over us; we were thrilled with the realization that at last the long-hoped-for occasion was at hand. The older soldiers, however, seemed dismayed at the idea of going back into the lines.

Chapter 3

Ypres, 1916. From Archives Canada

It was dusk when we arrived at Ypres. In the murky twilight, the town had the aspect of a graveyard. And such it might well have been. Everywhere there were signs of the destruction caused by heavy shellfire. We saw jagged rows of houses, once beautiful, but now wrecked almost beyond recognition, only a few odd sections of walls were still upright, and piles of bricks, rafters and broken furniture were strewn about. Some great buildings, which may easily have cost fortunes, were torn asunder, reduced to a crumbling mass of ruin. We passed a large pile of bricks, at the side of which was an opening with steps leading down into the earth. I saw a flicker of light below, and smelled the strong odor of chloride of lime.

"Smells like a hospital", Ted remarked.

"That's the dressing station of the 9th Field Ambulance." Ribbons explained. "It's the first place the wounded are taken to, and from here they are taken by ambulance to the hospitals."

We were billeted in a long building, partly shot to pieces, with only half the roof remaining. Orders were to stay at hand, as some of us would be called on a working party to bury the dead in No Man's Land.

It was our platoon that was picked for the burial party. The sergeant ordered us to take only gas masks and rifles and to follow him. We stopped at an engineer's dump on the outskirts of Ypres, where each man received a spade. In single file the party passed through the Menin Gate and started across country toward the front.

Our progress was slow and difficult, impeded by loose wire, broken tree trunks, and treacherous shell holes that were partially concealed by long grass. Every little while orders were passed back from the head of the party – "Watch for shell hole to the right; shell hole to the left; wire overhead; wire underfoot." We had to stoop and go slow, or sometimes deviate from our course; else we should have become entangled in wire or have fallen into a hole. After winding our way over the broken country for some time, we came to a well-paved road, and were ordered to fall out for rest. Ribbons explained that we were back on the Menin Road, which would lead us straight to the front.

Beyond a low ridge, about half a mile distant, the front line was now visible, illuminated at odd intervals by momentary flares, which shot up into the air, burst into bright incandescence, then faded slowly, while descending to earth. With each rise and fall of the flares, long shadows crept alternately back and forth behind the tree stumps and mounds that covered the shell-torn country. A light breeze from the front brought us the strange odor of dead men; it reminded me of an ill-kept slaughterhouse, but it was more sickening. The night was quiet; we could hear the faint rumble of motor lorries and transports, moving about far behind us and beyond the German line. Occasionally the stillness was broken by rifle shots or the vicious tapping of machine guns. Stray bullets whizzed over our heads, and there was a dull smack when an odd one struck a tree stump. There was a dull flash on our left, beyond the enemy line, followed by the report of a field gun. The shell came over with a light moan, which lasted but a few seconds and was drowned by the loud roar of an explosion on our right.

A profound silence ensued; everything became unnaturally quiet, as if the stillness of death were creeping over the lines – a terrible, awe inspiring silence that made my flesh creep. And yet I was filled with an overwhelming excitement that made me want to get closer to the novel and mysterious seat of war. The spell was broken by the loud boom of a gun back of us. With a wail like a siren, a big shell sailed high overhead, towards the enemy line; after it passed, the sound grew faint until it sounded like a distant waterfall. A bright, red flame leaped up on the far-away horizon, lighting up the eastern sky for a moment, died down for a second, then flared up again. Ribbons turned to me and said with some satisfaction. "A direct hit on an ammunition dump that time!"

The order came to fall in, and soon we were moving forward again. The road showed many signs of a recent shelling, and these became more numerous as we went along. We had to pick our way carefully around the black, yawning holes and the big chunks of clay of the ridge, trenches stretched at right angles away from the road. In one of them, I saw a number of dark figures pressing closely against the side. On coming down the slope, the flares seemed suddenly closer and were almost startling, as each one ascended in a brilliant arc of bright showery sparks. As a precaution against being seen by the enemy, we remained motionless while the flares lasted, and moved forward only during the intervals of darkness. We came to a culvert at the lowest cross-section of the road; on both sides soldiers crouched low in shallow trenches. Ribbons leaned over to me and whispered, "This is our front line. We are now crossing into No Man's Land."

A machine gun burst forth ahead of us; sparks flew from the stone road as the bullets struck and ricocheted into the air. A man cried out in pain, and there was a low call for stretcher-bearers – one of our fellows had been shot through the ankle. As the wounded man was carried back, I heard an old veteran mutter in an envious tone, "A nice Blighty for that guy."

The platoon was divided into two groups, going right and left into the shell torn No Man's Land. We stumbled about in parties of four men, keeping close together lest we should become separated and lost. An uncanny sensation of helplessness crept over me; all my training seemed to drop away. Knowing that in anything should happen, I should be at a loss to act, and I kept close to Ribbons. He seemed so sure, so confident, such a veteran.

Mist was rising from the water-filled shell holes, and the moist air was heavy with the awful odor of putrescent bodies; it was horribly nauseating. Dead men lay everywhere. In the semi-darkness, the faces seemed to leer and mock with demoniacal grimaces that sent icy shivers up my spine. After removing the identification discs from about their necks, we rolled the bodies into shallow holes and covered them up. One corpse was cut in half; we buried the upper part, and then searched for the lower part, but in vain. I was hazy and stupefied. It was uncanny – these dead men. It was almost impossible to believe that the cold bodies had been alive and active short days ago; I shuddered as I realized that my turn might be at hand – my body might soon be lying here, disintegrating in the hot sun and moist atmosphere. It was all a grim business. My imagination has tricked me, for after all war was not beautiful; it was deadly and terrible.

Our ghastly work finished, the sergeant rounded us up and in single file we started back. The fresh air seemed sweet and pure after we had inhaled the horrible stench of No Man's Land. I was glad to get away from there – Death hovered too near!

We approached a long row of piled-up sand bags, called China Wall. A salvo of shells came screeching over, a deafening explosion rent the air and a burning white flash almost blinded me. I rose, dazed and trembling with fright. What would happen now? My foremost instinct was to run, but I was powerless to act. I saw that the old veterans had flopped: we inexperienced, in our sudden terror, had only stopped – the result was one man killed and two wounded. The dead man was buried, and the wounded carried to the dressing station at Ypres.

Such was my first experience at the front. I was now a veteran, and already I understood why veterans could not adopt the light boastful attitude of raw recruits. One night under fire made the difference.

It was daylight when we reached our billet. After a warm breakfast, which we prepared on our Primus, we lay down to sleep. But we did not fall asleep for a long time; our experience had been too harrowing, and for hours we were busy talking. Some claimed to have seen a sniper in No Man's Land; others had seen pieces of human bodies hanging from barbed wire. Ted told us he had heard some Germans talking in a nearby shell hole. J.C. passed around a Luger pistol and belt he had taken from a dead German. We inspected it very closely, and Ribbons showed us how it worked. J.C. had many offers from the fellows, but he valued his prize too highly and would not sell.

We were awakened by a terrific din – the town was being shelled. Deafening explosions burst forth one after another. Our building shook violently from the heavy concussion, threatening to collapse and crash down upon us any moment. We lay frightened and trembling, expecting every minute to be our last. I shut my eyes, yet the raging inferno continued: shells screeching madly overhead: terrific roars that echoed and re-echoed throughout the town: loud crashes, as buildings were blown to pieces and toppled to the ground.

At last the shelling ceased. I had not expected to survive the living hell, and for a few minutes was too stunned to collect my senses. I arose, still trembling, and went outside. A grey smoke hung about, and the air was heavy with the acrid fumes of burnt Sulphur. The large town had previously suffered from heavy shellfire; now, however, it was over half demolished. Everywhere lay new piles of bricks and rafters in smoking ruin from the heavy bombardment. It seemed a miracle that we had survived unscathed.

At dusk our platoon was ordered on a wiring party. We arrived at the engineers' dump and were loaded down with heavy rolls of barbed wire and iron screw stakes. When all was in readiness, we started off once more for No Man's Land.

On arriving there, Ribbons selected Ted and me, along with four others to be the covering party ahead of those stringing the wire. He stationed us in extended order along No Man's Land, about ten yards apart. Our instructions were to lie still and watch carefully; should a German party approach us, we were to run back and warn our party.

I lay flat on the ground, silent and tense, and listened carefully. My heart beat rapidly and nerves quivered with excitement. A flare shot up high in the air in front of me brightly illuminating the surroundings for a few seconds. My body trembled, and I crouched lower, wondering if it were a signal for enemy action.

"Miller! Miller!" a voice called in a loud whisper on my right.

"Here! What's the matter?" I whispered back. I saw Ted crawling on all fours toward me greatly agitated.

"Are you scared?" I whispered nervously.

"No," he answered with teeth chattering, "But there is a German sniper in front of us, and I can see the sparks fly from his rifle every time he shoots."

"Are you sure?" I asked doubtfully, as the only shots I had heard had been from a distance.

"Yes, and when the flares went up, I could see his head move."

"Better report it to Ribbons when he comes around," I said, not knowing what to do.

"Yes, I will" he replied, still shaking, "but I wish you would come and see for yourself."

Silently and stealthily we crawled over to Ted's post.

"Over there!" he whispered excitedly, pointing to a mound a short distance away. A flare went up in front, and I saw that the object was a mound of earth with a peak resembling a man's had. Greatly relieved, I gave Ted a sharp dig in the ribs and told him what it was. After the flare had burned out, I crawled back to my post.

Ribbons came around and asked if I had seen anything. I reported that all had been quiet, and he went on to Ted. In a few minutes, Ribbons was back.

"Say, what's wrong with that guy over there? Is he blind or seeing things?"

"Why?"

"Oh, he just told me that he saw someone crawling towards him with a big knife. He must be blind in one eye and unable to see with the other."

"I think he is a bit scared, that's all," I said. "And furthermore, I can see everything from here that he can."

"Then you keep our eyes open. I shall be back every few minutes," he said and he went on.

Ribbons had hardly gone, when Ted came crawling over again. "I can hear the Germans whispering their trench!" he whispered breathlessly.

"Just your imagination," I chided him.

"No, no! It was as plain as could be! I am not going back there again."

"Well, stay then and keep an eye on my front. I shall watch yours from here."

But I had to watch Ted most of the time. Every little while he startled me by saying that he had seen something move. He stared at every object continually until he imagined it moved. At last I became exasperated and told him that if he should see anything move he should look away from it or close his eyes for a while and then look again; and to be positive it moved before telling anyone else and getting their wind up. He was quiet after that and brought me no more hair-raising reports.

Taking everything into consideration, however, Ted could hardly be censured for his ability to create imaginary, lurking foes. To lie in that dreadful No Man's Land, ever-vigilantly watching for an invisible enemy, was a severe strain on nerves and senses. With a little imagination, the queer, startling sounds and grotesque shadows became convincing evidence of enemies creeping stealthily towards us with murderous intent. I was glad when the order came to retire, and we were permitted to go back to our billets at Ypres.

The following night our battalion moved to the front. "C" company was stationed in the support trench along the ridge, behind the front line. The trench, though quite shallow, was well built up in front with sand bags to form a parapet, which screened us from the enemy. Under the parapet were shelters, constructed of sand bags and sheets of corrugated iron, which served as living quarters when we were off duty.

Our trench duty was to stand guard, one hour on and one hour off. There were two at each post; one standing on the firing step, watching; the other sitting below, resting or dosing. At the end of every hour we changed about – and so on throughout the night.

The night was very quiet. Occasionally a few rifle shots came to us from the enemy line on a ridge a few hundred yards ahead; but somehow, they were not at all frightening: there was a sense of security in knowing the position of the enemy.

At dawn, the usual hour of attack, everyone was ordered to stand to. The command, one that we well understood, was taken up with great alacrity. There was even some hope that the Germans would attack, because we were confident that from our redoubtable position we could easily drive them off; and, moreover, it would be an opportunity to dispel from the minds of the older veterans the idea that we were merely raw recruits. Nothing happened, however, and there was some disappointment.

In the cold grey of early morning, we had our first clear view of No Man's Land. The strip of hollow between the two ridges was bleak and bare, without any natural features, pounded and churned into a desolate waste, and covered with shell holes, each of which was half filled with stagnant water. The Menin Road, leading down the slope and up over the next ridge, was hardly separable from the devastated surface on both sides, smashed and torn, with only a few ragged stumps along the roadway. Our front-line trench wound its way along the bottom of the hollow, curving in behind us on both flanks. In it, with bayonets fixed, soldiers crouched low, concentrating on the ridge ahead where the enemy lay entrenched: from our position, looking down, they seemed dangerously exposed. The German trench, marked by a parapet of earth along the opposite ridge, showed no signs of activity; it was hard to believe that there were men standing behind that parapet, watching and waiting as we were. It left with me the impression of two great physical forces contending for possession of that scarred strip or battlefield, yet hesitating to strike, each waiting to "see the other fellow's hand" first.

A little after sunrise we were ordered to stand down, only a few men at intervals remaining on watch for the day. The sergeant-major came around with the rum issue, giving each man a drink. When my turn came, I told him to go easy because it was the first time for me. He poured out a tablespoonful into a shaving-stick holder, which he used for a measure, and handed it to me. I drank it, almost choking as the fiery liquor burned by throat. The sergeant-major, a little Scotchman, laughed at my distress.

"What's wrong with ye, lad? Kin ye no drink a wee drappie without choking?"

I explained that I had never drunk anything stronger than wine.

"Sir," Ted spoke up, "may I have Miller's share?"

The sergeant major was astonished for a moment, but after sizing Ted up, he smiled and said, "well, ye're a big mon, and I suppose ye kin stand anither." Whereupon he poured Ted a second drink.

The following days were quiet and uneventful. We spent most of the time in our dugout, talking or playing cards. J.C. was very fond of liquor and ever tried to inveigle someone into a gamble for the drink of rum in the morning. Being a good gambler he often succeeded in his purpose – the sergeant-major willingly agreed to the arrangements, apparently unconcerned as to who drank the issue of rum. Sneezigs' one incorrigible weakness was sweets. At

Goddersvelde we had not been affected by his craving – he had been able to steal from the quartermaster's store, or if that failed, from the cooks. But in the line his only chance of appeasing his sugary want lay in acquiring, rightfully or otherwise, someone else's share of jam. Often after having helped himself – for at night he sometimes went back to the dugout on some pretext – he tendered his share of bread, cheese or cigarettes, to compensate for the jam. I believe that if tempted by a tin of jam, he would have risked a trip across to the enemy line. Thus J.C. and Sneezigs bartered with each other or with the rest of us. And Dad, on whom we had conferred the honor of dividing the rations that were issued to our section, kept a record of all transactions during the day so that he might dole out even justice in the evening when the rations arrived.

Ted and J.C. seemed to be naturally opposed to each other; neither had much regard for the other's opinions on any matter. They furnished us with hours of amusement, engaging in ceaseless controversies that ranged from women – J.C.'s favorite topic – to war. J.C. complained bitterly about the scarcity of the fairer sex and the meagerness of the rum issue; and made lengthy speeches in which he advocated certain changes in the military system whereby soldiers would be assured of a more voluptuous life.

When not wrangling with Ted, J.C. picked on Sneezigs. Sneezigs was unable to pronounce his "j's" which was very amusing; and J.C. purposely asked him to repeat words that would make us laugh. But one day he overstepped himself –

"Sneezigs, which would you sooner have – an extra drink of rum or a tin of jam?"

"A tin of yam," was the reply, as expected.

J.C. started to laugh. "You know Sneezigs, your name should really be 'Tin of Yam'."

"If you call me '*Tin of Yam*' I will call you '*Yug of Rum*'."

Everyone laughed. "What's the yoke?" Sneezigs asked, perturbed. J.C.'s face took on a sober expression.

"Can't you really say Yam? Try it again, slowly."

"Jam." Replied Sneezigs. J.C. burst out laughing.

"All right, Yay See. You laugh at me. I will give you a Swedish word. Say 'Syltetoy'."

J.C. made a noble try. "Sil-t'tow."

"No. *Syltetoy*", Sneezigs corrected him.

"Aw, you can't say a word like that anyway. You just have to sneeze it out. By the way, what does it mean?"

"Yam", was the quiet rejoinder.

We laughed, but this time at J.C. Ted roared so loud that we were afraid the enemy might hear him and send over a few shells to stop the racket. J.C. tried to smile, but his red face betrayed his chagrin; it was once that his ready wit failed him. No one questioned Sneezigs' pronunciation after that.

For making tea, we got water from a shell hole behind our trench, usually filling our mess-tins and water bottles there in the morning while it was still dark; it was too dangerous to go out in the daytime – some friendly sniper might take us for a target.

One morning, much later than usual, I went out behind the trench for water. It was dawn when I crawled to the edge of the shell hole. The water was very clear; and I was about to dip in my mess-ten when I perceived a pair of boot sticking out of the soft mud at the bottom. On closer inspection, to my great horror, I saw the outline of a dead body, covered lightly with a fine sediment. I drew back quickly and returned to the dugout.

"Where is the water?" asked Ted, on seeing my empty mess-tin.

"There is a dead soldier in the shell hole," I replied, "and by the looks of things he has been there for some time."

"What" cried Skinny? "The shell hole from which we get water for tea?"

I nodded, sickened at the thought.

"Oh shucks," Ted broke in grinning, "I never tasted the difference anyway. This of all the good tea we've had. The thought doesn't bother me any – what a fellow doesn't know never hurts him."

Although Ted was right in his philosophy, it was not at all comforting.

One night we moved ahead to relieve D company in the front line. Dug in low, soggy ground, the trench was very shallow and it was equipped with poorly constructed shelters, all of which afforded us little protection and less comfort. The outline of the enemy ridge seemed to tower menacingly above us. The night was very quiet, yet I had an uncomfortable feeling that something was about to happen.

Shortly after sunrise, a red flare suddenly shot up in front; and a second later the enemy started to shell us. Overhead shrapnel shells came screeching over, six or more at a time, bursting in mid air above us, and leaving dense clouds of black smoke. Large trench mortar shells burst thundering all along our trench. Columns of earth shot up on every side. Large sections of trench collapsed or were blown in. The earth heaved and groaned as if it were in the throes of a terrible earthquake. The whole surrounding areas was a maze of lurid flashes that put the very daylight to shame.

We had orders to stand to, with the expectation that the ever-increasing fury would culminate in a personal attack by the enemy. With a sense of utter helplessness, we watched the trench mortar shells tumbling and twisting through the air with no apparent definite direction; we tried to judge the erratic, sudden descent of each deadly projectile, uncertain which way to flop. Cowering low, we pressed closely against the side of the trench, vainly hoping to absorb from the moist, quivering earth some steadiness for the awful moment when we should be forced to defy death. Every nerve – every fibre of my trembling body was taut. My stomach seemed to contract with a queer, panicky sensation. It was a feeling of terrible growing suspense, augmented by each explosion until it became an insane dread that the next shell would make a direct hit and blow us to pieces.

The shelling ceased as suddenly as it had begun. There was no attack, and I was filled with immeasurable relief. Everything was quiet, but the roars of the explosions still sounded in my brain, and my body still trembled. Our company had suffered a number wounded, but fortunately no one had been killed.

The trench was wrecked, but we had to wait until dark to repair it. Many corpses, previously buried in No Man's Land, had been blown up and exposed by the shellfire; these unfortunate victims had to undergo a second burial.

The battalion was relieved and went out for a few days' rest. Everyone was glad to get away from the dreadful front. The faces were more serious now; no one expressed any desire for excitement.

Chapter 4

A crater on Hill 60

Strange thoughts come to a man when he is face to face with Death. In the mortal distress of the moment, the past events of life, as a representation of the future, are vividly recalled to the mind, and one already has vision of a happy or unhappy Great Beyond. It is a supreme moment in which the fearful hope for the mystic, infinite future supersedes all the reasoning powers. Such was my first experience at Hill 60.

The next turn at the front took us to this ridge some miles southeast of Ypres. The whole hillside was a gouged mass of mine craters with white chalk scattered here and there over the surface, and looked ghastly in the murky twilight. The battalion, which we relieved, lost no time in starting back – they were relieved in more than one sense of the word.

Our company had hardly occupied the front-line trench when the order came to line up. The officers went along the trench selecting a man about every twenty-five yards with orders to stand guard for the night and keep a sharp lookout. I was one of the chosen ones and quickly mounted the firing step. The rest of the company filed out and retired to the support trench some fifty yards behind, leaving only a few of us to guard the front line.

Standing there, gazing over the parapet into the surrounding gloom, I was filled with an uncanny feeling of apprehension. What if the Germans should attack? I shuddered as I thought of our weak defense. Yet surely our officers must have known what they were doing, even though it seemed so unwise to me.

I went down the trench to the left to see who was on guard next to me. To my surprise, it was Ted. I saw that he was very pale.

"What is the idea taking the rest of the fellows further back?" I asked him in a low voice.

"I don't know for sure," he replied weakly, "but I heard a rumor that this place is 'under-mined' and loaded by the Germans. Headquarters expects it to be blown up towards morning."

"Then what are we supposed to be doing here?" I asked, startled.

"We shall have to stay until it's blown – and we'll be blown up too", he faltered.

Overcome by a feeling of hopelessness, I left Ted and returned to my post. The dreadful significance of his words made me shudder. It meant death – certain, fixed death, with no chance of escape – a sealed fate that was approaching nearer and nearer every minute. I felt suddenly sick. I didn't want to die. I was too young. Surely there must be some mistake; maybe Ted had merely been trying to get my wind up. But then he had been unmistakably nervous himself; therefore it must be true!

A light mist settled over the trenches. It became denser and denser, until it was almost impossible to see. A flare went up on the left, showing a dim white outline. I stood motionless at my post, trying to remain calm in spite of the cold awful sensation that was creeping up my spine.

Corporal Ribbons came around with some rum for us fellows. When he came to me, I related what Ted had told me and asked if it were true.

"Yes," he replied nervously, "but don't mention it to anyone. How are you taking it?"

"I feel the same as him."

"Well you are not showing it. Just try to stay cool."

The whole scheme was quite clear to me. The Germans would blow us up to make a gap, through which they would rush, in an early morning attack. Our fellows, however, would be lying in wait for them.

Buy why did I have to be picked for this job? Was it really my deathwatch? I thought of our first burial party at Hooge, and a convulsive shudder went through my body; vaguely I wondered if they would find enough of me for a burial.

A flare went up directly in front. I braced myself against the side of the trench and could almost feel myself going up. Nothing happened, and I realized that it was only a little after midnight; the mine would not go up for a couple of hours.

My entire life passed in review before my eyes. Father – Mother – Anne. How sweet life had been with them! But it was all over now; not even in memory could I cherish a thought of them, unless – unless that power was extended into eternity. My father was stern and resolute, yet I knew he would forgive me when he heard of my death. My mother – the shock might kill her. It had been hard for her to say, "Do your duty, my son...." How much harder it would be for her to bear the news of my death. My sweetheart pledging herself to await my return – poor Anne! – brokenhearted, she would now wait forever. I should not see my loved ones again. I should not return the shining hero, covered with glory. I should not even die fighting in battle. I was going ignominiously to my ill-fated death, without ever having seen an enemy – without even having struck one blow for my dear country. In an hour or so I should be helplessly killed, tormented only by my own thoughts.

Killed – what a strange word! It struck an ominous chill in my heart. My breath came in short gasps as I thought of it. Soon the inevitable would happen; inexorable Death would swoop down on me; my body, following the immutable law of Nature, must relinquish the soul and turn back to common clay. Oh that it would only happened quickly and be over with! This suspense was awful, and the end was sure to come anyway.

To the soul in agony, time passes slowly. It became lighter. A bird twittered behind the lines. Dawn was approaching. My heart beat rapidly. I became weaker, leaned heavily against the side of the trench for support. Any minute now. Each fleeting breath might be my last. It was the end of life. Death was at hand. Death and Eternity. The thought was unbearable. This must be a horrible nightmare! I passed my hand over my eyes – my forehead was cold and wet.

Then I heard a voice, the sweet, soft voice of my dear mother. It said, "Pray to God in Heaven" – I flung myself down on my knees and prayed earnestly to Him. Come what may, I was placing my life in His Hand. My nerves were quieter. My soul was at peace.

A red flare went up ahead. I braced myself. Swish – Swish – something passed through the air. A light explosion. My heart stopped beating; I strained and trembled. Again the same sound. Hand grenades, I thought, but no, the explosions were not loud enough. I had a transient glimpse of something flashing through the dense mist, followed by a long tail. Rifle grenades – it was the first time we were shelled with these things.

The attack was coming now. The mine would be blown any second. The strain was beyond endurance; my body grew limp and insensible – the rifle grenades falling thickly about me seemed only like light feathers floating around as compared to the greater doom impending.

Daylight filtered through, gradually dispersing the gloom. Yet nothing happened. Ribbons came around with another drink of rum.

"When shall we be blown up?" I asked weakly.

"I don't think it will come off today – I believe it was on account of the fog."

The words rang again and again through my befuddled brain. At last the meaning was clear: we should not be blown up? Again I heard the voice of Ribbons beside me – we were relieved. A warm feeling surged through my body; I felt strong, yet I was weak. My heart ached with a queer sensation – God had answered my prayers and spared me!

We joined our company back in the support line. Everything was quiet, but I could not sleep. The memory of that awful night haunted me.

Three days later we were relieved and marched back to Goddersvelde. After supper that evening, J.C. invited me to go down to the estaminet for a drink of wine. On entering the place, we found Ted already there, sitting at a table with a bottle of champagne before him, staring gloomily ahead. We approached and sat down at his table, but he seemed unaware of our presence. And elderly woman hastened to serve us.

"Vin blanc, Madame." I ordered.

Ted looked up suddenly and restrained her. "Champagne, Madame." She brought another bottle of champagne and glasses.

"Never Mind, boys, this is on me," said Ted, and he started to pour the drinks.

We drank to one another's health, though I noticed that Ted's manner was constrained.

"Come on, Ted, snap out of it!" I slapped him on the back, "You aren't standing on the mine at Hill 60 now."

"Please don't talk about it," he said seriously. "That night was just plain hell. I will not forget it as long as I live, and I hope I never have another like it."

"Oh cheer up, Ted" J.C. comforted him. "You wouldn't have been hurt even if the mine had gone up. There were four of us ready to catch you in a blanket, and Sneezigs had a cup of tea ready to steady your nerves. We thought you might need a new suit of underwear too, but we didn't know what size you wore."

I had to laugh, though a minute later I was sorry. Ted did not crack a smile. He drew his receding chin back further than ever, looking sober as a judge.

"J.C. your turn will come some day. You may have to go through the same thing. I'll get one on you, and you need not expect any sympathy from me."

We finished our drinks and went back to the old barn for a good night's rest.

Our rest was a life of great ease after the hectic experience at the front. To J.C. it was more than that – almost a state of perfect felicity. He paid numerous visits to the estaminets and drank liquor there to his heart's desire. On one or two occasions, notwithstanding the fact that he was handicapped by being unable to speak Flemish, he was successful in carrying on flirtations with Belgian girls – what he lacked in speech was easily made up by gesticulation, for I may say that J.C. was a born actor.

All good things come to an end sooner than one desires. So our respite terminated. One day, about the end of July, we heard that we should leave shortly for Sanctuary wood, between Hooge and Hill 60. From the expressions of the older fellows who had been there, we judged that it was a bad place.

J.C. came up to me, seeming quite worried. "Miller, I just hate the idea of going back in this trip."

"Well, nobody is exactly in love with the idea."

"It's not that, it's my nerves. I can't stand the shelling."

"Nerves?" I laughed. "You shouldn't have it so hard. I've given you my share of rum almost every morning in line."

"What's an extra drink of rum when I can get all I want at the estaminets when out of the line? I am going to try to stay out this trip."

"It can't be done," I told him.

"Oh yes it can be done quite easily." Then he lowered his voice. "You and I shall report sick tomorrow morning; and if the scheme works, we shall be left out with the transports.

"O.K. and what is the scheme?"

"Just this. When the Medical orderly makes his round, we shall report sick. Then, when we come up before the M.O., you can tell him you have a severe pain in the back and a bad headache; I'll let on my throat is swollen and that I can't talk."

I readily saw through J.C.'s shrewd plan. Having an accomplice would greatly lessen his own culpability, should he fail. The plan sounded rather foolish; yet in view of the result if successful, it was worth trying. J.C. was quite sagacious in such things anyway; he was one who, in civil life, would not have to depend on the sweat of his brow so long as he had a cunning idea in that prolific organ behind his brow. And Lady Luck usually favored him. So I agreed.

Next morning, when the medical orderly came around I reported sick.

"Name and number?" he asked.

"Jacob Miller, 425084."

J.C. had his bayonet out and was hammering against his mess-tin to attract the orderly's attention. His face actually had an expression of acute pain. Pointing to his throat, at the same time whispering faint, inarticulate sounds, he tried, in the most pitiable manner, to make the orderly understand that he wished to report sick.

"Your name and number?" asked the orderly.

J.C. gazed at him helplessly for a moment, then pulled out his pay book and showed him.

We followed the orderly to the medical inspection room located in a farmhouse a little way down the road. We had to wait for some time until our turn came, because the sick parade was much larger than usual that morning – apparently others had designs similar to ours. Most of the fellows were getting Medicine and Duty, and I began to wish that I had not reported sick. At last our turn came.

"Miller, you are next," said the M.O. "What is your trouble?"

"A bad headache, sir."

"Hm-hm, were you drinking last night?"

"No, sir."

"Let me feel your pulse." Then after a while, "Ah normal. Sergeant, take this man's temperature."

The medical sergeant brought a thermometer, shook it and stuck it in my mouth, with orders to keep it under my tongue.

The M.O. took up the sick list. "Brown, you're next. What is your trouble?"

But poor J.C. was unable to speak. He pointed to his throat and made a gurgling sound as if he were choking.

"Throat trouble, eh? Let me have the tongue depressor."

One of the orderlies handed him a chip of wood shaped like a spoon.

"Open your mouth and let me see what is wrong with you. There, now hold still for a moment." It only took a few seconds to convince the M.O that there was nothing wrong with J.C. Turning to the sergeant, he said: "Give this man a pill Cath Co (meaning a number 9) and paint his throat with iodine. You might also mark him M and D.

J.C. looked at me, and there was a faint smile on his face. I had to turn to the wall to keep from laughing and almost swallowed the thermometer. "Normal, eh? Sergeant, give this man a pill Cath Co and mark him M and D."

The sergeant produced a little brown pill and asked me to open my mouth. I had hardly done so, when he threw the pill, so accurately that it landed way down my throat and I had to swallow it whether I wanted to or not.

I went outside to wait for J.C. who was having his throat painted with iodine. I had hardly finished rolling a cigarette, when he appeared, coughing and spluttering.

"How does it feel?" I laughed.

"Can't explain," he gasped. "just seems to draw everything together and tastes as if I had my mouth full of rotten wood. I didn't have a sore throat when I went in there, but I sure have one now."

"Oh never mind J.C.," I comforted him. The joke is on us. You can sling the lead to that old boy."

On approaching our billet, we met Ted and Sneezigs coming out with their mess-tins to get breakfast."

Ted grinned at us. "I heard you two fellows reported sick. How did you make out?"

"Medicine and Duty," I told him.

"I thought so," he laughed. "You can't pull the wool over that baby's eyes. You know, I went to see him yesterday about an ingrown toenail, but he only gave me a dose of castor oil and told me to report back to my platoon."

"That's nothing," said Sneezigs. "Yesterday morning I reported sick with bronchitis. He asked me to take off my shirt, then he pull out a riga-ma-jig with a rubber hose and put the ends into his hears. The other end, which looked like a telephone receiver, he put on my chest, told me to say 99, 99. I said it about ten times, and then he said to me 'You can go now'. I asked him 'where – to the hospital?' He was much surprised and said 'No, back to the ranks'."

"Aw this is rotten business," said J.C. philosophically. "Now take civil life for instance. All you have to do is see a doctor and tell him what is wrong with you. He sympathizes with you immediately. Then the first question is 'Are your bowels moving freely?' If you say yes, he will ask 'Are you a big eater?' If you say 'no' he will tell you to eat more; and if you say 'yes' he will tell you not to eat so much. After you pay him five dollars he grins at you and tells you to take it easy for a few days."

But all our mutual sympathy did not help us any. That afternoon we packed our kits and started off for the front. The day was very warm. The fields of grain along the road were tinged with yellow by the hot sun. Beads of perspiration glistened on our faces as we went along, heavily loaded down with equipment and extra ammunition. Someone started to sing:

"We are going to the farm,

With our milk pails on our arms

You'd better watch old Fritz, or

He will send a whiz-bang there,

Stealing softly through the air.

The lobster wants you

His memory haunts you.

So keep away from Zillebeke,

Stay away from Zillebeke,

Keep away from Zillebeke Farm."

We learned the song and joined in. Soon the entire battalion was singing. But it was too hot, and we could not keep it up for long. Pale and exhausted, one fellow dropped out and lay down at the side of the road. The doctor examined him and sent him back to a hospital. Later we learned that he had died of heart failure.

In the distance, white puffs of smoke appeared in the sky; our anti-aircraft guns were shooting at a German Taube aeroplane. We halted and waited until the plane disappeared.

The progress became slower and slower under the heavy loads. Our throats were parched by the burning sun and dust. Our officers warned us to go easy on our water bottles, but few of us had any water left. At last, weary and exhausted, we reached a number of wooden huts, where we made camp until sundown.

After winding our way for some time in single file around shell holes and tangled wire, we came to Sanctuary Wood. What had once been a dense copse of luxuriant growth was now a ravaged area of stripped tree trunks and stumps and hummocks. The front line trench, shell torn and ragged, zigzagged through the middle. The battalion which we relieved filed out in silence; I asked one of the fellows what it was like, but he merely shrugged his shoulders.

I took up my position on guard beside Ted and looked over the parapet. The same old odor of dead men, which was part of every front, pervaded the air; but here it was stronger, more abominable and more sickening. A flare went up, and by its illumination, I had a look ahead; in the bright light the earth showed torn and yellow; the broken trees and stumps seemed to move about like silent, grey ghosts. As the flare slowly descended, grotesque shadows crept here and there, lending greater weirdness to the ghoulish surroundings.

The interval of darkness that followed was a terrible strain on the nerves. Horrors! A strange apparition suddenly appeared, in the form of a light, luminescent glow, which rose and fell vaporously near a large mound.

Ted grasped my arm and whispered nervously, "Do you see that?"

"Yes", I replied. "I wonder what caused it."

"By God, Miller, it must be a ghost!"

Although I did not believe in the existence of such roving spirits, yet I experienced an uncanny feeling of uncertainty. I tried to be calm and rational. "Maybe it's just an optical illusion."

O'Reilly, an American, on guard next to us, offered a probable explanation – "No, it's not an optical illusion. You'd likely find a number of dead buried under that spot, and that's only gas escaping from the decaying bodies."

It was rumored that O'Reilly was a graduate in science. There was some consolation in his scientific explanation, yet a lurking superstition persisted in leaving an eerie feeling that the strange phenomenon might possibly be a soul lingering over the body that it had left so recently and so unwillingly.

All was quite until morning; then the enemy started to shell us. We stood to, and faced the shellfire, as a raid was expected. Explosions thundered deafeningly all around. Some shells made direct hits on our trench, and killed or wounded men and blasted the trench to pieces. Pale and trembling we watched the scene of destruction, as each deadly missile landed with a terrific roar, striking terror into our hearts.

One of our observation planes came roaring over, and the shelling ceased suddenly. Enemy anti/aircraft guns, however, tried to bring down the plane; we could hear the reports of the guns and the shells whistling through the air, followed by explosions overhead; clouds of black smoke opened up all around the plane; but each burst was too far away to do any damage.

Evidently the observer located some of the German batteries, for our guns opened fire. But our shells hardly ever exploded; we counted eight duds out of the first ten shells. Ted turned to me disgusted.

"They might as well use a pop gun!" he said savagely. "Those shells must be loaded with sawdust."

After everything was quiet, we learned that we had suffered thirty casualties, wounded and killed.

Fortunately, there was no more shelling during the rest of our turn at the front. We followed a quiet routine of watch by night and sleep by day. Every morning after stand down, we received our issue of rum. I was beginning to enjoy it now – much to J.C.'s disappointment; it warmed and livened one up after a strenuous watch.

We were relieved and went back to the huts where we stayed in reserve, enjoying again a life of ample leisure. We had now made three trips into the line and were beginning to feel like old soldiers. The only thing we could not yet boast of was having seen an enemy, as Ted expressed one day –

"Here we have made three trips into the line, and haven't had a chance to draw a bead on a German yet."

"War is much different from what we thought when we were watching from Mont-des-cats." I remarked.

"Yes," said Ted, "it sure is. You know, when we were standing on top of that Cat Mountain, I imagined that we should stand in the trenches and shoot at the Germans; and that the side that had the best marksmen would win. But so far, I don't even know what a German looks line."

"Well, for my part, I am not very anxious to find out", said J.C. "Not after the way some of the poor fellows we buried at Hooge looked – they must have got an eyeful of the Germans – yes, more than an eyeful, some of them."

On August 11th, 1916, we moved up to the front at Mont Sorrel. The ground here was so soggy that it was impossible to dig below the sod surface without getting into soft mud from which the water seeped continually. The trench, therefore, was very shallow: a breastwork of sand bags in front protected us from direct shellfire, but we had no protection from any shells that might land behind. Our front line and the German front were very close together. At one place, on our right, they were only fifteen yards apart, and the German flares landed behind our lines.

The enemy opened up on us with a barrage of rifle grenades. We dreaded these things more than heavy shellfire; one could hear them coming quite plainly, but there was no way of knowing their direction. All night long we were harassed by them, and by daylight we had several slightly wounded.

After our rum issue and breakfast, I went back on guard. The chap on my right turned to me, saying that he was going to look over the top. I warned him not to try it, because the snipers were very active. But he paid little heed to my advice. Turning his head sideways he raised one eye cautiously over the edge. A rifle cracked near by, and he fell back unconscious. A dum-dum bullet had entered his forehead above the eye. At the call for stretcher-bearers, the M.O. rushed up, and after a hasty examination, he ordered the wounded man to be carried to his dugout where he attended him. He was still breathing that night when he was taken out, although the M.O. expressed little hope for him.

All was quiet. The larks were singing high up above us while I kept guard on that morning of August 12th. The sky was clear. Everything was so calm and peaceful that I could hear a German brass band playing far behind their lines. Looking through a crack in the parapet at the German trench about a hundred years away, I caught an occasional glint of a bayonet as some sentry shifted the position of his rifle. But there was no sound coming from there, not even the rattle of a mess-tin.

Suddenly a red flare went up on our left, where A and B Companies were stationed. The whole German artillery opened up in full blast; and the air was full of screeching shells. The earth quaked and thundered when the heavy barrage struck our line; the ear-splitting roars of the explosions continued as more shells kept coming;

everywhere flying death poured in on our front. Our officers shouted the order to stand to, and the men sprang to their positions with ready rifles. The shells were now exploding in our trench, and men falling all around. I became dizzy as the earth rocked and heaved before my eyes. Above the thundering din of the explosion, the cries of wounded men in terrible agony, was faintly audible.

Someone shouted hoarsely: "They are coming." Dim, grey forms with flashing bayonets were leaping up on the left and running toward our trench. Our officers shouted: "Fire, rapid fire!" We started to fire as fast as we could. My rifle grew hot and kicked like a mule at every shot: my nose was bleeding profusely from the heavy recoil. Our Colt machine gun started to spit fire, and the grey line fell down like grass before a mower. A second wave came over, running from shell hole to shell hole, carrying bombs. We kept firing until we saw no more coming. We had repulsed the attack.

With fixed bayonets, faces pale and streaked with sweat, nerves strung to a breaking tension, we trembled at our posts while shells continued to burst around us.

The shelling lasted until noon, and then died down. After everything was quite we learned that our battalion had lost a hundred and twenty-five men, killed and wounded.

Around me lay many dead and wounded, who could not be moved until night on account of enemy snipers. We were relieved from the terrific roars of the shells, but now we were tortured by the moaning of wounded men; their groans of agony cut through me like a knife – it was almost unbearable. The medical staff was busy, administering whatever first aid was possible in the trench; but this did not allay their distress very much. Some of them died and were forever relieved of their suffering.

I felt sick and weak, with a sharp pain in the chest from the heavy firing, and tried to get some rest. But where could one find rest? Where could one find relief? Nowhere. There was no place in the trench where one might recline without bodily contact with the dead. The touch of the numb bodies sent icy shivers up my spine – it seemed that the death in the corpses was conductible. My mind was in turmoil – these boys who short hours ago had lived and smiled at one another now lay in the cold rigidity of death – their bodies mangled – their faces distorted in last agony – their breaths forever stilled.

That night the wounded were taken out to the dressing station and the dead were carried back for burial. This was some relief to us, although the incertitude of our fate kept us in a state of constant trepidation. All night we stood on guard, nervously waiting for morning and whatever it might bring.

Morning dawned, and my heart quickened as I tensely waited, expecting a repetition of the previous, sudden attack. All was quiet however, and we were able to get some rest.

We finished our turn at the front without further casualties and went back to the huts where we stayed in reserve. There was a rumor about that the battalion would go south to the Somme front. We hoped that it would be a quieter front than Ypres. Anyway, as Ted expressed, it could not be any worse than standing on a loaded mine at Hill 60.

One evening when the mail arrived, I received two letters, one from my mother and one from Anne. I was overcome with joy, and too happy to eat. Going down the road a little way, I lay down under a hedge to read the letters from my loved ones. As I perused the contents of each page, my heart filled with intense longing, a feeling that can only be inspired through the love and anxiety of a mother and sweetheart. My thoughts carried me back to the bright cheerful scenes at home in Canada. Oh, how I longed to be back there instead of out in the wilderness of Flanders where Death lurked constantly!

After reading each letter a number of times, I folded them gently and placed them in my breast pocket for future comfort. With a light heart I went back to my billet. That night, for the first time in weeks, I slept peacefully and dreamed that I was home; the war was over and loved ones surrounded me again. So lovely were the faces, so sweet were the voices, so happy was I, that when I awoke to find myself in a stuffy, overcrowded hut in Flanders I could have wept.

Next afternoon I was sitting under an apple tree (the remains of an orchard) writing letters home to Mother and Anne. Beside me sat Ted, also with pencil and paper, though I noticed that his thoughts were far away, for he was gazing listlessly up at the small apples.

I continued writing, mentioning that we had been in the line and that we were now out on a rest. I described the country and told about some of the strange things I had seen. I finished my letters and looked up. Ted was walking up and down in front of me, stopping at intervals to gaze up at the tree.

"What's on your mind, Ted?" I asked, lighting a cigarette. "Don't you feel like writing today?"

He grinned foolishly. "Well, the trouble is, I don't know what to write."

"Your school ma'am?"

"No, not her. Betty I mean."

"Betty? Who the devil is Betty?"

"Betty is the little blond – don't you remember the two girls who came to see us a Caesar's Camp?"

"Yes." I replied, "But you had nothing to do with her."

"Didn't I though?" he laughed exultantly, reaching in his pocket for a letter. "Just read this, old man, and see if she doesn't love me."

I read the letter. It was from a girl in England who, apparently cared a great deal for Ted. She mentioned that she would never forget the night they had sat on the bench in the park: a thrill went through her every time she thought of the wonderful question he had asked her. I started to laugh, and Ted snatched away the letter.

"What was the wonderful question?" I asked.

Ted stuck out his chest proudly. "Just leave it to this kid. I told you it was a case of love at first sight on her part."

"But when did you see her alone?"

He started to laugh. "I slipped one over on you when we were in quarantine at Caesar's Camp – I told you I could step with the best of them. One night when you were asleep I got up and went to see Betty."

"How about the guard?"

"Oh, that was easy. I crawled out the back of the tent and when the guard wasn't looking, I wriggled through the fence and started off for Folkestone. You know Miller, love always finds a way."

I gazed at him dubiously. Ted continued: "In Folkestone I looked up Betty and took her to a show. After the show, we went for a walk in the park. We sat down on a bench and talked for a while. She kept moving closer all the time and I thought she was trying to push me off the bench, so I hung on tight. But she kept on pushing against me until I could not figure out what she wanted – and of course with a girl like Betty a fellow can't be too free and easy. At last I put my arms around her, and she didn't seem to mind at all. She kept asking me about Canada. I told her all about back home and asked her if she cared to go to Canada. 'Yes' she said, 'I'll go with you if you marry me.' I told her I would as soon as the war was over. Then shell fell around my neck – and, of course – I had to kiss her." Ted squeezed his eyes shut and grinned happily in memory of the blissful occasion.

"Well, you old son of a gun!" was all I could say, overcome with astonishment.

"Yes, Miller, I am a real kid if I ever get going. Now you beat it. I am going to write, and a real hot letter it will be."

I glanced back over my shoulder as I wandered off. Ted was busily scribbling away, his face beaming with happiness.

Chapter 5

Canadians at the front in the trenches

One morning, in the first week of September, we received orders to pack our kits. The battalion would move south to the Somme front. Our first move was to Goddersvelde where we were joined by our transports and pipe band. With transports and band in the lead, we marched west along the Ypres- Poperinghe Road, followed by a horse-drawn ambulance to pick up the sick, lame and the lazy.

As we gradually drew away from the front, the country showed fewer signs of destruction. The road was flanked on both sides with tall, green trees. Along the road were fields of grain that showed signs of approaching harvest. Everything seemed calm, and the day was beautiful.

Ted, who was beside me, appeared to be in very good humor.

"Quite happy over your letter the other day, eh Ted?" said J.C. who never missed a chance to start an argument. "Another girl seems to have fallen victim to your charms."

"You are right, J.C." Ted returned good-naturedly. "And a finer girl you never went out with in your life."

"How about the one in Canada?" asked J.C.

"I don't know just what to do about her. She sends me a parcel every two weeks, and I hate to throw her over, but the one in England is much better looking."

"In that case I'd go easy for awhile," advised J.C.," or you may be sued for breach of promise after the war is over."

"Well she is much older than I, though I hate to give her the slip now", Ted stated.

"No, don't give her a slip," advised Sneezigs. "That was a sweet cake she sent you the last time, and we wouldn't want her to cut off your rations."

The battalion halted, and we fell out for a rest. I removed my pack and lay down beside J.C. He pulled out a box of nerve tablets, and took out two tablets and swallowed them.

"What are those for?" I asked inquisitively.

"My nerves," he answered. "You know I am getting to be so nervous that I almost went crazy the last trip in the line, when they were coming over on us."

"Do the pills help any?" asked Skinny.

"Finest thing out," replied J.C. "I have only been taking them for a short time, and they have already helped me. Here, try them fellows."

Skinny, Dad and I each took one. Sneezigs was busy eating bread and jam. Ted waved away the proffered tablets in an emphatic gesture. "No thanks J.C. I wouldn't trust you that far. Those little brown devils look just like No. 9's to me. I had one from the doctor the other day and haven't got over the effects of it yet."

The order came to fall in, and soon we were back on our way. The pipe band started up, playing snappy Scottish airs. Bagpipes were new to me, and I asked Ted what they were playing.

"Don't ask me," he grumbled. "I can't understand that noise."

Dad overhead the remark and laughed. "What's the matter, Ted, don't you like Scottish music?"

But Ted was not to be humored. "The music may be all right for a Scotchman to march to," he returned, "but it sounds like ----- to me!"

Within a few miles of Poperinghe, the battalion turned south. After the shell torn Ypres Salient, the country through which we were passing showed no signs of destruction, and seemed so peaceful that one would scarcely have known that there was a war. But there were some unmistakable signs of war. There was an absence of men: women were engaged in heavy tasks in the fields – at one place we saw two women operating some kind of a farm implement, having a horse and a cow hitched up. There was the morose attitude of every civilian that we passed; each face was indelibly stamped with a solemn look of depression. Passing through the villages, we created no stir. The sullen feeling was even prevalent amongst the children; it was evident that these youngsters also knew only too well, the disastrous results of the war. I could not help wondering how it would affect their future: passing thought the adolescent stage of life with their country steeped in horrible bloodshed and calamity, they would, in all probability, bear the stigma of the cruel war as long as they lived. The gloomy outlook on life was one of the peculiar and certain signs of war.

It was late in the afternoon when we arrived at a small village near Hazelbrouck. There we halted and made camp until next morning.

After the long marches along stone-paved highways, through villages and towns, we were again approaching the front. Again we could hear the guns in a steady roar, and the distant sky was dotted with white and black puffs of smoke from anti-aircraft shells.

While going along the road on the last afternoon of our march, we met hundreds of German prisoners marching in fours, with mounted guards on each side, in front and behind. Some were looking dejected and sad; others were smiling, glad to be out of the war. One of our fellows shouted to them in German: "Hello Fritz! Wie geht's!" Like a flash their heads turned our way to see who had addressed them, but for an answer they received a loud "Ha, ha!" We passed battalions of Imperials coming out of the lines, loaded down with souvenirs. They had German helmets tied to their packs, Luger pistols and small daggers strapped around their waists.

It was sundown when we arrived at the large town of Albert. We were placed in bivouac encampment on the outskirts of the town. After the long day's march, we were all in, and notwithstanding the uncomfortable quarters, we slept soundly.

Next morning, we moved on toward La Boisselle. As we went along, the country gradually became rougher and showed more signs of destruction. We came upon a number of blown-out mine craters, trenches and deep dugouts, which had been the front line before the Somme Drive on July 1st, and halted to prepare for our turn at the front.

On Sunday, September 10th, 1916, we were ordered on church parade, and assembled in one of the large mine craters. After we had sung the hymn "Onward Christian Soldiers" the brigade chaplain delivered his address. He outlined the evil intentions of the Germans and depicted the unutterable cruelties they had inflicted on innocent women and children. He said that, unless we overcame our enemy, the world would be dominated by these fierce and merciless tyrants; it was our Heaven-sent task to overthrow these "Huns" and teach them such a lesson that the world would be rendered safe for democracy.

These words made me sad. I could not believe that Heaven had chosen for us this task. It seemed to be the designs of a man that we, the highest form of God's creation, were made to hate and destroy. Were we really carrying out the will of Christ? "Vengeance is mine, I shall repay", said the Lord. I could visualize my mother, with a Bible in her hands, saying to us: "Love thine enemy as thyself; do good unto them that despitefully use you; love them that hate you; feed and clothe them when they are in need and distress – and pray for them...." Ah, yes, but this was different. One nation was fighting to exterminate another. Self-preservation was the primal law of Humanity. This was war.

After the service we were lined up for inspection and again addressed, this time by some red-capped general. At the conclusion he said: "The Canadians are wonderful fighting men. I know that you shall not allow yourselves to be beaten. You are fighting for your sweethearts and mothers, for your King and Country..." I was quite impressed by his speech, but Ted made a grimace and muttered "What does that old boy know about the front line?"

On the afternoon of September 13th, we moved northeast. We arrived at a ration dump near Posieres in time for supper. We were now very close to the front line, and I saw that the surrounding vicinity was even more shell torn and more devastated than the Ypres Salient; as far as one could see, was the same ruinous waste, pitted and pulverized, without so much as an unbroken tree to give some relief to the eye. There was a nervous tension among the men; they hardly spoke to one another.

After supper, we were loaded down with Mills bombs and extra bandoliers of ammunition. We waited until dusk, and then set out for the front line, traveling in platoons about a hundred yards apart. On approaching the front, we broke up into single file. Everyone was silent. I could feel the oncoming disaster; it seemed that the very atmosphere was charged with something oppressive.

We reached the front about midnight and quietly proceeded to establish ourselves. The trench was very shallow and broken, and had small funk holes dug in the side, each one large enough for one man to sit in. In places the trench ran out to the surface, and there were only shell holes for protection. Dad, Skinny and I found part of a trench equipped with funk holes and immediately settled down for the night. All was still, yet we could not sleep – this was front line duty. The impenetrable darkness hung heavy with doom. We were very restive.

Towards morning the enemy began to shell us. Tired and weary after a sleepless night, we stood to, as an attack was expected. The hours dragged painfully on. The scorching sun and bursting explosions became unbearably monotonous. So utterly exhausted that we scarcely noted the raging fury of the bombardment, we stood to at our posts like wooden soldiers.

At sundown the barrage lifted from our line and began to rake the reserves and transports further back. With knowing stomachs, we waited for our ration party. The shellfire was so heavy, however, that they were unable to get through to us and we were forced to appease our hunger by nibbling hard tack. Feeling miserable and too hungry to sleep, we sat in our funk holes through the dark night.

At 3:00 A.M. our sergeant appeared and told us that we were to capture Moquet Farm at daybreak. C. Company was to follow him into No Man's Land, which would be the jump-off place. At these words, he climbed out of the trench and set out. Silently we arose and followed.

After we had proceeded for some distance, the order came in whispers to secrete ourselves in shell holes, three men to a hole, until the appointed time – 5:02 was the hour of action. We quickly extended ourselves along No Man's Land and crawled into shell holes.

The shell hole I was in was quite large and held four men. We lay down with our bombs in position for instant use, and with bated breaths and fast-beating hearts, awaited the awful zero hour. Time stood still! It seemed an age before faint streaks of light, stealing slowly across the sky, began to dispel the surrounding gloom.

When it was light enough to see, I raised myself on my hands and peered over the edge of the shell hole. My heart almost stopped! There, before me, not twenty-five feet away, sitting in a small shell hole were two Germans. I dropped back quickly and whispered what I had seen to the fellow beside me.

He decided to have a look also, and I warned him to be careful. He raised himself cautiously and looked over the edge. Turning to me, he whispered, "Where are they? I can't see any..." A rifle cracked, and he fell dead beside me. I thought surely that we should be charged upon and killed. The other two became excited and one of them wanted to call the sergeant.

"Stay where you are", I advised him, "or you may bet the same."

I asked what time it was. Ten minutes to five; another twelve minutes of suspense. Would the time never come?

A red flare shot up, and an enemy gun in front of us opened up. A terrific explosion burst forth all around us. Myriads of blazing lights floated before my eyes. I was suddenly without feeling or thought. I tried to raise myself, but there was not response to my efforts. Slowly my brain began to clear itself.

My senses returned, and I saw that I had been thrown completely out of the shell hole; near me lay one of my comrades, badly wounded, his tunic was dripping blood in several places. Slowly, and with painful effort, I dragged myself to him and pulled him back into the shell hole. His eyes flickered open for a moment, and I beheld the most intense expression of pain. Weakly he asked for water. I have him some, though, to my sorrow I saw that there was little hope for him. He lapsed into unconsciousness, and a moment later his body twitched spasmodically as death seized him. Another mother heart-broken!

The shell hole was strewn with fragments of flesh and bone that were covered with bits of clothing. The bodies of my companions had taken up the greater force of the explosion and thereby saved my life. With shaking hands, I tipped up my water bottle for a drink. Then I chewed a cigarette, which steadied my nerves somewhat, although I had to hold myself together by sheer force of will.

A red flare went up on the right and another on the left. Then the whole German artillery opened up simultaneously. The Air was full of flying death; shells landed and burst all around. The roars of the explosions were deafening. Our own artillery opened up in full blast, and the din became more terrific; large shells, small shells, overhead-shrapnel shells and trench mortars – the sky was full of shells – came from every direction and burst everywhere. Columns of black earth were thrown high in the air, like the spouting of geysers. The cries of wounded men became a prolonged screech. The whole surrounding area was a tumultuous sea of death and destruction – ready to engulf me at any moment. I began to pray.

I looked up. The Germans were rushing in extended order toward us. Dad rose out of a nearby shell hole, and pointing to the enemy, he shouted: "Come on boys! They are coming! Let's go up ---- and at 'em". His rifle slipped from his hands. With a look of pain, he staggered and fell back into the shell hole.

Our machine guns began to sweep the entire front. I had to duck. When I looked again, the Germans were nowhere in sight; our fellows from No Man's Land were going back to our front line. I rose quickly and ran over to Dad's shell hole. Dad was sitting there alone, with an expression of great pain, gazing at his bloody right arm, which dangled, loosely at his side.

"Come on, Dad!" I shouted.

He looked up at me, somewhat dazed, and then arose without speaking allowed me to assist him back to our trench where he received first aid. His arm was broken in two places.

Our trench was full of dead and dying; the bottom was covered with a red, sticky mud and little streams of blood were flowing from the mangled bodies. There were three brothers: one was dead, another wounded so badly that he was slowly dying, the third was almost desperate – with tears running down his face, he was beseeching his wounded brother not to die, "If you go Frank I want to die too. I want to go with you and Bill…" My heart was full of pity at the sorrowful sight, and I had to choke back a lump in my throat. Poor chap! Maybe it would be better to die. How could he face his mother and tell her about this bloody mess? But his mother! In her terrible grief, he would be her only consolation. I hoped that god would see fit to spare him for her sake.

As we could not remove the wounded until dark, I sat down in a funk hole to wait. The bombardment, continued, and I was dazed from the steady roar. After remaining in this position for about three hours, I decided to change and moved down the trench about fifty feet. I had scarcely sat down, when a terrific explosion shook the ground – the part of the trench I had just left was blown to pieces.

I began to wonder why it was that although men were being wounded and killed on all side of me, always I was being spared. Surely it was a miracle of God! Then I remembered the words of my mother while she had clung to me in the last embrace – "May god protect you, my son, and send you back to me alive and well..." Her prayers were being answered, and I was being spared. I fell down on my knees to thank God for having spared my life once more and to pray for protection. My nerves were quieted; a great peace settled over me. In spite of the intense shelling, I was aware of the Omnipotence of God.

I felt hungry. Having left my rations behind me in No Man's Land, I opened a dead man's haversack. It contained some bully beef and hardtack. After consuming some of it and taking a drink of water, I felt better.

Towards dusk the shelling died down. Our sergeant came down the trench and told us that we should be relieved that night. The battalion would go back to some chalk pits near a ration dump for reinforcements.

At ten o'clock we were relieved. All those who were fit were ordered to help carry out the wounded. A big, husky fellow, named Cook, and I carried a stretcher. We picked up the first wounded man we came to. To my surprise it was Dad. He had been hit again and was suffering so intensely he couldn't speak.

We started off, following a communication trench leading back from the front. It was hard for us, being loaded down with equipment, rifle and carrying a wounded man. The Fritzes were sweeping our back lines with machine gun fire and as the trench was only four feet deep, we had to stoop. In some places the trench was too narrow to admit passage of the stretcher, and we were compelled to make a portage overland, which, aside from being dangerous, was very tiring. At last I was exhausted and could go no farther. We set the stretcher down. Cook through off his equipment.

"Help me hoist him on my back", he said.

I assisted him, and he stumbled on down the trench, carrying Dad. It was the last time I saw them. Dad, after spending some months in a hospital, finally recovered and went back to Canada where he was discharged from active service. Cook, I believe, was killed on the way out, for nothing was heard of him. The memory of his brave act, however, shall remain with me as long as I live.

Crawling along on all fours, we continued on and found the trench becoming shallower, until it ran out to the surface on the face of a ridge. Ahead of us was Death Valley, dark and sinister with machine guns raking it from all sides. We stumbled ahead into the dark night. In some places we had to flop and creep along on all fours. There were dead men piled up all along the path forming a long parapet. Most of them had been stretcher cases that had succumbed to their wounds or had been shot on the way out. While creeping along behind this unusual defense, I was weirdly aware of the hundreds of dead bodies. Yet I was thankful – their unfortunate deaths saved other lives, for this human parapet was our only protection from the seething fire of enemy machine guns.

After some hard work we landed at a large mine crater in which the dressing station was located. There were a number of ambulances waiting to pick up the wounded, but not nearly enough, and many wounded had to wait until the fifth and sixth trip. One could hardly bear their feeble cries for help and water.

After a little rest, we continued on to the chalk pits. On arriving, we found the cooks waiting for us with a well-prepared meal of mulligan and tea. We were lined up and numbered off. Only one hundred and twenty-five men answered the roll call; it was all that was left of a whole battalion. Ted and Sneezigs were there, but I could not find Skinny or J.C. When I learned that they had been sent back to the transports, I was greatly relieved.

The order came to line up for the rum issue. As we passed the sergeant major, we received our little snort. Some of the boys fell in a second and third time, until the jug was dry. Then we went for a warm breakfast. Having eaten little during the last forty-eight hours, we had voracious appetites and enjoyed many helpings of the beef mulligan.

The mainland arrived with a load of letters and parcels. I listened hopefully for my name to be called. At last it came - a letter from Anne. I hoped for another letter or parcel from my mother, and waited patiently. There was none and I was disappointed. Many unclaimed casualty parcels were left over, and these were distributed amongst those of us that had not received any. I was fortunate in getting one, and hurried away to a place where I should be alone to read my letter.

The message of love and encouragement filled me with happiness. It was the happy occasion that every soldier looked forward to; the occasion when in the blissful memory of his sweetheart, the terrors of death were momentarily forgotten.

After reading the letter, I placed it in my breast pocket and opened the parcel. There was a note, 'To Harry – from your loving Mother". Laying it gently aside, I proceeded further. It was a large parcel and contained everything that a poor soldier could desire: a pair of woolen socks (which I immediately put on), a tin of Old Chum smoking tobacco, some chocolate bars, chewing gum, a bottle of Bovril, a tin of Oxo Cubes, and a small cake. I surveyed all these in happy anticipation of the enjoyment I should derive from them; and mentally expressed my sympathy for the kind mother who, no doubt, at this moment was unaware that her son had been wounded or perhaps killed. I sincerely hoped that he had been only wounded and that he would be safely returned to her. I decided to save the eats to take to the front and stored all my newly received presents in my pack. After rolling a cigarette from the Old Chum, I lay down on the sunny side of a shell hole and was soon asleep.

When I awoke the sun was sinking in the west. Seeing the rest of our company lined up for supper, I got out my mess-tin and fell in line. There were many strange faces about, as reinforcements had arrived.

I finished my tea and took a stroll around to see if I knew any of the new men.

"By cripe, if it isn't Miller!" a voice cried close to my side.

I turned to see who had accosted me, but failed at first to recognize the newcomer. After gazing at him for a moment his identity dawned upon me.

"Giese!" I cried, grasping his hand. Where in the dickens did you come from? I thought you were discharged at Winnipeg."

"So I was", he said. "But after hanging around home for a while I got tired of it and re-enlisted in the Black Devils Battalion. We stayed in England so long that I thought we'd never see any excitement. But at last they shipped us out, and here we are."

"You'll get all the excitement you want", I told him.

We talked for a while about things back home. Then he asked me numerous questions about the front. I explained to him some of the rudiments of self-preservation such as the various sounds of shells, how to tell their directions by the reports of the guns and how to flop away from bursting shells or bombs.

A husky well-built fellow, who was standing nearby listening to our conversation, interrupted me: "We'll show you what the little Black Devils are made of. Wait until we see the Heinies; we'll make them run."

I sized him up for a moment and thought: you will make a nice target for a sniper's rifle.

That night we were ordered on a working party to dig a support trench. Carrying picks and shovels, the whole battalion set out. Two engineers guided us to the location of the work near the front line. Each man had a section of trench two feet by four feet assigned to him.

To some of the new fellows, this sort of manual labor was not at all consistent with their idea of warfare, and they were quite indignant about it. One of them remarked: "I thought we came up here to fight, and now they want us to dig ditches."

"Don't worry at all", one of the old-timers grunted, "you'll get all the fighting you want."

Our work was almost finished when a machine-gun lashed out ahead and we were struck by a hail of bullets. The call for stretcher-bearers rang out; one man had been killed and seven wounded. We finished our work in silence, and returned to the chalk pits. After a warm breakfast, we went to sleep.

The whole of the following week was devoted to nightly working parties in order that the new men might become accustomed to trench life and shellfire.

One morning we received word to pack our kits. The Germans were to be driven back beyond Regina Trench which was our first objective; and our battalion was to move up nearer to the front, so as to be at hand if reinforcements should be needed.

The front line being a considerable distance from the chalk pits, we started out in the afternoon. After going for some time we were halted and ordered to entrench. There we stayed for a few days, enjoying the short respite of comparative ease and safety.

A steady bombardment began at the front. Many rumors drifted to us, from which we concluded that, after a fierce encounter, the Canadians had forced the Germans to evacuate Regina Trench, the long-desired objective.

In accordance with these new developments, our battalion prepared to move ahead. We were loaded down with extra rations and many bandoliers of cartridges. It looked as if we were in for a long stay in the lines. At dusk we set out.

Stretcher-bearers coming from the front line filed past us. I asked a wounded soldier –

"What is going on up there?"

" The Germans counter-attacked, but we drove them back", he informed me.

"What is the front like?" I inquired again.

"Nothing left of it. It's blown in all over."

I caught up with Ted and told him what I had learned. He merely shrugged his shoulders in a hopeless manner and remained silent. I missed the cheerful presence of Skinny and J.C.

We came to a large trench below a ridge and were ordered to occupy it. By the light of the flares beyond the ridge, I judged the front line to be a considerable distance away. The bombardment died down, and all grew quiet. I sat down in a funk hole and dozed off.

At daybreak I awoke. The guns behind our lines were opening up. A large shell came whistling like an express train; and from the sound I knew that it would fall near us. A sudden rush of air swept me off my feet, and a heavy concussion knocked the wind out of me. I arose, dazed and trembling, and saw that the shell had struck the side of our trench – not six feet from me – with such great impact that it had completely buried itself. Through some kind of fate the shell was a dud and did not explode.

I was still trembling from the effects of the sudden jar, when another shell came over. It landed a hundred yards behind us but did not explode. An officer came down the trench, and I immediately reported the incident –

"Our shells are falling short."

"I think they are trying to find the range", he said, "I shall try and get in touch with headquarters." With these words he turned and walked back.

I heard another shell coming and ducked again. This one landed about two hundred yards ahead of us, but did not explode either.

"What the heck is the matter with our shells?" cried one of the new recruits. "They are all duds!"

"Thank your lucky stars that they are duds, or we shouldn't be here to tell the tale", said a veteran who had also been knocked down by the impact of the first shell.

Later we heard more shells; but they went high overhead and landed far behind the German line.

On the afternoon of the following day, we received orders to move to the front. We started out, following a communication trench, which led up over the ridge. The sun was quite hot, but the trench was cool. All went fine until we came down the ridge toward a sunken road. We smelled the odor of dead men, which became stronger as we approached the road.

When we reached the sunken road, we were shocked beyond control. What a sight met our eyes! The whole road was filled with dead men. By the uniforms I recognized Germans, Canadians, Australians and Scottish Kilties. This must have been the scene of terrific hand-to-hand combat some four days previous. The bodies were piled four feet high, and the strong odor that emanated from them was most sickening. We had to pick our way over the gaping mouths and puffed blackened faces that stared with unseeing eyes at us. As we stepped on the heads and chests of dead men, the black blood oozed around our boots – we had to force all our will power into action. Gazing to the right and to the left the same heart-rending sight. O God! Why were men ever born to die thus on the battlefield, and to be strewn around as carrion! My throat tightened, and a horrible sensation sent shivers through my body. As long as I live, awake or asleep, I shall still see in memory that horrible sight.

On the other side of the road we entered a deep trench, which was half filled with dead. As I stumbled over the bodies, I looked around to see how the new reinforcements were taking it. Some of them, coming over from the sunken road, were vomiting; they were no longer joking and laughing. I felt sorry for them, poor fellows! –

That on their first trip into the line they had to encounter such a gruesome spectacle.

We followed this open grave for a short distance and came upon another sunken road. Thank goodness this was clear of dead! We found some dugouts and shacks and settled down to stay until dark. After supper, we lay around in groups, smoking and talking. Occasionally a light breeze wafted to us the odor of putrescent bodies. To the older fellows, it was not so bad because they were used to it; but the new fellows turned up their noses, and there were many expressions of "Phew".

Ted turned to me and muttered: "Some soldiers, these fellows."

"Oh, I don't know about that Ted. We were just as bad at first."

"I don't thing so", he protested.

"Remember, Ted", I reminded him, "the night of our first wiring party at Ypres?"

"Yes. Why?"

"Remember when you and I were lying in the shell hole, and how your teeth and knees rattled when you told me there was a German sniper in front of us and that you could see the sparks fly from his rifle. And Ted, that was only three months ago."

"Yes, but it seems like three years."

I lay down with my head on my haversack and watched the moon rise in the east. Now the moon was shining over a shell torn country enveloped in destruction and desolation and death. In a few hours that same moon would be seeing my home. What a contrast! There that golden disc would shed its soft rays over a beautiful landscape of silver-crested prairies with houses here and there nestling against dark backgrounds of trees and hedges: here the moon was looking down upon dead bodies, ragged trenches, shiny gun barrels and bayonets, and crouching soldiers. There, all would be calm and peaceful: occasionally the solitude would be broken by the hoot of an owl or the long drawn-out howl of a lonely coyote; then all would grow quiet again – the serene tranquility of midnight in Canada. Here, the nights were filled with the roars of cannons and the cries of men in agony. There, moonlit nights were nights of romance; there was that sweet, nocturnal fragrance in the air, there was that magnetic charm of moon light which softened lovers' hearts and filled them with redundant happiness; - the plenitude of love over all. Here, moonlit nights were charged with weird influences that made one shudder. There, the moon was a blessing; it was a friend to lovers and a guide to lonely travelers. Ah for the sought-after moon of Canada! But here! Here the moon was a curse; it was the bane of a soldiers' existence, for it revealed him to the watching enemy – and revelation meant death! O blessed Moon of my Homeland! O thrice-accursed Moon of France!

Ted, pulling my belt, shook me out of my reverie.

"Come on Miller. Fall in."

"What time is it?" I asked.

"Past midnight."

We started off in single file across country towards the front. We stumbled over dead bodies, crossed sunken roads and shell holes. At last we arrived at a trench, and the word was passed back in whispers, "Remain silent."

Ted and I nodded to each other. We were in the front line once more.

Chapter 6

Canadians dead at the Somme – 1916 – Ontario Archives

A and D companies moved to the left; B company moved to the right, and our company crossed the trench and continued on in silence. We followed an old communications trench leading at right angles from the front line trench into No Man's Land. We had gone about fifty feet when the order came to file in. The company we were relieving made haste to get out and beat it back as quickly as possible.

Our sergeant took the machine gunners out and stationed them right along the parapet. Then he returned to us and explained:

"This is an old German communication trench which leads right from our front line (which is called Regina Trench) to the enemy frontline. About a hundred yards down this trench there is a blockade. The Germans are holding the trench on the other side of the blockade." He stationed us along the trench and went towards the blockade.

After the sergeant left us, I cleaned my rifle, slipped two clips of cartridges into the magazine, and fixed my bayonet. I was ready.

The moon had vanished behind a cloud. It was too dark to discern any objects more than fifty feet away. I climbed out of the trench to have a look around. Our Colt machine gun was posted about twenty-five feet to the right; the gun and gunner were barricaded with sand bags. At that moment a flare shot up on the left. By its illumination, I saw tree stumps and piles of bricks farther ahead, which I concluded to be the ruins of a farmyard and orchard. According to the path of the flare, the enemy was not more than a hundred and fifty yards away.

The moon was breaking through the clouds. It was time to get back into the trench. As I let myself down, I heard a sound behind me and on turning I saw a number of men coming towards me from the left of the front. A machine gun burst out ahead; at the same time a man jumped into the trench beside me. He had four fingers shot off one hand, and at the sight of it he started to cry. The first aid man led him away.

Flares were going up on the right and on the left, but there were none going up in front. I became suspicious; something was wrong. Then it dawned on me; the enemy was going to make an early morning attack. I mentioned it to Ted who was on my left, but he merely nodded. The new recruit on my right said grimly: "Let them come. I am ready."

Red flares were going up now, followed by green ones. "What does it mean?" I asked Ted.

"I think they have changed their signals", he offered.

It was becoming faint in the east. Our captain came through, and I saw that he was troubled. His face was pale and had the peculiar expression, which I later learned to know so well. It was the sign of a soldier's premonition of death.

"Every man stand to", he ordered in a strained voice and passed on.

Dawn was breaking when a red flare went up ahead of us. It was not followed by a green one. I knew that something was about to happen, and I began to tremble. At that moment the whole German artillery opened up, and shells began to fly overhead; there was a steady roar and the shells exploded back in our support lines. All of a sudden the air was full of enemy hand grenades. Some fell in our trench, exploding and wounding men; others burst on top, causing no damage other than raising clouds of dust. The captain came running around the corner. He was about to give us an order when he fell dead at our feet.

The sergeant ran up, shouting, "They're coming!! Fire!"

The Germans were charging us from the right. I could hear a German officer shouting, "Vorwärts! Vorwärts!" as they came rushing in extended order. We all began to fire. The machine gun above us opened up, spraying bullets right and left. At the same time our artillery opened a barrage in No Man's Land, and we could scarcely hear the reports of our rifles above the din of the explosions. I was shooting as fast as I could; my rifle was so hot that I could smell the wood around the barrel burning.

I looked up and saw that the barrel of the machine gun was red hot. Suddenly the gunner pitched forward, shot through the head.

With blood running out of his sleeve, our sergeant came back from the front of the trench. He was followed by a number of others, also wounded. Soon everyone began to push back toward the front line.

"What is going on up there?" some one shouted.

"The Fritzies are in the trench, this side of the blockade, and are bombing this way!"

Bombs were flying and exploding ahead. As everyone was moving back, we were forced to retreat to Regina Trench.

After we were all in our own front line, we were ordered to block the communications trench at the point of its intersection with the front line trench. I ran back into the communication trench for a spade. Stumbling over a dead body, I recognized it as Giese. His uniform was blown completely from him, and his body was bleeding from head to foot. Poor Giese! – the excitement he craved had been but short.

Three of us started to dig, while a fourth man with a periscope watched the trench ahead. We had almost finished blocking it, where there was a ring of a steel helmet and our observer fell dead at our feet. I quickly grabbed some Mills bombs and threw them over the blockade into the communication trench. After the explosions I stuck the periscope on the end of my bayonet and looked over. Except for the naked body of Giese still lying there, the communication trench was empty. On turning around, I saw that the rest of our company had disappeared. We finished the shoveling and I took another look –

all was as before. I turned my periscope to the left. Crack! went a rifle and the bullet smashed my periscope.

The other two fellows were new recruits. I ordered them to remain at the blockade and keep a sharp lookout, while I went to the left to see where our company had gone.

About a hundred feet to the left there was an old communication trench leading up a hill toward our back line, and I decided that this was the way our company had gone. I looked over the parapet, into No Man's Land, and saw a German Machine gun posted a short distance away, with the barrel trained on our block. It would be useless for us to follow the communication trench back, because we should be spotted as soon as we got up the hill. We were trapped!

On returning to the blockade, I found only one of the fellows were still there.

"Where is the other fellow?" I asked.

"After you left, he became frightened and started to cry. Then he got up and beat it over the top to the back. But I think he was killed because I heard a machine gun firing as soon as he went over.

"Well, we had better stay here. There is no chance of getting away now", I told him.

The sun was beating mercilessly down upon us. My throat was parched; my tongue seemed to fill my mouth. I tipped up my water bottle for a drink, but it was empty; a small hole at the bottom showed where a bullet had passed through. I threw it away. There was a can with some water in it standing at the side of the trench. I took a drink, but it was very warm and smelled of gasoline.

"Here come some of our fellows!" my companion called out.

I turned and saw about twenty fellows dashing toward us from the left. The enemy machine gun burst forth – poor fellows, they were all shot down.

There was nothing for us to do buy lie down. I had no hope of getting out alive. About three o'clock the Fritzies began to shell our block with whiz-bangs. I watched the trench from both sides, expecting the enemy to come over any minute.

The sulphur of the bursting shells compounded with the smell of dead men made me sick. I began to vomit and crawled nearer the wall of the trench. The young recruit looked at me and started to cry – I suppose he thought I was done for. He cast a speculative glance behind and said:

"I am going to try and get out of here."

"Stay where you are until dark; then we shall make a get-away." I ordered.

He was just a young kid, not more that eighteen or nineteen. He had no right to be here at all.

A shell burst directly above me. The roar of the explosion was deafening; and I thought that the concussion had blown the insides out of me. A shower of earth almost buried me. I had a hard time extricating myself, and with painful effort I dragged myself away. I crawled to the right to a short distance and came upon a dead machine gunner. His water bottle was half full, so I took a drink and slung it over my shoulder. Then I lay still. I was feeling giddy and weak; my ears were ringing; my body was like a knife; the perspiration was rolling off my brow in a steady drip. A wave of nausea and blackness swept over me. I strained against the unseen forces, trying in one last supreme effort of will to rally my faculties and rise. The giddiness increased; slowly I felt myself slipping; and finally I was overcome by the strange waves of darkness.

When I opened my eyes it was dark. My youthful companion had disappeared. I climbed out of the trench and staggered across country. After going overland for about half a mile, I was exhausted. Wearily I crawled into a nearby trench and dragged myself inside a dugout. There I immediately fell asleep.

I awoke much refreshed and hungry. It was still dark, so I lit a match to view my surroundings. My hair almost raised the steel helmet off my head! There, lying beside me, were two German soldiers! My breathing contracted; I lay back stiff and trembling. With shaking hand I noiselessly drew my bayonet from the scabbard and held it poised, ready to strike at the slightest stir. The dugout was still as death; only my overwrought heart pounded against my ribs so, that I thought the Germans would heart is and wake up. I strained my ears to catch their breathing. All was quiet; there was not the slightest sound. Could it be possible that they were dead? On the strength of this hope, I risked lighting another match. This time I surveyed them more closely, and to my great relief, I saw that they really were dead. I arose and beat it as fast as my legs could take me. There might have been other Germans (live ones) in the locality.

I did not stop running until I reached the sunken road. After stepping lightly over the horrible mass of dead men, and going a little farther, I sat down for a rest. The pangs of hunger came to me, and I pulled out my last tin of bully beef and began to open it. The ineradicable picture of the sunken road recurred to me. My hunger forsook me. I could no longer eat. In disgust I threw my bully beef away.

Missing my rifle, I remembered that in my fright I had left it back in the dugout, and passing a dead man, I picked up his. An officer and two men, carrying a field telephone and a bundle of wire approached me. I asked the officer if he had seen my battalion.

"I do not know where they are now, but we passed some of your outfit going out this morning", he informed me.

Thinking that they would be in the first trench we had occupied since leaving the chalk pits, I hurried on. When I arrived at the trench, I found a different battalion there. Again, I asked if anyone knew where my battalion was.

One young fellow spoke up: "Your outfit has been passing in ones and twos all morning. I thing they are out at the chalk pits."

I went on to the chalk pits and found the battalion there. As I made my way to the field kitchen, I saw that most of the old soldiers were still left, but only a few of the reinforcements. Seeing Scotty, one of the cooks, I asked "How about a little tea, Scotty?"

"Sit down Miller", he answered in a friendly tone; "I shall make you plenty."

While I enjoyed about half a gallon of tea, Scotty informed that we were going back to the Albert-Bapaume Road for reinforcements. "I don't think we shall come back here. I heard a rumor that we shall be going to a quiet front for the winter."

This was good news. After thanking Scotty for the tea I went out to lie down for a little sleep. But I could not sleep for joy. The words, "a quiet front for the winter", kept ringing in my ears; happily I anticipated a nice long rest – no shells for a while – no machine guns – no sickly odors. This was good news indeed!

I arose and went in search of some of my comrades. A familiar figure stood near a battery of 4.5 field guns. On approaching I saw it was Skinny. He saw me at the same time and came forward. After a warm handclasp, we inquired about each other. I told him of my experiences and asked about Dad.

"He is in hospital at Etaples. His arm was badly splintered and he was afraid of losing it, but it is coming along fine now. I received a letter from him the other day, and he asked about you."

"I am glad that he is better. It looked as if it might be worse than that."

"By the way Miller, I received a parcel and have some cake left over for you. Come on over."

I went over to his cubbyhole and ate some cake and toffee. Ted came along. He looked at me and grinned. "Well, I see that you are still alive."

"Yes, but not by much. Say, what happened to you after the bombing began back at the blockade?"

"Leave it to this kid," he grinned. I get out of the way when anything turns up. – That is, if I can."

"Where did you go?"

"After the captain was killed, and our sergeant wounded, we were recalled and hoofed it back here."

"Was the sergeant wounded badly?" asked Skinny, who always sympathized.

"The last I saw of him," explained Ted, "he was high-tailing down the trench, carrying his alarm clock in one hand, and holding down his helmet with the other. I suppose he was so scared that his hair stood straight up, and he had to hold down his helmet for fear of getting hit on the noodle."

"We must have suffered quite a few casualties," I remarked.

"Yes, but mostly the new fellows," said Ted. "The poor fellows were really unprepared when they got into the jam, and the result is that most of them are pushing up daisies by this time. Oh, let's not talk about it. Fellows, I have a parcel."

"From Betty?" I said teasingly.

"Yes, from Betty, and she's a damned fine girl too. If I ever get out of here, I'll marry her and take her back to the old homestead in Canada."

He invited us to his funk hole to enjoy some of his sweets. We accepted. After we had eaten everything, he handed us each a Woodbine. We smoked and talked all day. The boys were lining up for supper when we rose. There was an odor of frying onions.

"Hamburger steak for supper," Skinny remarked.

"You mean bully beef disguised," said Ted. He was right.

After supper, we rolled into our blankets and tried to get some sleep. But after we got warm, the "cooties" became lively.

"I hope they give us a bath and some new clothes soon, said Skinny as he tried frantically to reach the inaccessible part of his back.

Scratching until our skin bled, we finally dropped off to sleep.

Next morning we formed what was left of the battalion and set out for the Albert-Bapaume Road. After an hour's march we arrived there and made camp. Four hundred new men arrived to join the battalion too. After they had been place in the various companies, among us, we started north.

At odd intervals our pipe band played. Ted had a natural aversion to the weird music, and scowled every time it started up. His annoyance amused me.

"What's the matter, Ted; don't you like music?"

"Say", he growled at me, "the guy that invented that noise must have been in an asylum."

A Scotchman turned to Ted. "That's fine music –"

"Fine music, my eye!" Ted snapped at him. "It sounds just like a bunch of cats squalling."

With a shrug of superiority the Scotchman turned away. From his manner it was apparent that he had little regard for Ted's opinion of music.

At last the music stopped. Ted heaved a great sigh of relief, and said, "I hope those guys are played out forever."

In the middle of the battalion, someone with a more cheerful disposition started to sing. For an hour or more we sang steadily – every song we could think of, including the soldiers' famous grasshopper song. Ted roared so loud that he drowned out the rest of the battalion.

Everyone was happy. We did not know where we were going and did not care, so long as we did not have to live in constant dread of death. The pleasant words still rang in my ears – "a quiet front for the winter".

Chapter 7

A Canadian soldier returning from the front - Ontario Archives

It was late afternoon when the battalion arrived at a small village. The village was, in its true sense, a community settlement of farmers and consisted of a dozen or more houses, each having the barn and lesser farm buildings in the background adjoining its respective strip of farm.

After we had been billeted in the barns, J.C., Sneezigs, Ted and I went for a stroll around the place. Autumn was well advanced. Behind the barns, in long rows, stood stacks of grain on which flocks of crows were feeding ravenously. The trees were almost bare, and the ground was covered with a yellow blanket of eddying swirls at the corners of the buildings. Some of the walnut trees still had nuts hanging from the upper branches. By throwing sticks and stones up into the trees, we brought down some of the nuts. After the dark husk was removed, there was the hard yellow shell of the walnut, which, on being cracked disclosed the sweet, edible kernel. We came to an orchard behind one of the houses. Apples were strewn about on the ground under the trees.

"How about some applesauce for supper?" J.C. suggested.

"It's a good idea", said Ted. "For once the little boy has used his head."

We all agreed that it was a good idea, and picked up some of the apples. When we arrived back at our barn, Ted went in search of something in which to cook the apples. He returned in a few minutes with a cooks' dixie. I started the Primus and heated some water, while the others peeled the apples. In less than an hour we had them well cooked and mashed up. But something had been overlooked – we had not put in any sugar. J.C. and Sneezigs went out to get some from the cooks, but they returned with long faces – we were out of luck. J.C. felt the disappointment most keenly; for he sat on his pack and held his head in his hands in a hopeless gesture.

"Yes", he sighed heavily, "if we had some sugar now, we could have a nice feed of applesauce; but as things are always against us, we shall have to eat the darn stuff sour."

"You are right again J.C.", said Ted. "And if we had some ham, we could have ham and eggs – that is, of course, provided that we had the eggs."

Sneezigs laughed and started to sing:

"What do we do with eggs and ham?

Where there is plum and apply yam?

Left turn? Right turn!

What do we do with the money we earn?

Oh, oh, oh, - it's a lovely war!"

After a meal of bread and sour applesauce we turned in for the night.

When we awoke the next morning, it was raining heavily. We hoped that we could stay and rest until the rain stopped. To our dismay, however, we were ordered to fall in, and had to march all day in the dismal downpour. Everyone was silent and glum as we went along. We were soaking wet and felt miserable. At odd intervals, someone started to sing, but we were not in the mood and the songs died down.

Someone shouted: "When shall we go back?"

"Soon, I hope", another returned.

Ted raised his head and bellowed: "Do we like apple stew?"

"Not without sugar!" J.C. yelled back.

Sneezigs spoke up: "Are we ever going to get paid?"

Everyone laughed at this – even the officers allowed their grim-looking visages to soften.

"We hope so!" we all shouted.

It was dusk and still raining when we arrived at the small village of Etrun. We stopped on the outskirts of the village, in front of a large, dilapidated warehouse. Apparently the building had suffered from the concussion of a shelling, for all the windows were blown in; but there was no sign of it having been struck. We were ordered to stay here; and crowding in, we soon quartered ourselves.

"This is a fine barn to spend the winter in – not enough air holes," grumbled J.C., as he looked around at all the open windows.

"I wish they would have blown if off the map completely before we go here," said Skinny.

"Well, let's get out of here and see what we can find", I suggested.

J.C., Skinny and I went out and turned into the one long and crooked street of the little village. It was still raining, and the street was quite muddy. We entered the first estaminet we came to and approached the counter. A fat, old dame sat behind the bar, grinning at us. J.C. pulled out a twenty-franc note and slapped it on the bar.

"Three vin blancs, Madame!"

"Vin blanc fini, Monsieur", she answered apologetically, and then mumbled something about beer.

"We don't want beer," said J.C. We are cold and wet. Have you any cognac or rum?"

"Cognac, oui, oui," she said, and quickly served us with three small glasses of brandy.

J.C. tasted it. "This is about one percent brandy and ninety-nine percent water. I'd like to tell the old girl about it, but I cannot speak French very well yet."

"That's the trouble with this war," he sighed. "I was just getting along fine with the Belgian girls when they shipped us out here, and I shall have to learn to speak French now. I suppose that when I get these women to understand me, they will ship us to Russia or Palestine.

The door opened, and two Imperials entered. Striding up to the bar, they ordered champagne.

"That is the real stuff," said J.C. when he saw the pale liquor sparkling in their glasses. He quickly ordered a bottle.

We soon finished the first bottle, and I ordered another. We were beginning to feel hilarious by this time and started to sing – "It's a long, long way to Tipperary..." Skinny ordered another bottle. I saw that he was becoming intoxicated and indicated to J.C. that we had better take him back.

"Oh he's all right," J.C. laughed. "A few drinks won't hurt him; it'll build up his intestinal fortitude."

After finishing the third bottle, we decided that we had had enough and went out. It had stopped raining, and the moon was shining clearly above us. Skinny was staggering from side to side. Gazing up at the moon, he started to sing –

"O lovely Moon! Up in the sky,

You shine so bright the long, long night..."

J.C. and I joined in; and with much singing, we happy three plodded through the mud and slush towards our quarters. Skinny became more and more unsteady; finally he fell headlong into the mud. J.C. and I picked him up. He was a sorry sight, but we couldn't help laughing – we were in the mood to laugh at anything. His face and uniform were covered with soft mud. We carried him to the side of the road and wiped some of the mud from him. He was as slippery as an eel, but with much pushing and pulling we managed to get him up to our quarters where we put him to bed.

When I arose next morning, the battalion was lined up in front of the quartermaster's store; the boys were being outfitted for the winter. I fell in behind and had to wait a long time.   When my turn came, there was not much left but I was fortunate enough to receive a pair of boots and a pair of trousers.

Back in our quarters, I tried on the trousers. They must have been made for some big fat giant, for when I pulled them on the waist came well over my chest. Ted, who was sitting near me, started to laugh.

"They seem to be a little tight for you under the arms. Better take them back and exchange them."

"This was the last pair they had," I said. "But I am going to shorten them."

"Why do that and waste a good pair of pants?" J.C. interposed. "It would be better to trade with Ted. His are a little too tight, and these would be more likely to fit him."

After sizing them up for a moment, I took them off and began to make a few alterations. I cut about ten inches off the bottom and hemmed them over.

"They should be well made to measure now," I said to J.C. who was watching me.

I tried them on again. I had to lengthen my braces to allow the pants to come down. The waist was now in the right place; and the legs were now the proper length – I was quite pleased with my handiwork.

There was a roar of laughter. J.C., Ted and a dozen others were holding their sides and shaking with mirth. I became confused and looked behind me. The seat of my pants stuck out and hung down way below my knees.

"Just hold that pose", laughed J.C. "All you need is a long cigarette holder and a towel wound around your head, and you'd be a real Turk."

Feeling quite embarrassed, I quickly took off the trousers, flung them in a corner and donned an old pair.

"Well, the pants are not totally wasted," said J.C., picking up the two pieces I had cut off the bottom; "These can be sewn on Ted's sleeves to him some protection for his wrists."

Ted glowered. "J.C. you'll do well to take a good jump at yourself."

In the Battle of the Somme the battalion had lost a number of officers and N.C.O.'s; consequently there were some promotions. Our section leader, Ribbons, was raised to the rank of sergeant of No. 11 Platoon, C Company. Ted, J.C. and I decided that his promotion should be marked by a celebration. We found him sitting on his pack, polishing his buttons; on his sleeves were three new stripes.

"Congratulations, Sergeant Ribbons!" we spoke with one accord.

"Thanks, boys." He rose and shook hands with us. "You are not looking for an extra snort of rum already, are you?"

"No, not that," laughed J.C., "but we should like you to come down to the estaminet and celebrate."

"Yes," I added, "we should like to wet those new stripes a bit."

"All right boys," said Ribbons. "I'll be with you in a minute."

On arriving at the estaminet, J.C. kicked the door open and shouted: "un bottle of champagne, Madame."

"Now go easy," Ribbons restrained him. "Don't start off in a hurry. We're not going to get tight and make fools of ourselves. We shall have only one bottle, and that will be on me."

We sat around the table while Ribbons poured the drinks. Ted proposed a toast to the new sergeant of No. 11 Platoon, C Company, and we all drank. There was some champagne left over, so I poured it over Ribbons' stripes – afterwards J.C. bawled me out for wasting good champagne that way.

That evening the mail brought me a letter and a parcel from my mother. Ted and Sneezigs were likewise fortunate. By putting together the contents of the three parcels, our section enjoyed what we termed a feast in honor of Ribbons.

On the fourth day of our stay at Etrun, orders came to move to the front. We were told to prepare for an eighteen-day stay in the lines.

The battalion set out, following the stone-paved Etrun-Anzin Road. On the left of the road ran a small river, whose banks were covered with bunches of large willows. Beyond, the ground rose to a ridge along which there were a number of old trenches and dugouts, which had been used by the Germans in early 1915. On the right, a narrow flat stretched along the road toward Anzin. Across the flat, on the eminence beyond, was an army cemetery, with its white-painted crosses looking like a patch of lilies in the distance.

We soon came to Anzin. The little village was in ruin; only an army bathhouse constructed of corrugated iron was still standing. Nearby was a supply dump consisting of iron screw stakes and rolls of barbed wire. We came upon a wide and deep trench along the bottom of which were trench mats to facilitate walking, and followed it in single file. There was a bit of bush along the right of the trench, so we were able to go along without much danger of being spotted by the enemy.

After going for some time, we came to the front line. The trenches were well built up with bags of earth. In some places the ground was still muddy from the recent rains. However, the weather was quite fair now, and we hoped it would remain this way to dry things up.

C Company was ordered to file into an immediate support trench, well equipped with dugouts, about a hundred feet behind the front line. After we had stationed ourselves, I removed my pack and laid in on the firing step. The Imperials whom we were relieving began to file out. As one of them passed me, I asked: "What kind of a front is this?"

"Ow," he answered with a broad accent, "Jerry is quiet in this 'ere sector. Don't disturb 'im, and 'e won't 'urt yer. The last shell 'e put over was about six days ago."

I turned to Ted and found him grinning at me. His receding chin was almost out of sight.

"Yes," he mimicked, "if only the blinking fat 'eads in the artillery 'ave the brains to leave 'im alone, we shall be all right."

After the Imperials had gone, we mobbed our stuff into the dugouts. The one that we were allotted was quite shallow, the top only being about four feet below the surface. Above the entrance someone had placed a skull – it was quite yellow and fresh; and its teeth, one of them gold-filled, were yet intact. The death's head leered at us menacingly. I wanted to tear it down, but Ted restrained me.

"This thing gives me the creeps," I argued.

Ted laughed. "It won't hurt you. Leave it up there. It will bring us good luck; and furthermore, it will show that the dugout is occupied by a bunch of real, tough guys."

"Well, for my part, I ain't so tough," said Sneezigs. "You take it down, I'll hate to look at it in the moonlight."

However, the skull remained; and to make it look lifelike, Ted stuck a half-smoked cigarette between the large teeth.

Our underground compartment was large enough to hold seven men. As there were only five of us, Ted, Sneezigs, and two new men and myself, we had a little extra room. Ted ordered the new men to the rear of the dugout, and whispered to me: "Those greenhorns don't need to know everything. Let them find out the way we did."

Ted and I were ordered on night duty. Our line was in the heavily rat-infested area; and there were thousands of the sneaky rodents scampering here and there or rummaging about in the tin cans and other rubbish that lay on top of the trench. Their frolicsome activities kept us in a nervous state, because half the time we did not know if a bombing party was sneaking up or if the rats were making the racket. We spent a watchful night.

The next night was the same. We were under a continual nervous strain. And did start and tremble at every sound. At last I thought of a plan to exterminate some of them, and sent Ted to our dugout for a piece of cheese. He brought me a fair sized chunk. I stuck it on the end of my bayonet and held my rifle over the parapet. In a few seconds a rat began to nibble, and I pulled the trigger. Soon another one began to nibble, and I pulled the trigger again. This was great sport. We were beginning to enjoy it when Captain Clarke came on his nightly rounds.

"What's all the racket about?" he asked anxiously.

"Killing rats sir," I told him.

"Stop this nonsense!" he said sternly, though with undisguised relief, and went on.

After he had gone, we tried it again. It was one way of killing off a few of the sneak little beasts and gave us great satisfaction.

One morning Sergeant Ribbons issued a large chuck of grease to each dugout. One of the new fellows brought our issue of grease into the dugout; and not knowing what it was for, he handed it to Sneezigs. We thought it was margarine and divided it among Ted,

Sneezigs and myself – the two new fellows wanted some, but we told them it was only for old soldiers. We put it into a mess-tin and set in on our brazier to melt. When the grease was hot, we dropped in slices of bread and fried them until they were nicely brown. They tasted very good. This went on for a few meals until our grease was all used up. I went to Ribbons to get some more.

"Have you any of that grease left?" I asked him.

"Why? Did you use it up already?"

"Yes, and it tasted real good."

"Your darn fools, Ribbons laughed. "That stuff was not to be eaten. That was whale fat to rub on your feet so that you wouldn't get trench feet."

I went back to the dugout and told Ted and Sneezigs.

"Oh well, I don't mind," said Ted. "I always did like whales. They are such nice little things you know."

The joke was on us, but we did not tell the new fellows about it; nor did we eat any more of the grease.

That night Ted and a new man went on night duty, and I remained in our dugout. I intended to keep my quarter loaf of bread, which was our ration every evening, for the next day.

On the two previous nights the rats had eaten all my bread, so I conceived a plan to conserve it from the thieving rodents. I rolled my bread into a sand bag, placed it under my pillow, and went to sleep confident that I should have bread for breakfast.

Next morning, when I arose, I opened the sand bag. There was a large hole in the bag, and all that was left of my bread was the crust and a few crumbs. I was exasperated; this was final proof that our bread could not be saved from the rats. Henceforth I should eat all my bread as soon as I receive it and do without until the next allowance.

After breakfast I went on duty. A heavy mist had descended. The air was cold and raw, and penetrated our scanty clothing; the first signs of winter were in the atmosphere.

The enemy started to shell us with "pineapples" (small trench mortar shells). Some of the shells landed in our trench, and we suffered a few casualties. We were ordered to stand to because it was an ideal morning for a raid. I expected to see the Germans break through the mist any moment. War was a reality once more; and each misty shadow seemed to be a grim tentacle of death, reaching forward to grasp us and crush out our lives.

The fog lifted, and it started to rain. The shelling ceased – the Germans must have been too taken up with their own discomfort to add to ours. Our trench had been blown in at two places, and we were ordered to repair it. After digging away at the surplus earth, and filling new sandbags, we built it up again. By the time we ere finished, everyone was soaking wet.

The rain continued steadily for several days. The bottom of the trench was covered with water, and it was coming into some of the dugouts. The earth, which during the dry season had been crushed and beaten and pulverized by shellfire, now readily absorbed the moisture, gradually becoming a jelly-like substance. Parts of the trench collapsed. Long rows of sandbags, which served as a revetment, were continually sliding down. We kept picking them up out of the soupy mire and replacing them; sometimes they slid down as soon as we had them up! What a job this was!

At last it was over. We were relieved and started back for six days rest. The trench mats were completely submerged. Large chunks of earth had slid down and blocked the way. We waded knee deep in thick mud.

We arrived at two large tunnels near Anzim, and two companies of us prepared to stay. The tunnels were equipped with bunks along the insides, evidently having been used as a place of rest before. We split up, one company to each tunnel, and soon made ourselves at home.

The first four days were devoted to rest. We played cards, wrote letters, or sat around talking. On the fifth day we were ordered on a working party to lay a narrow gauge track. I was about to fall in, when Ribbons approached me –

"Miller, you don't have to go. We are going to give some of the older fellows a break. There will be three others and yourself staying back today."

I thanked him and crawled back into my bunk to continue a letter I was writing.

"Aren't you going out today?" asked Stacey, who occupied the bunk above mine.

"No. Ribbons let me off this time," I answered.

"Gee, Miller, I wish I could stay here with you," he said regretfully.

He started to pace back and forth, and it was apparent that he had something on his mind.

"Say, Miller", he stopped in front of me suddenly, "would you mind going out in my place today?"

"Not at all, Stacey", I said. "It's O.K. with me so long as Ribbons doesn't mind."

Stacey ducked out. After a few minutes, he returned, his face beaming. "It's O.K. with him. Thanks ever so much, Miller. I will pay you back some day. There is something else I simply have to do today." He gratefully squeezed my hand.

"Oh, forget it, Stacey, that's nothing. I don't mind," I said as I picked up my gas mask and helmet and went out.

We followed a narrow trench for a little distance, and then went overland to a railroad dump about half a mile from the tunnels. It was a little misty, and we thought the Germans would not spot us. But we were mistaken. We had scarcely begun to string out the rails when five shells burst around us in a diamond shape, the nearest one landing about a hundred feet away.

"Everyone scatter!" shouted Ribbons, and we all sought shelter.

More shells came over, but fortunately no one was hurt. Soon the shells ceased to land in our immediate vicinity and began to drop away in the direction from which we had come.

Ribbons got up to see where they were bursting.

"Boys," he said excitedly, "they are landing somewhere near the tunnels!"

A few minutes later Major Caswell came running up.

"Come on!" he cried breathlessly. "All of you hurry up! The tunnels are blown in and four men are buried alive."

We gathered some spades and ran back with all haste, hoping to be able to dig our comrades out before they would be overcome by suffocation.

The tunnel I had occupied had been blown in at both ends; the other had collapsed in the middle. We immediately started to dig from the top down. The ground was so soggy from the recent rains that every time a spade was pulled up it had to be scrapped off. The Germans spotted us and started to shell, and we were forced to abandon our work until dark.

We dug steadily all night, but did not reach the entombed men. About midnight of the second night we found them, or rather what was left of them. Evidently, they had been playing cards when the catastrophe had descended upon them, for bits of cards were strewn about with the mangled pieces of flesh and bone. One fellow's watch, penetrated by a small piece of shrapnel, was found; it was taken care of by the Captain who later sent it to the next of kin.

We buried the remains in the little cemetery between Etrun and Anzin. After the interment, Major Caswell said sorrowfully:

"There lie four of my best men: a sergeant, two corporals and a private – and I would willingly have given my life for any one of them."

We all shared his feeling.

My heart was filled with sorrow as Stacey's last words came back to me – "Miller, I will pay you back someday." He had believed that by substituting for him, I had been doing him a great favor. Poor Stacey! Unknown to himself, he had been doing for me the greatest act that one man can render unto another. He had saved my life. My remains should have been buried there, and he should have been alive and well, walking around my grave, instead of me around his. He had been grateful to me for taking his place on a working party – what did I owe him for taking my place in the grave?

Oh, Fate!

Chapter 8

Canadian soldiers playing games at the front

On returning to the front, we heard that things had been quite lively; the Fritzies had made a few nightly raids on our trenches.

Ted and I occupied the same dugout as on the previous trip. Sneezigs was stationed in another, a little way down the trench. The skull was in its place, above the entrance to our dugout.

"See", said Ted, "our good luck charm is still here."

We had orders to lie low, because the last battalion had suffered heavy casualties. We worked by night, building up the blown-in trenches; and stayed in the dugouts by day. I wondered what fate had in store for us this time.

It was now late in November, and we had to keep our braziers burning all day. They were to be lit in the early morning, so that the enemy would not see the smoke; and after the coke became red hot, it burned all day without smoke.

One morning, Ted went to put some more coke in the brazier. The fire being very low, he put in a few wood chips to give it a start. It began to smoke so badly that he had to set the brazier out in the trench. This was very dangerous, as it was now daylight, and the enemy could easily see the smoke.

"I think you had better put the fire out altogether, as the Germans can see the smoke", I advised Ted.

"Go on Miller", he remonstrated, "those fellows are too busy making breakfast, the same as we are, to be out looking for smoke. Can't you smell the sausage?" He pulled his chin out of sight with a grin and proceeded to fry some bacon.

Sneezigs came down the trench, sniffing the air.

"By gosh, that smells good," he remarked. "Bacon, eh?"

He looked into the mess-tin at the frying bacon and started to laugh. "You fellows call that bacon, huh? Why, one of those slices wouldn't fill my hollow tooth; and besides, it only has one strip of red meat."

"That's why the boys call it Lance Corporal bacon – it has only one stripe," I responded.

"Yes," grumbled Ted, "our officers get all the good stuff; they get the sergeant bacon with three stripes; while we poor devils have to eat sow belly."

"You are wrong, Ted. I'll show you what the officers get for breakfast", Sneezigs said and went back to his dugout.

"Did you see Sneezigs' face?" asked Ted.

"Why, what is wrong with it? I countered.

"Didn't you notice the jam on his chin?"

"Yes, but there is nothing wrong with that."

"Yes there is. I'll bet he was into our share of jam. Wait until he comes back; I'll ask him."

"Oh, I don't think so, Ted", I returned. "He must have some of his own left yet."

"No he hasn't." Ted said firmly. "I was right there when he cleaned up on the whole works for supper last night."

He removed the lid of our jam tin and showed me. It was empty. At that moment Sneezigs reappeared with a small package.

"I'll show you some real bacon, and it's not one striped stuff either," he said as he opened the package.

Ted's eyes nearly popped out at the sight of the contents: there, before us, lay three slices of ham.

"I'll be darned!" I gasped in surprise.

"Where did you get the ham?" asked Ted.

Sneezigs grinned boastfully. "Well, seeing that you are so darn nosey, I'll tell you. I was hanging around the quartermaster's store to pinch some yam, and I saw one fellow slice this ham. I waited for a long time, until at last he turned his back. It was just the chance I wanted: and like a flash, I stuck three slices in my pocket and beat it."

Ted pulled a long face. "So that is what the officers are getting for breakfast. No wonder they are getting fat in the trenches."

"Well, there you are," Sneezigs broke in. "Remember the bugle call: 'the officers' wives get pudding and pies; while the privates' only get skilligallee'."

"By the way, Sneezigs", said Ted, pointing inside our dugout entrance, "is there any more jam left in that tin down there?"

Sneezigs' face turned a fiery red as he took a look. He shook his head and stammered: "No, it's empty. I think the rats must have eaten it; or else, maybe, the new fellows have cleaned it up."

Ted's face lit up in a broad smile. "Yes, Sneezigs, I believe there was a rat at it. You are all right. Miller and I shall starve, but don't let it happen again. We are forgiving you this time, seeing that you are giving us two slices of ham." He picked up two of the slices of ham and dropped them into the mess-tin.

Muttering to himself, Sneezigs walked off with his one slice of ham, while Ted and I chuckled happily.

I took off the bacon and put on some potatoes to fry. Looking at Ted, I saw that he was very dirty from handling the brazier.

"You better go down to the shell hole for a good wash, and quit digging around in the grub with those mud hooks," I ordered.

"Yes," he said, looking at his dirty hands. "I was beginning to think it a good idea myself." He went into the dugout and reappeared with soap and towel.

"Watch the ham," he grinned at me, as he went on down the left of the trench.

The potatoes and ham were well done, so I took them off and put on some water for tea. I heard the faint report of a trench mortar gun and saw a "Minnie" wobbling through the air toward me. Instinctively I turned and dived head first into the dugout. A terrific explosion burst forth at the entrance, and I was hurled to the back of the dugout. All was dark. I found myself covered to the waist with earth.

"How are we going to get out of here?" a voice wailed beside me, and I realized that one of our new men was buried in with me.

"Find the shovel and pick that are in here somewhere!" I cried.

I dragged myself out of the loose earth and crawled to where the implements had been. Bumping into my companion, I snatched the pick from him. The dugout was over half filled with earth, there was only about a four-foot square in which we could move. My companion started to dig frantically in the direction where the opening had been. I stopped him.

"Its no use to dig in there: We'd suffocate before we'd make it. We have to try the top."

We pried away two support planks from the ceiling and started to dig for dear life. Chunks of mud fell down on our faces, and small particles filled our eyes. Our arms tired quickly from this over-head exertion, but we kept on.

The air was becoming stale. My breath came in gasps. I was worrying desperately: we were buried alive. We should die before getting out. They would dig us out after. We should be reburied beside Stacey and the others.

Slowly we dug the cavity upward, and had to reach higher. The air was getting closer and closer. My lungs were beginning to ache. My throat was tightening – it seemed that the tentacles of death were already choking me. My companion was sobbing with fear; and I could hear his breath sucking in between sobs, as he slowly and painfully wielded the spade.

"Come on, mate! Hard at it, and we'll make it!" I cried with hope and picked away with renewed effort.

We heard voices from above: "they are still alive and digging up..." followed by the pleasant sound of spades digging down toward us. This gave us new hope, and we dug faster than ever.

Pains shot through my head, and lights danced before my eyes. A shower of earth descended upon me, and light broke through. We were saved. We had cheated death!

We stuck our head up and inhaled deeply of the air that rushed down to us. Then we withdrew our heads, while the fellows from above dug the hole big enough to admit our shoulders.

I was about to pull myself up out of the hole, when there was a faint report, and a "Minnie" came streaking through the air toward me. Everybody scattered. I tried to get back into the dugout, but was stuck; and with horrified gaze, I watched the shell come over. I closed my eyes. There was a terrific roar overhead; the earth trembled; the roar continued to echo in my head. I opened my eyes, and seeing a large cloud of smoke above me, was aware that the shell had burst about a hundred feet in the air. In all my years at the front, this was the only trench-mortar shell which I saw explode before hitting the ground. My life was saved by a miracle!

I quickly pulled myself up and assisted my companion in getting out. His face was dirty and streaked with tears. We drank deeply of the fresh, cool air for a moment, and then staggered back into the trench. Weakly I sat down on the firing step, and did not move.

"Were you buried, Miller?"

I looked up and saw Captain Clarke standing before me.

"Yes, sir", I answered.

"Are you hurt?" he asked.

"No, sir."

"Here, take a drink of this. You had better lie down somewhere for a while; you don't look any too well." He handed me his water bottle, and I took a small drink- it was rum.

I had been sitting there for some time when Ted came up.

"Hello Miller, how are you coming? Have you cooked breakfast yet?" he grinned at me.

"Yes, it's all done", I answered weakly.

"Where is it? Let's go and eat."

"Go ahead. It's all over there; and all you have to do is get a shovel and dig for it."

Ted started to laugh. But I was not in the mood for laughter. My nerves were quivering so badly that my whole body was shaking. I could not control myself.

Ted was aware of my condition and said sympathetically: "Say Miller, you had better watch out. The first thing you know you will be shell-shocked. Come over to Sneezigs' dugout and have some tea. It will steady your nerves."

His suggestion failed to stir me at first. I felt miserable and sick; and I knew that it was not tea that I needed, but peace: peace and a long rest. Ted urged me again, so I started over with him to Sneezigs' dugout. I was so shaky that I could hardly walk. I sat down, while Ted related our predicament: we were without shelter and had not yet eaten breakfast. Sneezigs was sympathetic and immediately began to prepare tea.

"It's your fault Ted, that the dugout is blown in," he said. "I'll bet that the Yermans drew a bead on that darn skull over the entrance. So much for your crazy good luck idea."

"Oh no," Ted grinned. "That was just because you fellows did not believe in it. You see, I had faith; and it was good luck for me: I wasn't in the dugout when it blew up."

Sneezigs served us with hard tack and tea. "Now, if you fellows had not pinched the two slices of ham, I could treat you to them. I bet they would taste darn good to you right now, huh?"

"Maybe so," said Ted, "but under the circumstances, they would have tasted much better – if that shell hadn't come along."

I drank some tea and felt slightly relieved. After our light breakfast we sat around for a while, smoking and talking.

"I hear the C Company is chose to pull off a raid about the end of the month", remarked Ted.

"That's the reason we were put in supports the last two trips." I pointed out. "What platoon is to do the dirty work?"

"I don't know", he answered, "but I suppose it will be we old war horses again."

It started to rain and lasted all day and night. Next morning a working party arrived with rubber boots for the entire company and many rolls of barbed wire for wire entanglements. We were each issued with a pair of rubber boots with instructions to wear them until we were relieved, and then to leave them for the next battalion. We dried our feet carefully and rubbed them with whale oil before putting on the boots. What a relief to have dry feet again! We were a happy as school children and enjoyed walking in the water without getting wet.

I was thinking of the rolls of wire that had been brought down, and hoped that I should not have to go out on a wiring party. But my hopes were short-lived. The next evening we were told to prepare for a wiring party. One consolation, however, J.C. and I were to be the covering party ahead of those stringing the wire.

After supper, J.C. came over to our dugout, and we made preparations to go. We took our rifles, and one bandolier of ammunition and two Mills bombs each. Our instructions were to go ahead of the party into No Man's Land, until we came to a large mine crater near the enemy line; we were to go around it to the side nearer the enemy and stay there on watch; if one or two Germans approached, we were to shoot them; if a party came over, we were to throw our bombs and beat it back to warn our party which would be working about fifty yards behind.

This looked like a ticklish job. With Ribbons in the lead, we set out, followed by the rest of the party, some carrying a roll of wire each, others carrying iron screw stakes.

J.C. and I soon arrived at the crater and carefully picked our way around. Suddenly a flare went up ahead. We stood stock still until it burned out, and then crept forward. Another flare shot up, so close that we saw the sparks fly from the flare pistol. We flopped on our stomachs on the edge of the crater and waited.

We were so close to the enemy line that we had to talk in whispers, and smoking was out of the question entirely. J.C. pulled out a handful of tobacco and put it in his mouth.

I poked him in the ribs and whispered: "What's the matter, J.C.? Have you got the wind up your neck already?"

"Yes", he whispered back, "that flare man is darned close for comfort."

At that moment another flare went up, and landed right beside us. We held our breaths and dared not move until it was burned out. We expected to hear a burst of machine gun fire directed at us any moment. I was getting nervous. Putting a cigarette in my mouth I began to chew it. J.C. gave me a sharp dig in the ribs. I merely nodded to him – I knew what he was about to say.

Around midnight sounds came to us from the inside of the crater – plop – plop – plop – the sounds of many feet trudging stealthily through the mud. I looked over the edge and saw the faint outline of nine or ten dim forms approaching us from the bottom of the crater. I nudged J.C., and we waited breathlessly while the steps drew nearer. They approached within ten feet of us and stopped directly below, thus cutting us off from our own line. There was a faint whisper in German, then, all was still. J.C. started to pull the pin out of a bomb. I quickly reached over and stopped him: even if we should wound, or perhaps kill a few of them, the rest would shoot us down before we could escape. We waited.

After what seemed an age, the steps began to recede from us and slowly faded away in the depths of the crater. Evidently they had been a raiding party; and having heard our wiring party at work, they had gotten cold feet. We could not figure out where they had gone; and we spent a nervous three hours. (Later we learned that the Germans had a tunnel leading from their front line to the crater.)

At last the flare, which was the signal for our return, went up behind us, and we lost no time getting back to our trench. J.C. went on down to his quarters, and I retired to Sneezigs' dugout where Ted and I were now staying. Ted and Sneezigs were preparing a lunch when I entered.

"Well Miller, how goes the wire stringing?" asked Ted. I related our experience.

"You are some soldiers," he laughed. "Why take me for instance; if I had been there, I should have captured the whole lot, single handed."

"Never mind what you should have done," Sneezigs interrupted. "Tea is ready, and we may as well eat." He produced some light biscuits and a can of peaches.

"What in the dickens, Sneezigs," asked Ted, "another parcel from your Swede girl?"

"Not this time," Sneezigs answered soberly. "The Y.M.C.A. is in the front line now, you know."

"In the front line?" Ted echoed.

"Yes, they have a little dugout store near battalion headquarters. You can buy anything you want, cigarettes, fruit or yam."

"That makes life a bit easier," said Ted, "but by the looks of things, the war will last forever."

"Yes," sighed Sneezigs, "you know what they say – 'The first seven years is the hardest'. After that we shall be used to it."

Ted and Sneezigs were ordered on night duty. Having been out on the wiring party, I was excused and went to sleep along with the four new fellows in the dugout.

Next day all was clear and sunny. We spent most of the time playing cards or sleeping. In the evening, when the rations and mail arrived, I received a letter from Anne, and quickly retired to a secluded corner to read it. I was surprised at the brevity and tone of the letter: this time she expressed no anxiety for my return, but asked only how I was getting along. It was strange; I thought that she should suddenly turn so cold toward me. I put the letter in my pocket, intending to write to find out what was the matter.

"What is the trouble Miller? Doesn't she love you anymore?" asked Ted jokingly.

"Yes" remarked Harv, one of the new fellows, "they only love you as long as you are with them; as soon as you are away they start to run around with someone else. I'll bet you ten francs, Miller that she is out with someone else this very minute."

"I suppose you are right," I said gloomily.

"Never mind, Miller" Ted spoke up. "I had hard luck too. I received a letter from an old friend the other day, telling me that my school ma'am is running around with another guy. But I never cared for her anyway; and besides she is too old for me."

"How old is she?" I asked.

"Well, she is seven years older than I, - and I am no spring chicken myself, you know."

The new fellows thought this was a good one and started to nag Ted –

"Does she wear glasses?"

"Has she got her hair done up in a knot on top?"

"Does she comb it straight back?"

"Is she bow-legged or knock-kneed?"

These implications did not please Ted. He turned to the new fellows angrily, "Who the dickens asked you fellows for a song anyway? Just because you were on a wiring party last night, you think you won the war. You're nothing but a bunch of greenhorns!"

Two of the fellows resented this remark, and began to talk back.

"Keep your mouths shut!" Ted growled at them, "or I'll lick the two of you."

He could have carried out this threat, I am sure; and there was almost a fight, but Sneezigs poured oil on the troubled waters, by interposing brusquely –

"What's the matter with you fellows anyway? In the first place you'd have to whittle Ted down to your own size, see? And in the second place, you'd be crazy to fight over a skirt, see? Sometimes I think that's what started this war – just a petticoat…"

We all had to laugh at Sneezigs' humor, and the quarrel was soon forgotten.

About nine o'clock we were ordered on another wiring party. Ted and I constituted the covering party. We did not go to the mine crater, but secreted ourselves on a little knoll to the left of it.

The night was very dark and quiet. We could hear the Germans walking back and forth in their trench, swinging their arms against their sides to keep warm.

After we had been there for some time, it started to rain. Soon we were soaking wet and ice cold. Ted grew very restless and moved from side to side. At last he could stand it no longer and began to curse.

"To hell with this job! he said aloud, "I don't give a damn if the Germans capture the whole works! Let's go back."

I jumped forward and clapped my hand over his mouth.

"For heaven's sake, shut up!" I whispered through clenched teeth. I was certain that the enemy had heard him and expected a bomb to be thrown at us any moment.

Ted rolled over on his back, removed his helmet and put it over his face to keep off the rain.

"All right then," he grumbled resignedly, "we'll stay for a while."

We remained silent until the signal for our return.

"Thank goodness it's over!" said Ted aloud, again sending shivers up my back.

We returned to our dugout and dried ourselves in front of the brazier.

Ted and I were ordered to stand guard for the night. It had stopped raining and a light mist was hanging over the trenches. Our support trench was only a hundred feet behind the front line; therefore, as it became lighter towards morning, we could see into No Man's Land quite clearly. All of a sudden, as if they appeared from nowhere, ten Germans came stumbling in single file across No Man's Land, straight toward us. They seemed as unconcerned as if they were out for a stroll.

I stooped down and whispered to Ted: "The Germans are coming!" He jumped up quickly, grabbed his rifle and drew a bead on the foremost one. They were quite close now, almost upon our front line trench.

"Don't shoot Ted!" I said quickly. "They are lost and will walk right into the trench."

A shot rang out on our left, and the Germens ducked back – all except one who, in his confusion, jumped right into our front line trench. He was quickly surrounded and taken.

A minute later a runner appeared and asked for Miller.

"Here," I answered.

"The major wants to see you at headquarters."

I threw off my equipment and went down to the major's dugout. On entering, I saluted and asked why I was wanted.

"We have a prisoner here, Miller," Major Caswell indicated the German who was nervously sitting on a box in the corner. "I want you to ask him the following questions: what regiment is he from; how long have they been in the trenches; where they came from; what rations they are getting; what training they have; and how many men they have in the front at present?

The major took a pencil and paper, drew the empty whiskey bottle, which held the candle a little close, and motioned me to begin.

"Zu welchem Regiment gehören Sie?" I asked the prisoner.

He hesitated for a moment, and then answered: "Erstes Jäger Regiment." I translated it and went on –

"Wie lange seid ihr schon in dem Graben?"

He realized that we were trying to get information, and refused to answer. I repeated the question, but he remained silent.

"Here, give him a few snorts of this," said the major, handing me his water bottle.

I poured out a stiff drink of rum and handed it to the prisoner. He took it and gulped it down. After a few minutes I gave him two more, then I handed him a cigarette. After he had taken a few drags I again questioned him. He was feeling lively by this time, and responded quite readily to my inquiries.

They had come here from the Somme for a rest, but would be going back soon; their food was very poor, and they were only getting half rations; they were getting many recruits who only had a few weeks training; and their army consisted of many useless civilians in army uniform.

After we had all this information, the major called a couple of men and an N.C.O. and ordered them to take the prisoner to a battalion headquarters.

I went back to my dugout, Sneezigs was there, drinking tea and heating hardtack and jam. I joined in; and while we were thus occupied, I told him about the prisoner.

"I hope that puts the kibosh on the raid that they are talking about", he said with his mount full of hardtack and jam. "They must have all the information they want now."

Chapter 9

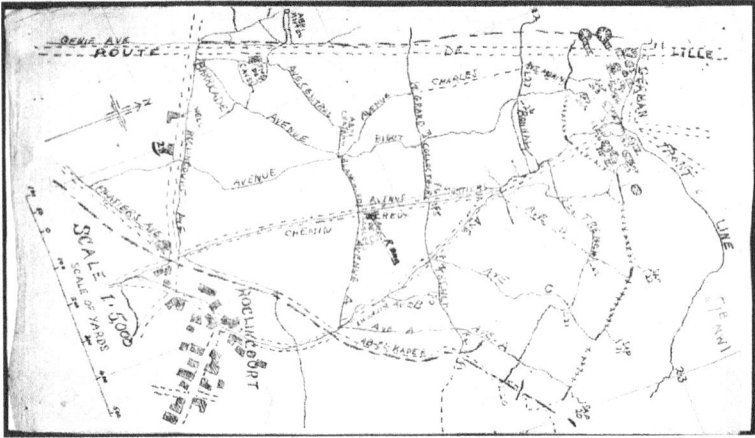

1st Canadian Mounted Rifles map, Dec 1916

Rain and more rain. Day in and day out, the same cold downpour – we were sick of it. The water was mounting higher in the trench, and the entrances to the dugouts had to be built up to keep it out.

Ted looked up at the sky one day, and watching the everlasting drizzle, he remarked soberly: "Another few days of this Heavenly barrage and we'll be drowned out entirely."

"Then we'll yust stand in the trench and sleep with water up to our necks," Sneezigs prophesied cheerfully.

"That reminds me of a story I heard the other day," said Ted. "An Imperial battalion was relieving a Canadian battalion in the front line. The Imperials arrived sooner than they were expected, and found one of the Canucks sitting on the firing step washing his socks. One of the Imperials said to his pal, 'Strike me pink, Bill! Look, that blighter over there is washing his socks in the water we have to sleep in tonight!'"

Fortunately, we did not stay to wait fulfillment of Sneezigs' prophesy. We were relieved and went back to our old quarters at

Etrun, where, notwithstanding the rain and sleet blowing in through the broken windows, we were much more comfortable.

Orders came to No 11 Platoon, C Company, to prepare for a raid on the German trenches. We were called together to study maps showing the exact location of dugouts and communication trenches in the German front line – these had been compiled by our scouts after they had prowled around in No Man's Land for many nights. Our captain outlined the details of the coming raid; the artillery would be on a barrage in No Man's Land in the afternoon to blow up the wire entanglements so that we could get through; at three o'clock we should go over the top and cross No Man's Land to the right of the mine crater; some would carry high explosives to throw into the dugouts; others would go right and left to round up prisoners; O'Reilly, the American, and I were detailed to remain at the point of the trench were we should land, and keep guard. The whole show would not last more than ten minutes. After every man knew his part, we were dismissed. The date of the raid, however, was withheld from us.

The boys spent most of the time playing cards or visiting the estaminets. Although it had stopped raining, I remained in our quarters most of the time. I wrote a few letters home, saying that I was still well and enjoying life.

One sunny day I could not resist taking a stroll in the country. Everything seemed so calm and beautiful. I wondered if I should enjoy many more such scenes. When I thought of the coming raid, my mind became uneasy; I had had so many narrow escapes that the law of averages was against me; and I feared that something would happen this time.

Returning to our quarters, I met Ted.

"Where do you think you are going?" he asked.

"Back to the billets," I responded.

"Why go to that icebox? Come with me and have a feed of eggs and chips."

"Where are you going to get it?"

"Just leave it to this kid," he grinned. "I can dig up anything."

"Lead on then, Brother."

He took me to a house on the outskirts of the village. After knocking, Ted pushed open the door and we entered. An elderly woman greeted us with a smile. "Bonjour, Messieurs."

"Bonjour yourself," said Ted. "We want some eggs and chips."

"Pardon?" she looked up at him inquiringly.

"Never mind pardon; we are buck privates," said Ted laughingly. "Hurry up with the eggs."

The old lady stood before him hesitatingly. Ted thought desperately for a moment, and then cried: "Ah, now I've got it! Ooves – that's it. Bring us some ooves and chips!"

She was bewildered for a moment, but finally she got the drift of what he wanted. "Des oeufs et des pommes de terre?"

"Yes, I guess you are right, old girl," Ted said. Then turning to me, "So that's the word for chips – bum de tears?"

"Yes, I think so," I answered.

"Well, then, hurry up. Bring us some ooves and bum de tears. Come on, get busy!"

"Oui, oui," she cried excitedly. And motioning for us to sit down, she hurried away to prepare the eggs and chips.

"What do you think of the raid?" Ted turned to me.

"I don't like the thought of it. I have been through so many narrow escapes that I'm afraid something will happen to me on this trip."

"Yes," he signed, "I guess you and I are the only ones left who haven't missed a trip in the line yet."

The old lady served us, and we set to, eating heartily.

"This reminds me of the good, old days at home," said Ted, as he speared a chip and stuck it away in the cavernous region under his moustache.

She brought us some fruit, biscuits and coffee. We had a delightful meal and felt quite satisfied.

"Combien, Madame?" asked Ted, as we rose from the table.

"Deux Francs," she said meekly.

"Deux, that means three." Ted counted on his fingers and winked at me.

"Oui, oui, deux francs, Monsieur," she repeated, holding up two fingers.

"All right, here you are Honey." Ted smiled at her, laying three francs on the table. He then pinched her gently on the cheek, and we made our departure.

We strolled back to our quarters and rolled in for the night. I could not sleep, however, and got up again. J.C. was sitting up, polishing buttons.

"Are you going on leave, J.C.?" I asked.

"No," he replied. "I have a new job now."

"Promoted to Corporal?"

"No, demoted to officer's flunky."

"How did you manage to get that job?"

"Well, remember when I was left back the last trip up the Somme? I was so darn scared to go back into the line that I worked up a temperature and reported to the M.O. He excused me from duty, and I was told to stay with the transports."

"Yes, but you were sick then."

"I know," he grinned. "I am all right now, but one has to fool these guys sometimes."

The next day No 11 Platoon, C Company, went into the line. As it was December 20th, my hopes of being on rest over Christmas were shot to pieces.

On arriving at the front line, we filed into a tunnel leading into No Man's Land, and waited. Our guns were shelling the wire entanglements; and we could feel the concussion of the exploding shells through the ground.

Crack! Went a rifle beside me, and one of our fellows cried: "I'm hit!" We moved him to the entrance of the tunnel and found that he had an ugly wound in his left arm.

"How did it happen?" the first aid man inquired.

"My rifle went off accidentally," the fellow answered soberly. He was excused from duty and sent to the dressing station.

When I got back to Ted, I told him about it.

"Accidentally, my eye! That was self-inflicted," said Ted. "That fellow sure knew how to get out of it; but I'll tell you a better one about J.C."

"J.C.?" I exclaimed.

"Yes, he's pretty slick. He chewed up a bunch of cordite and worked up a high temperature in order to be excused from duty; and now he is batman to the captain."

Sergeant Ribbons appeared and called out "Zero hour is three o'clock. The barrage will lift at two minutes to three."

We quickly filed out into the front line trench and lined up, ready to go over. I was about in the middle of the line. Ted was on my right and O'Reilly on my left.

Ribbons came down the line with some rum. I wanted to have a clear head for action, and refused my issue.

"Give me his share, if he doesn't want it," said Ted.

Ribbons gave him a second drink. "That feels better," Ted grinned at me after gulping it down.

I felt uneasy and began to tremble. Leaning against the side of the trench, I breathed a short prayer to Heaven.

The barrage lifted, and Captain Clarke shouted: "All right, boys!"

We went over the top like a whirlwind and ran towards the enemy line. I saw Ted's legs in front of me, taking about two yards at every step. We covered the distance across No Man's Land and sprang into the German trench.

O'Reilly and I stood guard, while our men ran right and left to round up some prisoners. O'Reilly climbed on top of the trench to have a look around. Turning to me, he said; "I can see them runn…" A shot rang out, and his helmet fell from his head. With a small hole drilled into his forehead he toppled back into the trench – stone dead.

German prisoners, with uplifted arms, filed towards me from both directions. I pointed to our trench and, in German, ordered them to beat it across. They went over, followed closely by our fellows. I was the last one to go back, and was scarcely half way across No Man's Land, when the last of them disappeared in our trench.

We were ordered to stay in the tunnel until dark. Our raid had been successful and had been carried out with clocklike precision. We had captured twenty-one men, including an officer; and we had suffered only one man killed and one wounded in the hand.

After the raid the enemy shelled our lines heavily for a few hours, and the battalion that held the front line suffered heavy casualties.

After everything was quiet, we filed out and marched off with our prisoners. I was called to the front of the party to accompany Captain Clarke and the German officer. The German officer was quite light-hearted, and I easily engaged him in conversation. He told me that, before the war, he had been a schoolteacher in Austria. He had received a parcel containing some smokes that very morning, and producing a package, he offered us each a cigarette. I thanked him and smoked it; it was a good smoke. I kept him talking all the way to Anzin, and translated our conversation to the captain. At Anzin, Clarke detailed a sergeant and six men to march the prisoners off in another direction to divisional head quarters. Then we continued to Etrun.

Captain Clarke told me that the battalion would be out on rest for Christmas; and after one more trip in the line, we should have six weeks rest. This was good news, and I went to the back of the platoon to tell Ted. He was in a sullen mood. I fell in beside him and tried to cheer him up.

"We shall be off for Christmas, Ted; and after one more trip, we shall have six weeks' rest," I told him.

"Who said so?" he growled.

"The captain just told me."

"Well, I won't believe it until we get it," he grumbled.

On arriving at our billet, we found the cooks waiting for us with a warm supper of mulligan made from fresh meat, potatoes and carrots.

After supper, Ted began to write a letter. I leaned against the wall to read a chapter from my Bible. The new fellows on both sides of us were still talking about the raid. It had been the first trip over the top for many of them, and they were remarking on how easy it was to slip over and bring back a bunch of Fritzies.

Ted turned to me, disgusted. "Listen to that noise. To hear them talk one would think they had brought back the whole German army." Turning to them, he shouted: "Say you guys, the next time you go over, be sure to bring back the Kaiser! Then the war will be over!"

"Oh, take a jump at yourself," one of them retorted. "Just because you were at Ypres and the Somme, you think you know it all."

"What's the use?" Ted muttered and rolled into his blankets.

Next morning we were lined up on parade. Colonel Andrews came around and addressed us. He congratulated us on our successful raid; and read messages of praise from the brigade and divisional commanders; complimenting us on the good work we had performed the day before. Some of the new fellows were all smiles – I believe they thought they were going to get a medal for their bravery.

We spent the next two days in rest. I was trying to figure out how we should spend Christmas, when I met J.C.

"The captain says that we shall go into the line tomorrow." He informed me.

"That means Christmas in the trenches after all," I grumbled.

"Yes, but cheer up Miller. I shall be there this time too. Of course, I shall be hanging around the captain's dugout most of the time, but I hope to slip down to see you once in a while."

"Don't forget to drop in on Ted and me on Christmas morning," I called after him as he moved away.

On the morning of the 24th, we made preparations to go to the front. The mail arrived in the forenoon, and Ted received a parcel from him school ma'am.

"By gosh!" he cried, as he opened the parcel, "the old lady still loves me after all!" He pulled out a small cake and put it in his haversack. "We are going to spend Christmas with the rats," he said gloomily, "so I won't cut the cake until tomorrow. By the way, Miller, have you any money on you?"

"About two and a half francs," I informed him.

"Well, here is another franc. Go over to the old girl's where we got the eggs and chips, and see if you can get wine for Christmas."

I took my water bottle and went over to the house. After I had knocked for some time, the door was opened.

"Bonjour, Monsieur", the old lady beamed at me.

"Avez-vous some vin blanc?" I stammered awkwardly.

"Oui," she said quickly in a low voice, and put her finger to her mouth while she mumbled something about a gendarme.

I entered and sat down. She went down to the cellar and returned with a pitcher of wine. After filling my water bottle, she poured some wine in a glass and handed it to me. I drank and asked how much I owed. Two and a half francs – I paid the amount. And thanking her as well as I was able, I took my leave.

We had our supper, and then set out for the front, following the same route we had traversed so many times. The night was very quiet. Occasionally the loud boom of a gun disturbed the solitude, and the swish of a shell as it sailed overhead.

About nine o'clock we arrived at the front. This time our company was stationed in the front line trench. Ted, Sneezigs and I were allotted a small dugout; it was a very flimsy structure, which was built up with sandbags and had a corrugated iron sheet over the top to keep out the rain.

While we were inspecting our new home, Ted remarked: "Well, there is one thing about it; they can't bury us alive in here anyway."

"No", I said. "They can only blow us out of here; then bury us."

Ted and I were ordered on night duty. We changed at 11:00 p.m. I took up my position on the firing step, watching; Ted sat below. We waited for some time. The night was very dark, only a few stars were visible. Everything was quiet, still as death. One would scarce have known that there was a war on, had it not been for the occasional flares lighting up the desolate strip of No Man's Land. But I knew there was no respite; even though everything was so unnaturally quiet. The fates of nations were at stake; to the world the war was too important to stop, even on Christmas Eve. All across France and Belgium, stretched that opposing line of trenches, where millions of men, from their latent positions, were warily watching and waiting with ready rifles. Thousands of field guns, camouflaged from view, were at had; and gunners were anxiously waiting for signals to release their deadly charges. Motor lorries, in endless trains, were running to and fro bringing up ammunition and supplies. Somewhere, far behind the line, generals were discussing and planning new maneuvers and juggling the destinies of thousands of soldiers; telephones were buzzing in active communication; and runners were rushing post-haste from headquarters to headquarters, carrying dispatches. And above it all, was the giant system of intrigue between the nations.   It was a labyrinthine problem, far beyond the understanding of a common soldier.

"I am going back to the dugout for a while," Ted said suddenly and went on down the trench.

I leaned against the side of the trench and watched the stars. My soul was filled with sadness. This was a fine way to spend Christmas Eve! Instead of having a cozy fire and a Christmas tree, here I was, out in the trenches, cold and numb, standing guard. No doubt the German sentries felt the same.

Suddenly I startled! I thought I heard the sound of music. I strained my ears and heard it again. It must have come from our support line; but no, there it was again – coming over from the German front line. I listened attentively and could hear the music was very soft; then it became a little louder, and I recognized the quaint, old melody of the Christmas hymn, "Silent Night, Holy Night". I stood very still, listening to the divine strains, which were wafted gently toward me; and I wondered whether the poor fellow over there, while playing, was thinking of his home and mother.

A gun boomed behind our line. A 9.2 went screeching overhead, and landed far behind the German line. This was war. While the German soldier over there – no doubt as miserable as I – was playing a hymn of solemn devotion to our Lord, Death yet stalked around us.

All was still. The faint chords again drifted through the night air. The music gradually became louder – it was now coming from our old organ at home and was softly blended with my mother's voice as she sang "Stille Nacht, Heilige Nacht…" Slowly the song and music died away, and mother turned to us. Joy and gladness radiated from her face; and the whole room was filled with Christmas spirit. Then we slowly knelt down, and my mother recited the Lord's Prayer. My heart was filled with divine thoughts and devotion.   Then the tree was brought in, a poplar sapling that my father had cut out of the bush, with green-fringed paper wrapped around the boughs to resemble a real Christmas tree – and a real one it was.   Candles were placed on the branches and lighted.   My mother brought in the presents and placed them around the bottom, with instructions that they were not to be opened until next morning. Then we all began to eat nuts and candies and oranges. I could hear the joyful laughter of my sisters, as they cracked open the nuts to see what they contained. Our little baby sister was crawling around on the floor, pointing at the lighted tree and gurgling in ecstasy. Oh, what a time we were having!....

I was startled. Someone was pulling my greatcoat.

"Hey, wake up." I heard Ted's voice, "or you'll be shot at sunrise for sleeping while on duty."

A stab shot through my breast when I realized my surroundings.

"What time is it?" I stammered.

"It's after one," said Ted. "You've been here over two hours. The officer has made the nightly round; it is a wonder that he didn't stop here and have you arrested. How long have you been sleeping anyway?"

"I wasn't sleeping," I protested. "I was waiting for you to come and was listening to the some music from over there."

"Music in the German line? Well, I guess those fellows are celebrating too. I hope they don't get too friendly and throw us over some bombs for Christmas presents." Ted chuckled happily. "By the way," he added, "J.C. is over here and he has a bottle of Scotch. I am sorry I did not come back, but I shall stay here and keep watch, and you can go on down."

"Don't fall asleep and let yourself be captured." I smiled at him as I turned to go.

"Don't worry about this kid," he grinned. "They'll never catch me as long as I have these long legs!"

"Well, good luck," I called back to him as I turned the corner and approached our dugout.

When I entered, J.C. and Sneezigs were talking and laughing.

"Good old Miller!" cried J.C. happily when he saw me. "Here take a good drink and make yourself at home. We have lots of eats - and drinks, too."

He pulled out a square bottle, which was half full of whisky, and set it on the ground before me. I was not in the mood for a merry party, but for the sake of J.C.'s feelings I took a small drink.

"Ted left some cake for you," said J.C.

"And have some tea and yam," added Sneezigs, reaching into his pack and pulling out a full tin of apple and plum jam.

"Where did you get that from?" I asked him.

"I went over to the quartermaster's store, before we left Etrun, and when he wasn't looking I took it," he answered boastfully.

J.C. started to laugh. "Are you still as fond of jam as ever? You know, every time I see you Sneezigs, your face resembles a tin of jam more and more."

There was a terrific explosion outside. We rushed out and saw that a large shell had landed near battalion headquarters. Ted was standing on the firing step, and when he saw us, he called: "Never mind fellows, that was only a Christmas message for Colonel Andrews."

J.C. left us with a "Merry Christmas" and I went back on duty.

"Be Careful, Miller" Ted warned. "There is a sniper around here somewhere. Better keep your head down, because he sent one bullet so darn close to me that the air pressure almost knocked me over."

I picked up two large pieces of chalk and placed them close together on top of the trench, leaving a small aperture to look through; and standing behind this improvised shield, I watched No Man's Land.

My thoughts drifted back to home – sweet, adorable home – filled with cheer, happiness and love. It was less than a year since I had been there, yet it seemed so strangely remote in the past. In contrast with my dreadful surroundings, that memory was vividly beautiful; it appeared as in a dream – a dream of many-colored visions that thrilled my blood and filled my heart with wonder. Oh what a strange sweet moment! It was that moment which was so dear to the lonely soldier on watch, when fanciful thoughts of the past dwelled in his mind as in the mind of a child. And that was almost all he had to look forward to – only those moments in the sacred hall of memory to nourish his aching heart.

I was still thinking of home and loved ones when faint streaks began to illuminate the eastern sky; and I realized that my watch was over – it was Christmas morn.

Christmas morning dawned with a heavy mist hanging over the trench. The air was cold. I felt numb to the bone and went to the dugout for something warm to eat.

"Merry Christmas, Miller," cried Ted.

"Same to you and many of them!" I returned.

"Well," he yawned. "I wonder where we shall be spending Christmas next year."

"Don't think about it. We are living only from one minute to another. Who knows if we shall see another Christmas?"

"I am not so darn anxious to see another one like this."

What a Christmas! I gazed around and was aware of the contrast between this and the Christmas back home. There the fields would be covered with clean snow; there would be a frosty tang in the air; one would go out sleigh riding across the fields – the tinkle of the sleigh bells was music to the ears, at home. Then there would be church – the message of good tidings: 'Rejoice! Our Christ has come!' But here there was nothing but mud and slush – with grim death overlooking all. Some of the boys were standing guard: others, half dozing in their dugouts. Every face, pale, with unsmiling lips and prematurely furrowed brow, was clouded with sadness. Memories of other days were foremost in every mind.

The following days were like a horrible nightmare – shells and more shells, a raging fury that gradually turned our trench into a veritable shambles. The earth heaved and groaned. Our bodies grew limp, inanimate, under the overpowering strain of the storm of death and destruction. At times the terrible roar was so intense that it seemed like a heavy blanket of silence floating invisibly about, enveloping and choking up sound, color, feeling – everything. And those deadly cylinders, the products of science, kept coming through the air like streaks of lightening. If only that accursed, invisible science, which was crushing our lives from us, would have taken shape, approached us as a tangible body, a live monster that one could have seen and grappled with – we would have flung ourselves at its neck and torn it to pieces. But this way – it was maddening! We had to remain at our posts, our nerveless yet operative bodies governed only by our sensory powers, which were gradually being developed to the efficiency of those of predatory animals.

There were gloomy hours during which my mind refused to follow the accepted grooves and channels. Prejudices were cast aside, and an attempt was made to discover the motives behind the acts. A rebellious feeling arose against the unfair principles of war. After all, what was war? A sanguinary, hate-filled struggle in which millions of hungry men, filled with a patriotic zeal often inspired by the agencies of greed, were fighting against an enemy whom, hitherto, they had never seen, and with whom they had no personal quarrel. All the diabolical inventions that could be designed and produced by the intricate art called science, were used to annihilate, in a wholesale manner, men, the highest form of God's creation: and they called it Divine Justice! There had been O'Reilly, the American, who had been a graduate in science. He had learned the laws of science; he and understood the mysterious chemical action of an explosion; yet, what had it availed him, his scientific knowledge? He was, as Ted expressed it, pushing up the daisies. He was dead, destroyed by the very science he had tried to master. The hopeless ness of it was appalling. The lives of men were governed by the very prejudices which men pretended to hate. Man was being destroyed by the works of man: where, oh where, was the world going?

There were awful hours during which my sight reached into the void deep beyond the horizon of worldly things; and I was alone with the universe and held communion with it as one mysterious presence with another. There, after the infinite hope of life after death, lay a promise. My soul would go on forever, above all this worldly contention, strife, war, death; seeking in another sphere, tranquility and rest. Then came the unanswerable questions. What was I? – this body, these faculties, this life of mine – what were they? I tried to reason amid the thundering din of explosions. In ordinary life my body could not have endured all this terrible suffering; here it was only my mind that still endured. My body was nothing, only an outer shell for my soul to creep into and seek refuge, whose existence was but ephemeral, born only to suffer and die. Education, Obligation, Ethics – all were in vain; men were born, lived, learned and died on the battlefield, torn to pieces by a shrapnel shell or a sniper's bullet. And yet there was Love. Could I call that vain also? I could not say. I did not know. Shell fell all around the trench, thundering, roaring. Involuntarily I ducked every time one landed near me. It was an instinct born of the desire to live. And yet I tried to reason that it would as well to die and leave it all – would not this be preferable to living and enduring the sufferings of this world? But there was my home, my loved ones – could I willingly part from these? Life! Life! Life! Was it really worthwhile? I could not judge. I could not think. It was beyond my grasp.

At last the shelling died down, and we were able to retire to our dugouts. For several days my body remained numb and cold after the hardships I had undergone. Cold spasms of shivering seized me, sending me into fits of desperation. Weary and exhausted as I was, I could not calm myself to enjoy a moment of peaceful slumber.

A fresh battalion arrived, and we went back to Etrun. After a day at Etrun, we started off for our long-promised rest. The sun was shining brightly; there was a light covering of snow on the ground, and the air was cold.

As we gradually drew away from Etrun, smiles began to radiate from the happy faces around me. Every step was taking us farther away from the terrible front. Six weeks rest – what a Heaven of bliss for a weary, shell-shocked, soldier!

Chapter 10

Canadian Artillery "Bringing up the guns" at Vimy Ridge

It was dark when the battalion arrived at a small village. The billeting party, which had gone ahead to procure quarters, met us on the outskirts of the village to guide the various platoons to their billets. Some were fortunate enough to get rooms in private homes; others had to occupy barns. Our platoon suffered the latter fate. Sergeant Ribbons led us into a farmyard; and pointing to a barn on the right, he motioned us to occupy it.

I went in quickly to get a good place and found Ted already there, holding a place in a corner with lots of hay to lie on. We removed our equipment and hung it on the pegs, which were driven into the wall to hang harness on. Ted and I decided to sleep together, because it was quite cold, and our barn was not very weatherproof.

After making a nice bed in the hay, we went out to get another issue of blankets. We received a blanket each and a brazier. On the way back to the barn we saw a sign in the window: "EGGS, CHIPS, COFFEE".

"They are more up to date here," remarked Ted. "Let's go in and see what we can get."

"Don't forget that we spent the last of our money at Etrun," I reminded him.

"Oh well, maybe we can borrow enough for a feed."

When we reached our quarters, Ted went out to borrow some money. He returned in a few minutes, a triumphant look on his face.

"How is this for a meal of eggs and chips?" he grinned at me, holding up five francs.

"No danger of you ever starving" I commented as we left the barn and made our way to the house.

A young woman of about twenty-five opened the door for us. She could speak a little broken English, which made us feel at ease.

"Eggs, chips and coffee, Madame," ordered Ted.

"Ze eggs cost mooch money, Messieurs."

"How much do you want for your eggs?" asked Ted. "You know we are almost broke."

"One egg for one-half franc," she replied.

"How many do you want?" Ted turned to me.

"We shall have to go easy," I said. "We haven't much money, you know. Two eggs will do for me."

"Two eggs each then; but if I had the money, I would order a dozen for myself."

We sat down beside the stove and watched the chips frying, while the young woman busied herself about the kitchen. Ted kept eyeing her up and after a few moments, asked casually: "Are you married?"

"Oui, oui, Monsieur" was the proud reply. "I get married before the war come. My man in French army. Sometime he come home to see me."

This news disappointed Ted, and he became silent.

"How do you like Canadian soldiers?" I asked.

"Canadian soldat tres bien, lotsa money. English soldat no money, yes – no?"

The eggs and chips were ready, and we set to. After our meal we went back to our quarters.

The night turned very cold. Ted and I cuddled up under our blankets and greatcoats, but we could not get warm; - the wind was blowing in through the cracks in the bricks and under the rafters. We got up and lighted a fire in the brazier. There was no vent for the smoke to pass out, however, and the barn was soon full of it. The rafters were quite high, though, so we did not entirely suffocate.

Some of the fellows rolled out of their pallets of hay and gathered around the brazier to warm up. We put water on for tea, and when the coals became red, we made toast, sticking slices of bread on the ends of our bayonets and holding them over the hot coals until they were a nice golden brown. Some of us stayed up all night, standing around the open brazier, eating toast and drinking tea. When daylight filtered into the barn, we were covered with soot and looked like chimney sweeps.

This was payday. An hour after we received our allowance there wasn't an egg left in the entire village.

That afternoon I began to get the shivers again, and my legs ached. Feeling cold and miserable, I went to bed. The pains increased, and my legs began to swell.

Next morning I reported sick, but was unable to get up to attend the sick parade. All day and night I tossed about restlessly. It was very cold, and I thought I should freeze to death. Ted kept the fire burning, but I could feel no heat.

On the second morning, the M.O. came around to examine me. He took my temperature and found it normal.

"We can't send you to hospital, because you have no temperature" he said and went out.

A few minutes later the medical orderly appeared with some pills. "Take four white ones and one brown one, every four hours."

After the medical orderly had left, Ted examined the pills and exclaimed: The white ones are O.K. Miller; but don't take any of the brown ones! They are No. 9's and you know what that means at night."

By dark I had taken twelve of the tablets, but I felt no effects from them. Ted brought me a mess-tin of tea. I tasted rum in it and could only take a mouthful; it turned my stomach.

The next day the M.O. came around again and examined my legs. They were badly swollen; and as he moved them around, I suffered excruciating pains in the joints and muscles. He brought me a bottle of liniment and some more pills.

Ted was roaring mad. After the M.O. had left, he cursed the whole army staff, from the highest commander down to our M.O. for not moving me to a decent place.

In the days following I ate very little and became so weak that I could not sit up. My legs throbbed with a dull pain and I had to lie still; it was agony to lie there in a helpless, crippled condition, hour after hour, day after day. Ted attended me constantly, bringing me some tea every little while and keeping the covers around me; he tried to relieve my distress by telling me funny stories.

One-day Skinny came to see me. "How are you Miller? He cried, grasping my hand warmly.

"Hello skinny. When did you get here?" I said, glad to see my young friend again.

"The transports just arrived. I heard you were sick, so I beat it right down here."

His presence cheered me considerably. I enjoyed hearing his pleasant voice again. We talked continually until it was time for him to go. I felt better and hoped to be able to join my old comrades soon.

Skinny came to see me everyday, and brought me a piece of cake, or some chocolate bars on every visit. He and Ted tried to induce me to eat, but no matter how I tried, I could not.

One day Skinny came into the barn – heartbroken. He had received a letter from home: his sweetheart at home had died. My heart went out to him. I tried to console him in his grief, but he stared unseeingly ahead; and I realized that he would not get over his loss for a long time, if ever.

The next few days I realized that the pain in my legs was lessening, and that the swelling was going down. One morning I awoke feeling much better, and tried to get up. I managed to get on my feet for a few moments, only to fall back on my bed again. I was yet too weak to stand, but the thought that I should soon be up inspired me with joy.

Orders came to move to another village; a different battalion was coming in to occupy our quarters. The boys packed all my things and loaded them upon a limber. I got up and found that I could stagger around. Ted helped me to a wagon and lifted me up.

The transports followed the battalion all the way. There was an inch of snow on the ground, and it was bitterly cold. I was afraid my legs might become affected again and kept rubbing them to keep up the circulation.

At dusk we arrived at a large village south of Lillers. I climbed off the wagon and started to look for my company and learned that we were billeted in another barn. On entering the barn, I found Ted had already made a bed for me.

"What day is this?" I asked.

"This is the 21st of January" Skinny informed me.

"The 21st?" I gasped. "Then I have been laid up for eighteen days?"

"Eighteen days is right," laughed Ted, "but by the looks of your beard, one would think you were laid up for eighteen weeks."

"How about a little cognac?" I suggested.

"I am broke," said Ted.

I pulled out my last pay and gave Ted money to get some brandy. He went out and remained away for a long time. Finally he returned.

"I couldn't get any brandy, but I found something better." He grinned and handed me a small bottle of rum.

"Army issue!" I said, greatly surprised. "Where did you get it?"

"Never mind where I got it. I had to do a lot of talking before he loosened up."

Ted heated some water and made me a hot drink. After I had downed it, I covered myself with blankets and began to perspire. This was the first warmth I enjoyed in three weeks; however the "cooties" livened up too, and nearly devoured me.

Next morning I awoke feeling fine. J.C. (who was the company barber) came around with his razor and gave me a shave. Ted heated some water and I enjoyed a good wash. I felt like a new man.

My appetite returned and I began to eat. Every day I became stronger, and soon was my old self again.

One evening, J.C. came into the barn. By the silly grin on his face and the happy sparkle in his eyes, it was evident that he had been imbibing at one of the estaminets.

He called me aside, and his demeanor suddenly changed to one of sobriety. "Say, Miller, have you any extra blankets?"

"Yes, J.C. I have a couple of extra ones."

"I'd like to borrow one from you. You know, I almost freeze to death these cold nights." He was actually shivering. I rolled up a blanket, wondering what new, wily scheme was afoot – I knew J.C. too well to believe him.

"Here you are J.C. This will cost you a drink of cognac."

"Right with me," he smiled and went out.

In about half an hour he returned, minus the blanket, but with additional signs of good cheer about him. "How are chances for another blanket?"

"What did you do with the other one?" I countered.

"Never mind the other one." There was a crafty gleam in his eyes as he moved closer. "Roll up another blanket and come with me. I'll let you in on a good deal."

I was determined not to be a goat. "What's the deal J.C.? You know I can't risk losing another blanket."

He grew impatient. "I'll tell you later. But hurry up. Stick a blanket under your greatcoat and come along."

At any rate, I thought, it was worth another blanket to find out what J.C. had up his sleeve. I put on my greatcoat and slipped a blanket inside.

We went along the street until we came to a large estaminet. J.C. led the way around the building, through the back yard and up to the back door.

"You stay here, Miller," he whispered. "I'll go in first to see if the coast is clear."

He knocked lightly at the door, and a moment later disappeared inside. This was a shady business, I realized. I was debating whether to turn back, or not, when the door opened and J.C. bade me to enter.

The room was part of the living quarters back of the estaminet. An old lady sat at a table in one corner, eating bread and corned beef. In another corner there were about fifty army blankets, neatly piled up, and many cans of corned beef. From the front of the building came strains of accordion music and sounds of feet shuffling about on the floor.

"Show her your blanket," said J.C.

I pulled it out and handed it over. After examining it closely – I wondered why – she made an offer. "Cinq francs, Monsieur."

"She wants to know if you'll take five francs for it" said J.C.

"I know" said I, "but what is it, cash or trade?"

"Trade. You can have anything from eggs and chips to army rum."

"That's fine. We'll start with rum and coffee."

We were having our second round, when a light tap sounded at the door. The old lady startled for a moment, undecided whether to send us out or keep us inside. Finally she ushered us into an adjoining room and locked the door. The room was in darkness. I lit a match and was surprised to find that it was a bedroom.

J.C., who was listening at the keyhole, whispered to me: I can hear a familiar voice."

I put my ear to the door and listened. It sounded like Sneezigs. I nudged J.C. "I think its Sneezigs."

"That's who I think it is, but we better make sure; it might be some high mucky-muck nosing around."

We listened carefully for a few moments. I heard the word "Petrol" than later "deux francs".

"It's Sneezigs," J.C. whispered to me; "I'll call his name". And before I had a chance to dissuade him, he shouted through the keyhole: "Sneezigs! Open the door and let us in on the deal."

All was quiet for a moment, and then we heard Sneezigs' voice, very timid and quavering. "Is that you, Yay See?"

"Yes," returned J.C. "And Miller is in here too. Open the door."

Steps approached the door, and the knob rattled. But the door was locked.

Open la porte, Madame," said Sneezigs. "Come on, tout sweet! Ma comrade in there."

The old lady came up and inserted the key. The door opened, and we stumbled out.

"What are you peddling?" asked J.C.

"I yust stole two cans of petrol from a motor lorry that stopped out there."

We sat down and enjoyed a few more rounds of rum and coffee. Than Sneezigs suggested that we have some eggs and chips. The old lady put on the potatoes to fry, and went into another room to get the eggs. J.C. got up quickly and tiptoed across the room to the pile of blankets. Taking two blankets, he went to the door, opened it noiselessly and tossed the blankets outside. He was back in his chair before the old lady returned. Sneezigs and I had to avoid each other's eyes to keep from laughing. J.C. put on his poker face and started a casual conversation.

After we had eaten the eggs and chips, J.C. turned to Madame. "Vous desire another blanket?"

"Oui, oui" she nodded.

"Deux blankets", said J.C.: and winking at us, he went out. About ten minutes later he returned, carrying two blankets. "Un bottle of champagne, et un bottle of vin blanc, Madame," he ordered.

While she was down in the cellar, getting the wine and champagne, J.C. purloined two more blankets. This performance was repeated until we discovered that we had reached the limits of our capacity. In addition, we had several bottles of champagne to our credit. Picking up these, we asked Madame to show us into the estaminet.

After going through two rooms and along a corridor, we found ourselves in the estaminet. The large room was crowed with soldiers and women, dancing merrily. In one corner sat two Frenchmen playing accordions.

We handed our bottles to the barmaid and asked her to keep them for us.

"How about a dance, Sneezigs," I suggested.

"Fine, but you go first," he said.

"Who would you like me to take?"

"That little, fat one." He pointed to a young girl sitting at a table with a French poilu.

"No, not her," I laughed. "She might be engaged to that fellow, and I don't want to start a row."

"What girl do you mean?" asked J.C. I pointed her out to him.

"Oh, that's easy. If you fellows are afraid to take a chance with the young lady, I'll show you how. Just a minute till I have another drink to stop this hiccup."

We each had another drink of champagne. Then J.C. made a beeline towards the charming young lady. He bowed very gracefully. Much to the displeasure of the poilu, the young lady accepted J.C and away they danced! J.C. was swinging here around like a whirlwind. The other dancers soon dropped out and formed a circle around them, to watch. The musicians played faster and faster. Suddenly J.C.'s foot slipped, and he fell with his partner landing on top of him. The wooden clogs flew from her feet and clattered across the floor. Everyone roared with laughter. The young poilu rushed up angrily, grabbed his girl, bawled her out in one long string of French, and started to drag her to the door. J.C. scrambled to his feet and retrieved her clogs. He handed them to her with a low bow, and said: "Excusez me, Mademoiselle." She accepted them somewhat sheepishly, and with her angry escort, went out.

The three of us went up to the bar for another drink. J.C. had lost his hiccup in the dance, and was quite heated up.

The music started up, and we went for partners. It was a gay night. We had numerous drinks of champagne, and danced everything from a fast polka to a twirl-and-dip. I remembered nothing after the twirl-and-dip.

I awoke to find myself lying in our barn, with J.C.'s legs across my face. Sneezigs was sitting up beside me, eating bread and jam. I pushed J.C.'s legs away, and asked Sneezigs what time it was.

"Eight o'clock. Better hurry or you will not get breakfast."

J.C. was sound asleep and snoring loudly. Beside him lay two blankets.

"Where did the blankets come from?" I asked Sneezigs. He started to laugh. "You are a fine bunch to go out with. Don't you know what happened last night?"

"I guess I drank too much champagne to remember. Tell me."

"Well, when we were ready to go home, you fellows wanted to steal some more blankets. So I yust took the old lady for a dance, and you and Yay See went back and stole four more blankets."

"Four, did you say? I can see only two."

"You are blind, Miller. Can't you see the two blankets that you are lying on?"

"And you got nothing out of the deal?" I asked.

He grinned at me and opened his pack. Inside were three tins of apple and plum jam.

The battalion moved on to the village of Burbure, situated within a few miles of Lillers. Our rest was gradually drawing to an end. We had been at Burbure less than a week, when orders came to move nearer to the front.

We arrived in Chateau de la Haie, and our company was billeted in the attic of a large building. After the cold barns we had occupied, this, the poorest part of the building, seemed a luxury.

New reinforcements arrived, lively young fellows, always talking and laughing. I could well remember when we had felt that way, but it seemed so long ago.

Ted turned to me and sighed. "Look at the innocent faces of those young fellows. They have no idea what they are up against."

"Yes," I agreed. "In about six months, if there are any of them left, there will be a great change."

We moved on towards Villers au Bois, following an old stone road. Again we were drawing deeper into the war zone, and the older men grew silent. To the new fellows, the terrible scenes of destruction were of great interest; and there were many exclamations of wonder. We reached a number of corrugated iron huts, and made camp.

The first few days were spent on working parties, carrying bombs, Stokes shells, and timbers from the munitions dump at Neuville St. Vaast into the lines, in preparation for the Vimy Ridge drive. Then we were detailed by night to carry chalk out of a tunnel leading into No Man's Land. After a week of this, we worked for a few nights, carrying gun cotton into the tunnel.

One day, towards the end of February, we were told to prepare to move to the front. A terror ran through my body as I thought of what we should have to go through again. We moved into the front line that night. The trenches were in poor condition; there were not dugouts at all, only a few funk holes covered with iron sheets. There was no other choice, and we had to make the best of it.

Fortunately for us, the front was very quiet. We were able to move around in the trench, unmolested by the enemy. It began to rain though, and the trench was soon transformed into a sinkhole.

On the sixth night we were relieved and went back as far as Neuville St. Vaast. The place had suffered a severe shelling some time previous; everything was entirely demolished and large piles of bricks, glass and rafters were strewn about. The only shelters we had were the open cellars; and about twenty of us were ordered into one of these cellars.

It was cold and damp. We found an old stove among the debris, and after piling up some bricks and sheets of tin in one corner of the cellar, we moved the stove in. However, when it came to fuel, we were at a loss; there was nothing to burn. Ted and I went up in search of wood, but could not find any small sticks anywhere. The large wooden rafters were too heavy for us to carry.

We wandered off to the left and came upon a cemetery. A few shells had landed in the midst of the graves, and pieces of coffins and broken crosses were strewn about. I judged that some of the French soldiers that had fallen in 1915 were buried here.

"Here is some firewood!" exclaimed Ted.

I was shocked at the idea of using for firewood a cross that had once marked a grave. We could not dare to commit such a sacrilege.

"Let's go on," I remonstrated. "I don't like the idea of disturbing a man's last resting place."

"What's the matter with you?" laughed Ted. "We are freezing to death up here and must have a fire to warm us; those fellows down below are hot enough already."

He began to gather some of the broken crosses. I joined in. When we each had a large armful, we started back to our cellar. Some of the new fellows stared at us, horror-stricken at our awful deed.

Ted started to burn some of his love letters. After a lot of blowing, we got the fire going. We made Bovril and tea, which warmed us up, and sat around the fire until we went to sleep.

On the night following, we had little rest. Every night we were ordered on carrying parties, to carry more ammunition to the front. This lasted about two weeks. Night after night we kept stumbling about, heavily laden with shells and bombs. We became so used to it, that we mechanically followed the orders that were handed back from the head of the party: "Watch for wire overhead; wire underfoot: shell hole to the right; shell hole to the left." Sometimes we fell out for a few minutes rest. It was a heavy grind. To us, the older fellows, whom the war had taught to accept any hardship without a murmur, it was not so bad; we were more or less broken to it. But the new fellows complained bitterly – and they had reason. I overheard a conversation between two of them – "Next time I see the transport officer, I'm going to ask him for a horse collar."

"A horse collar? What shall you do with it?"

"Wear it."

"And how will that help?"

"Well, since they make a guy work like a horse, he may as well look like one."

I told Ted about it.

"That fellow is right," he said; "only he doesn't know that he is considered even less than a horse. The other day I heard that in valuing men and horses in this war, they consider a horse worth five times as much as a man."

"That reminds me that in calculating the average life of a man in the trenches, they found it to be only seven months."

"We'll get ours one of these days," he said grimly.

At last we received orders to move back to Burbure for rest. On arriving there, were billeted in the same barn as before. It was now late in March, and the weather was much milder.

We were ordered to train for the Vimy Ridge drive, which was rumored to come off soon. Every day we marched out to a large open field, which was mapped out with white tapelines to represent the trenches as Vimy Ridge. The officers pointed out to us the relative positions of our trenches, the German trenches, communications and support trenches, and machine gun posts, as shown by the tape on the ground before us. We were shown the exact point of the trench where we should go over; ahead of us we should find a large mine crater; we should go around the crater and on, up over the ridge until we reached La Folie Wood, which would be our objective. After the whole scheme had been thoroughly explained to us, we went back to our starting point and formed a line. At a given signal we started out, charging over the tapelines. We went around the imaginary mine crater; and on, up to our objective. This performance was repeated three times daily, until we were thoroughly trained. We knew the large tape map like a book, and executed our sham drive as precisely as if the advance were actually being pulled off. The date and hour of the advance were withheld form us.

The landlady, whose barn we were occupying, was very kind to J.C., Ted and me, allowing us to sit in her parlour every day when we were off duty. We bought a great deal of cognac and coffee from her, and she liked us for spending our money.

But J. C. had other interests as well – the daughter, Amelia, a very pretty girl of eighteen. Having been appointed to the menial position of officer's batman, J.C. was excused from drill and had much spare time, which, however, was not wasted, for every time Ted and I went over to the house, we found J.C. there, drinking free cognac and coffee, with Amelia on his knee. It was obvious that she was falling in love with him.

Ted and I decided that things were going too far. We could not stand by and see our dear comrade fall victim to that ancient enemy of man – love: and there was Amelia to be taken into consideration too. Yes, we decided, we must do something before it was too late. But how could we save the situations? We held lengthy conferences and at last struck upon a plan: we should tell Amelia that J.C. was already married.

One day we saw J.C. walking down the street, carrying his barber's kit. The coast was clear. Ted and I went over to the house to carry out what we considered to be our duty.

After Amelia had served us with cognac and coffee, Ted asked her if she were going to marry J.C.

"Oui, oui," she cried proudly. "We get married; go to Canada, me have beaucoup piccaninny."

Ted and I roared with laughter.

"Why, your finance is already married," Ted said soberly; "and has a squaw with eight children in Manitoba."

"No, no!" she cried, alarmed. "You big lie! You no bon!" and slapped Ted's face.

"All right then, if you don't believe me, ask Miller," said Ted seriously.

I corroborated Ted's story. She blushed furiously and with a hurt expression on her face, ran from us into another room.

"I think we made a botch of it, Ted," I said.

"Yes. I didn't think she would take it that way. You know Miller, women are funny." I think I agreed with him.

Next morning, as Ted and I were eating breakfast, J.C. came storming into the barn.

"Say, what the devil have you fellows been spreading around here about me?" he cried angrily.

"Why, what's the matter J.C.? Have you been discharged?" said Ted innocently.

"Discharged, my eye! But what's the idea of telling Amelia that I am married? Yesterday, after you fellows left she called me in and raised the dickens. I had a heck of a time making her believe that you guys are a pair of first class liars."

Ted and I burst out laughing, and J.C. got over his bad humor.

One day, orders came to pack: the battalion would move up closer to the line. Ted and I went over to the house to say good-bye to Amelia and her mother. On entering, we found J.C. there, with his arms around Amelia. Evidently he had told her the news, for she was sobbing on his shoulder. We said good-bye hurriedly and waited for J.C., who glared at us for staying. He had a hard time tearing himself away, and had to promise faithfully that he would come to see her again if he got through alive.

We landed at Villers au Bois and occupied the iron huts that night. Next afternoon we were ordered to the front. We set out along the main road from Villers au Bois to Mont St. Eloi. The traffic along the road was so congested that we could hardly get through. There were loaded ammunition wagons going up the line and empty one coming back; battalions of men were going in and small parties coming out; officers were riding up and down.

It was dusk when we arrived at the front line. We moved to our positions, as had been shown us on the tape map we had studied at

Burbure. Ahead of us was Vimy Ridge, held by the enemy. We could discern the rim of the mine crater and other objects that were to guide the drive.

Every man's nerves were keyed up with excitement and fear at the thought of the oncoming drive. We did not know when it would come off and the suspense was awful. Every hour we dreaded the terrible news – it was time to face death!

Chapter 11

The Canadians attack at Vimy Ridge - Ontario Archives

At 4:00 A.M. on the morning of April 9th, 1917, we were ordered to stand to. We should go over the top a little after daylight: 5:30 would be the zero hour. We lined up in silence along the trench below the ridge, while the officers went up and down giving final instructions.

Every face was drawn and pale, and hands trembled as they nervously clutched the rifles. I looked around for Ted, and saw him standing down the line, between two new men; with open mouth and blinking eyes he stared ahead of him. I stood between Sergeant Ribbons and a new man.

Ribbons was very restless. Turning to me, he said, "Miller, I have a premonition that something will happen to me this trip. If I get hit, take my bandage and fix me up; a fellow would bleed to death before the first aid men come along."

I tried to cheer him: "don't worry at all, Ribbons. I think we all feel that way. We can only pray to God for protection."

"Yes, but sometimes God sees fit for us to die. And I can feel it coming – my sands of life are slipping fast." His face was ghastly, there was a queer light in his eyes – it was the unmistakable sign of death.

The sergeant major came down the line, giving us each a drink of rum.

"How do you feel now?" I asked Ribbons.

"I wish it were all over," he answered in a sickly voice. "It just seems as if my minutes were numbered." I felt sorry for him. He was such a friend.

Dawn was breaking. A dull red was showing in the eastern sky. Heavy clouds were hanging over the trenches, dark and gloomy, foreboding the imminent death. It grew lighter; the glow in the east became a fiery red, distending its soft rays on the masses overhead as if by its radiance it wished to overshadow the clouds of doom. Sweet, kind nature seemed so sympathetic. But what could the sympathy of nature avail us? Nothing could save us from the tide of battle which was about to sweep us ahead into the sea of death. And, light of morning! Thy soft glow, bright and comforting, would yet light up the path to the grave.

I gazed up into the eastern sky, and a heavy feeling clutched my heart:

"O light of Dawn! Thy transient wave.

Illumes but the path to the grave.

The bugle soon will sound the call;

Our lives we'll leave in Death's dark hall –

I and many comrades brave."

I leaned against the side of the trench and breathed a silent prayer to Heaven:

"O restless soul! Thy chafing cease;

Resign thyself to God's release.

So will I fight till my last breath,

And when I am embraced by Death,

May God give eternal peace!"

My nerves grew calmer, but my heart still pounded within my breast. A twelve-inch howitzer boomed behind me. Then, like a shot, our whole artillery opened up. I turned and beheld a spectacle which I shall never forget. I could see the flashes, long streams of fire like hungry tongues, spurting from each muzzle up into the sky.

The shells were landing like hail stones in No Man's Land, the earth quaked steadily from the force of the explosions; and flashes of bursting shrapnel shells lighted up the surroundings in a maze of burning light.

The barrage lifted, and our officers shouted: "over!" We were out of the trench like a flash and moved forward behind the heavy barrage. I kept close to Ribbons. As we were rounding the mine crater, an overhead shrapnel shell exploded above us; Ribbons staggered and fell. I stopped to see where he had been hit; but an officer, coming up from behind, ordered me to move on and leave Ribbons for the stretcher-bearers.

An enemy machine gun opened up on the right; another on the left. Our fellows were falling line ninepins. We dropped into shell holes; and running from shell hole to shell hole, we reached the machine gun post and silenced them with bombs.

German prisoners were coming forward in small parties. One young German came towards me, crying like a child and mumbling "Kamerad, kamerad, nicht schieszen!" I asked him in German why he was crying. He said their officers had told them that if they surrendered they would be killed by the English. I told him it was untrue and ordered to keep on going back.

A drizzling rain had descended upon us. The ground was becoming slippery. We continued up over the ridge until we reached our objective. The Germans were running down the slope ahead of us toward a railway embankment in the flat. A fresh battalion coming from behind leapfrogged us and followed up the German retreat.

We were to entrench ourselves at this point, but as there was an old German trench, we did not have to do much digging.

The air turned colder, and the rain turned to snow. Wet and shivering, we sat about in our newly constructed funk holes. All remained quiet until after dinner. Then the Germans began to shell us heavily, making a few direct hits and inflicting some casualties.

The heavy barrage moved to our left, and fell on La Folie Wood. At the same time the Germans counter-attacked the battalion that was holding the woods, but were repulsed.

I went down to the trench and found Ted sitting in a funk-hole eating bully beef and hardtack.

"Well, I see they didn't get you either." I said, approaching him.

He twisted his moustache at me with a grin and handed me a water bottle, an officer's water bottle containing rum.

"This is just what I need," I said, taking a drink. "But where the deuce did you get it?"

"I followed a captain over; and when the Germans started to sweep us with machine guns, I saw him fall into a shell hole. I dived in after him, to see if I could help him, but he was breathing his last. There was nothing I could do, so I took his water bottle and beat it."

The shelling died down in our lines, although those to the left of us in the woods were still getting it. It was getting late by this time so I dug myself a new funk hole and prepared for the night. I had scarcely settled myself when an officer appeared and order us to be ready to move back.

As soon as the fresh battalion arrived, we started back over the shell –torn ridge. The slope we had come up was now a terrible sight. Dead men lay everywhere. Our first aid men and German prisoners were still at work, carrying back the wounded. Some were blind and had to be led. I saw two wounded soldiers assisting a third around the shell holes; the three of them were staggering about piteously.

We landed at Villers au Bois at midnight and immediately crawled into the iron huts for some sleep.

Ted and I did not awaken until it was past noon. We decided that this was a convenient occasion to make a raid on the "cooties". We got some creolin, diluted it, and sprinkled it on our clothes.

"I hope to goodness that this stuff kills them all," said I.

"Aw heck, Miller," said Ted cheerfully, "we are not half lousy yet. I saw a big Scotchman the other day – he had nits in his eyebrows. Now that's what I call real lousy."

"Well, I don't envy the poor fellow."

Skinny and J.C. came along. "Hello," they greeted together. "You two old war horses back again, eh?"

"Yes, we are back again, safe and sound," I replied gratefully.

"How many did you kill this time?" inquired J.C.

"Over a thousand" Ted equivocated easily.

"A thousand!" exclaimed Skinny. "How could you mange to do that?"

"Oh that's easy," said Ted nonchalantly. "Just got a can of creolin – "

"You are nuts," J.C. broke in. "I wasn't talking about lice; I meant Germans."

"Oh, Germans? I didn't have to kill any. Sneezigs did all the work."

"Tell us about it," begged Skinny.

"Well, when we were going over, two German machine guns opened on us; and we crawled along from shell hole to shell hole to bomb them out. When we got close to one of them, Sneezigs threw a couple of bombs. He got up to see what damage he had done and one of the German gunners fired point-blank at him with a Luger. I saw Sneezigs spin around and drop into the shell hole. Then the German threw away his pistol and surrendered. Of course, I should have killed him, but I didn't have the heart to do it. I told him to beat it back to our line as fast as possible, or I'd give him about six inches of my bayonet. But poor Sneezigs did all the work. He put the machine gun out of commission. I told the officer about it, and I suppose Sneezigs will get a medal for his bravery."

"He deserves it," said J.C. "But where is he now?"

"He was hit in the arm and went back with the wounded," Ted explained.

"By the way, J.C., I see you have your equipment with you. Are you joining the ranks again?"

"Yes," he muttered. "Captain Bothwell was killed going over and I was told to report back to my company."

"Yes, I know," said Ted. "Here is his water bottle."

J.C.'s eyes opened wide at the sight of the water bottle, and he quickly reached for a drink. He threw it down, disappointed.

"Oh I'm sorry," grinned Ted. "I forgot to tell you that Miller and I just finished the last of it before you came, and it was real good rum too."

"Just my luck," J.C. grumbled bitterly.

"Cheer up, J.C." Ted comforted. "You can still fall back on your cordite stunt, you know."

"Yes, it works all right; but it nearly takes the top off my head every time I chew it."

Then I told the boys: "Ribbons – he is dead."

"Ribbons!"

"Yes, he went down in the drive."

The joking ceased. We were silent. What was there to say? Nothing. We had lost the best N.C.O. in the whole army. More than that: he had been a real friend. He had taken us up when we had been greenhorns; he had taught us how to take care of ourselves; it had been his instruction, admonition and steady guidance that had brought us through many a hard spot. Now he was gone. There was nothing to say.

Our battalion had lost heavily – over half the men, including many officers. We moved back a few miles to Camblain L'Abbe to be reinforced.

On arriving there that evening, we were in time to see a show given by the Third Divisional Concert Party (The Dumbbells). After we had been established in our billets, we went to see the Dumbbells. The show was a "scream" and we nearly brought the roof down with our roars of laughter.

While sitting there, watching the acts, I was really at rest. Yet it did not seem natural to see so many around me, at ease and enjoying themselves.

After the show ended, I realized that we were still in the war. As Ted and I were walking down the street, a gun boomed in the distance, thus reminding us of the stark reality of our position.

"Oh, I'm sick of it," Ted reflected bitterly. "I thought I was back at the Pantages in Winnipeg, with a little girl with blue eyes and corn-silk hair, beside me; but I woke up and found myself in this God-forsaken country."

"Let's go back to the billet and not think about those things," I muttered. "I'm fed up with everything too."

We received reinforcements next day, and on the days following we went on working parties to break in the new fellows. After a week of this, we were ordered back to the front. We set out in the afternoon, carrying bombs and extra rations as well as our regular equipment.

On reaching the ridge, we found that our line was now far ahead, on the other side of the railway embankment, in front of Mericourt. We followed down the slope for some distance, when about a dozen shells came over and landed all along the road. How fortunate we were to have escaped them! Some more shells landed around us and ahead, toward the railroad embankment. These were not high explosives, but burst with only a dull thud. Orders came from the front to don gas masks. We slipped on our masks and stumbled through the dense mist which had arisen from the exploding shells. We soon reached the railway embankment and were again in fresh air. C and D companies stopped here; A and B companies moved on to the front line, in front of Mericourt.

There was a shallow trench dug at the foot of the embankment, on the side away from the enemy. We were protected by the embankment and could only be injured by a direct hit, by a shell dropping vertically upon us.

The weather was quite mild now, and we did not mind the open-air quarters. Fritz was very quiet; sometimes, in the night, a few gas shells landed near us, but we did not suffer from then. High explosives were landing back of us, around an ammunition dump, which the Germans had been forced, to abandon during the drive; after much shelling, they finally succeeded in blowing it up.

Every day the sun shone brightly. We lay back in our trench, sunning ourselves and dozing. We spent many hours watching the aeroplanes fight overhead. Sometimes there were as many as thirty or forty planes engaged in aerial combat at one time. It was thrilling to watch them circle about and pepper one another with their machine guns. Some days we saw as many as six or seven planes come crashing down to the earth in flames. Once we saw a red Fokker come swooping down out of the clouds, darting about like a pigeon hawk. Later we learned that is was Baron Von Richthoven the crack German ace.

There was a cracked-up German plane, which had crashed before the drive, lying beside the embankment. Many of our fellows went over to it, to get souvenirs. They tore off the iron crosses and numbers; and some even ripped the canvas from the wings as removed parts of the fuselage to send home. When Ted, J.C. and I got there, the plane was completely dismantled; and we were obliged to remove the aluminum gas tank, the only movable part left on the wrecked skeleton. We cut it to pieces and made souvenir matchboxes. "Dad" Barker, the oldest man in our regiment, had a fine set of engraving tools and small files, and he would sit for hours, engraving our names, regimental numbers, and name of battalion on one side of the aluminum boxes, and the date and place on the other side.

In the early part of May, we moved up to the front line. The trenches were well dug and equipped with funk holes. Fortunately also there was no shelling and the front was very quiet. We slept by day and went on guard by night. It seemed more like rest than front line duty.

Everything remained calm and peaceful. The partridges were running about in great numbers, feeding in No Man's Land. Some of our fellows sniped at them and killed a few, but the officers soon put a stop to that. We lay back in our trench and watched the larks winging about high overhead. Their melodious singing filled our hearts with gladness.

One day Ted turned to me and said: "I wonder what brings the larks up here. Surely, if they had any brains they would fly back as far as Paris and stay there until the war is over."

"Yes, but they have no brains," I said. "And another reason is that they have been raised in No Man's Land. They have no fear of shells."

"That's all well and good – I agree with you there. But tell me, why weren't the first one's frightened away at the beginning of the war?"

"That's beyond me, Ted. Maybe God wished the little birds to sing for us every morning to cheer us up a bit."

"Do you really believe there is a God, Miller?"

"Yes," I responded. "I believe there is a God."

"But how can you prove it?"

"Well Ted, I'll tell you. Many times, when we were in a tight sport, I prayed to God for protection from the shells and bullets. It is what my mother taught me – to pray to God when I am in distress.

And he has answered my prayers, I know, else I shouldn't be here now."

Ted was silent and pensive.

"Didn't your mother teach you the same?" I ventured to ask.

His eyes were sad. He shook his head slowly. "She died when I was only five years old. I can hardly remember her."

He was thoughtful for a while, and then he said irrelevantly: "This is the kind of war I like."

Chapter 12

The view from Vimy ridge after its capture.

Notwithstanding the ever-present danger hanging over our heads, this duration of inactivity at the front was a pleasant redress. And our lease on life was further extended when, after it seemed that the action sure to follow this brooding quiet was almost imminent, we were relieved and went back to the reserve dugouts in La Folie Wood. Here we enjoyed a real rest. We lay around in the green underbrush, lazily sunning ourselves and daydreaming.

The big trees had been blasted to splinters. The short, broken stumps stood like statues, bearing evidence of the heavy shellfire that had swept over the woods. From one of them protruded a whiz-bang shell which had struck the stump and penetrated through the middle without exploding.

From our unrivalled position on Vimy Ridge, we had a wide view ahead. The railroad, coming along the flat from the south, deviated to the right at a point about a mile away, crossing the flat on its way north to Lens. Some three or four miles ahead, situated in the present No Man's Land, was Mericourt; and a little to the left of it Avion. On the right, scattered over the flat which stretched for miles east of the ridge, were many villages in ruin, laying in marked contrast with the green country surrounding them. I brought forth a pair of German field glasses, which I had picked up in the Vimy scrap of April 9th, and surveyed the landscape. My range of vision went far beyond the German line. Over there chimneys were smoking, and vehicles moved about peacefully. I saw a number of collieries in operation, and a small steam locomotive, with a few cars shunting around.

One day, as I sat with my back to the stump, enjoying the warm June sunshine, I heard some twigs crackling behind me. I turned and saw a man wriggling down the slope, holding his helmet up in front of him. When his face turned up, to my surprise I saw it was Ted.

"What did you find?" I asked as he drew near.

He held up his helmet and grinned. In a few minutes he was beside me. His helmet was full of nice, juicy strawberries.

"Where did you find them?"

"Over there, along the ridge," he pointed. "You can pick a hatful in about ten minutes."

I rushed to the dugout and told J.C. to take his mess-tin and come with me to pick strawberries. We started off on all fours, up the side of the ridge.

"Be careful!" Ted shouted after us. "Fritz has an observation balloon up, and can see every move we make up here."

We crawled up the hill, over shell holes and entanglements, until we came to the strawberry patch. Our mess-tins soon filled, we started back to our dugout.

Ted was eating mashed strawberries and bread when we entered. I began to mash mine up. Ted handed me an emergency ration bag, half full of sugar. "Make them sweet. They taste better."

"Where did you get the sugar?" asked J.C.

"Oh I went up to the old German gun emplacement, where the cooks keep their stores, and filled this bag."

"Yes, but don't the cooks sleep there also?" I argued.

"I know," Ted grinned. "But they were out hunting souvenirs, so I slipped in when no one was around."

"I believe you have learned some of Sneezig's tricks." I stated.

That night, when the mail arrived, I received a letter and a parcel from my mother. The letter contained six pages. She told me all the news at home; everyone was well, and waiting anxiously for my return. Finishing up, she wrote. "I have seen your girl quite often lately, out waling or car-riding with another fellow. I am afraid she is forgetting you."

Slowly I put the letter away. My heart was full. So, my suspicions were verified; she had been too busy going around with someone else. Yet, I thought, she had promised; and I must trust her. Likely she was lonesome and an occasional car ride would do her good.

I dismissed the thought and turned to the parcel. There was a lovely cake and some cigarettes. It was our first parcel in many weeks. Ted and J.C. began to jump around me like a pair of young roosters.

"How about some cigarettes?" begged Ted.

"I will be your friend for life, just dish out the cake," crowed J.C.

"All right, you two birds," I said. "But wait until morning; we shall have strawberries and fruit cake for breakfast."

"Oh that's too long to wait," J.C. complained.

"Yeah, we might get killed before morning," grumbled Ted. "Besides, there are enough berries and sugar left for a feed."

"All right then," I finally submitted. "Get the berries ready."

J.C. set up several German ammunition cases to serve as a table, and put three other cases around it to sit on. For a table cover we used an old lousy blanket. I started the Primus and put water on for tea. Ted finished mashing the strawberries and went outside, returning shortly with a handful of yellow flowers, which he placed in an empty corned beef can and sat in the middle of our improvised table. J.C. produced a new candle and whittled off the end for that it would fit into the long neck of an empty German wine bottle. With this perfect Ritz setting, we sat down.

"Just a minute boys – I forgot something!" J.C. ran over to his pack and pulled out three new khaki handkerchiefs. "Serviettes, boys," he laughed joyously, tossing us each one.

"Everything is fine," said Ted. "But there is one thing lacking. We should be dressed in evening clothes for the occasion."

"Yes, but it would hardly do in here," I said, indicating our crude surroundings. "Still, we might pretend that we are generals."

"That's it!" agreed Ted. "I always wanted to be a general, anyway."

Ted dished out the strawberries into our mess-tins, while I cut the cake. Then we started in, eating slowly, by tiny morsels, trying to appear very delicate and refined in our clumsy manner; meanwhile, formally addressing one another with the title "General" and facetiously discussing the war and expressing our deepest sympathy for the poor, ignorant infantrymen, so far below our exalted rank. We ate all the strawberries and cake with great relish. While drinking our tea, I passed around the cigarettes. We talked unceasingly, laughing gaily at the slightest intimidation of humor. It was a perfect evening. Our cup of bliss was overflowing.

"You know, fellow," Ted grinned and patted his stomach, "this wouldn't be a bad war at all if one of us received a parcel every day, and we could stay up here where it is quiet all the time."

"Yes," said J.C. "If we could have strawberries and fruit cake every day, but a fellow has to have a cast iron stomach to digest that bully beef and hard-tack."

"J.C.," I said, "I thought you were the one who boasted of intestinal fortitude."

"Intestinal fortitude, yes," he laughed. "When it comes to champagne, I can drink any general under the table; but I don't care to enter any bully beef contest."

There was a burst of explosions outside. We rushed out to see what was going on. Gas shells were dropping in the flat. A faint mist covered the flat and was creeping up the slope toward us. Orders came to stand to, with ready gas masks. There was a display of fireworks ahead of us, and at the same time a heavy bombardment started near Avion. Between the explosions of the shells, we could hear the faint rattle of machine gun fire.

Gas shells were landing closer. The faint odor of pineapples pervaded the air around us. We quickly cleaned the glasses and put on our masks. We could not speak to one another now, but had to stand like dummies. As we breathed through the chemical box, the cloths around our faces alternately inflated and deflated. The gas became denser as more shells came over. My vision was becoming blurred.

We had our masks on for an hour; my face was burning and smarting. Some of the new fellows pulled off their masks, but they started to cough and put the masks back on. Men were coming up the slope, staggering and coughing. As they approached, I saw white tags tied to their tunic buttons, and knew what was written on those tags – only a single word: "GASSED". They passed us in twos and threes; some were coughing and spitting and vomiting; some collapsed, suffocating from the deadly fumes. I heard someone shout: "Keep on going! You will be all right at the top of the hill!"

My lungs began to ache; red spots appeared before my eyes. I wanted to throw off my mask, yet I dared not, because I knew what the dire result would be. Perspiration ran from my brow into my eyes. The glasses were so sweated up that I could hardly see ten feet. I became weaker and weaker. Why did not the order come to go back to the top of the ridge? Were we going to stay here until we suffocated?

At last the yellowish mist became lighter. A light breeze sprang up, and the gas slowly disappeared. We threw off our masks and filled our lungs with fresh air. Ted lay flat on the ground and coughed until he was blue in the face.

We had hardly recuperated, when the order came to move to the front. Slowly we made our way down on the slopes and across the flat. On approaching the railway embankment, we ran into more gas and had to don our masks again. We passed through the gap where the railroad bridge had been blown out and kept on. Soon we were going up hill. The mist disappeared from before our eyes, and we removed our masks. The sky was red in the east when we reached the front line near Avion.

The trenches were shallow and afforded us little protection. We sat in funk holes all day, half dozing. In the evening Fritz started to shell us. Gas shells came over and we had to wear our masks most of the time. All night long we remained at our posts, coughing and trembling, with no hope of getting out of this hole alive.

Towards morning the shelling died down. With great relief, we settled back in our funk holes.

That afternoon I was peacefully dozing in my funk hole when suddenly; there was a rattle of machine gun fire, mixed with odd rifle shots. I jumped up quickly and grasped my rifle, expecting to see the Germans rushing toward us.

"Quick, Miller, look over there!" shouted Ted, pointing to the rear.

I turned and saw a German two-seater plane gliding down, straight at our trench. Our anti-aircraft guns were shooting at the plane and the shrapnel shells were bursting all around it. I noticed that the plane was out of commission. The pilot was frantically trying to reach his own line. But this he was unable to do, being forced to land right in front of our trench.

The plane was equipped with a swivel machine gun in the rear, which the gunner quickly swung toward us. But we had them covered with our rifles, and they realized that they had no chance. With hands held aloft, the two of them climbed out; they were quickly surrounded and brought to the trench. The gunner was quite angry because they had not been able to make their own line and cursed savagely. This did not help them any, for they were marched off to headquarters.

Everyone rushed over to the plane for souvenirs. Part of the propeller had been shot off and we judged this to be the cause of the plane's disability. We soon had the plane stripped of everything small enough to take away. The crosses were torn off and the instruments taken out. We were going to remove the machine gun also, but the Germans, seeing what was happening, shelled the plane until it was blown to pieces.

The next few nights were repetitions of the first, with gas shells and high explosives bursting around us. Men, pale and suffering from the effects of gas, stood at their posts clutching their rifles with trembling hands, expecting the enemy to come over any moment. This would last till morning, when all would become quiet again.

One morning we were sitting in our funk hole when gas shells again started to cover over. My eyes began to burn and tears ran down my cheeks.

"Tear gas!" I said to Ted.

"Tear gas is right! He cried excitedly. "This means an attack as sure as we are yet alive!"

We rubbed our eyes, but this made them smart hurt more than ever. We were ordered to stand to, and quickly donned our tear gas goggles. But they did not help much. My eyes were itching and the tears flowing so fast I could not see. I laid my rifle on the parapet and grabbed a bag of bombs: I couldn't see to aim anyway, and should the enemy come over, I was determined to throw bombs instead. Everyone was cursing and rubbing his eyes. One of our new men's eyes has swollen shut and bulged out like two chicken eggs.

A couple of our observations came roaring over, and suddenly, the shelling ceased. Everything was quiet once more. Ted kept guard while I lay on my back and bathed my eyes. They felt better and slowly returned to normal condition. I relieved Ted on guard and he treated his eyes the same way.

On the sixth day we were relieved and went back to La Folie Wood. We lay around for a few days as before, and were just beginning to enjoy life again when orders came to move north to another part of the front. Setting out at dusk, we arrived a few hours later at a sunken road below the ridge, in the Souchez sector. There we were ordered to stay in reserve.

Ted, J.C. and I were fortunate in getting a square-dug shelter with a tin roof, at the side of the road. The ground was all undermined by rats; and judging by the numerous rat mounds, there must have been many dead buried there.

We settled down in our dugout for the night, but could not sleep for a long time. As soon as things were quiet, the rats became lively and began to play hide and seek over our blankets. The incessant patter of tiny feet on the tin room, mingled with the startling squeals, was exceedingly unpleasant and annoying. Ted tossed about for a long time, growing and muttering curses at the unseen tormentors. I was almost asleep, when I was startled by a loud roar –

"You dirty…" Ted bellowed like a mad steer. And I hard some object strike the ground in front of our dugout.

"What's the matter, Ted? I asked, lighting a candle.

He was sitting up, glowering wrathfully towards the opening of the dugout. "Those damned rats!" he cried savagely. "I awoke to find one of the naked brutes sitting on my face."

"Did you throw him out?"

"No," he growled, getting up and crawling out. "I threw my boots after him, and now I suppose I'll have to find them again."

J.C. woke up, surprised and blinking. "What the dickens is all the racket about?"

"A rat was trying to choke Ted with its tail, and he is trying to find his boots now," I told him.

"It must have been looking for its mate in his moustache," laughed J.C. "I hope he doesn't find his boots."

Ted entered, carrying his boots. "Lucky thing for you that you found them again," J.C. piped up.

"Aw shut up," Ted growled.

"You know Miller, "J.C. turned to me, "it's pretty bad when the rats climb all over a man and start to chew his moustache."

"Yes," I jested. "I was going to grow one too, but now I won't because the rats would chew it off anyway."

Ted remained silent and sullen, so we quit our joking and again tried to get some sleep.

After breakfast the next morning, J.C. and I went for a stroll along the ridge. We came upon a pile of cordite sticks, each about ten inches long, resembling sticks of macaroni.

"Say J.C.!" I exclaimed, stuck with a sudden idea. "This stuff would be great for blowing up rat mounds."

"No, it's no good. It won't explode in open air; it just flares up like a match."

"I know, but we can put it in the tunnels and plug up the holes so that it doesn't get any air."

"By Jove, that's right!" he cried enthusiastically. "Let's take a bundle back with us."

Back at the dugout we found Ted sitting on the bank with his shirt off, cracking lice.

"Come on, Ted, we are gong to make a raid on the rats," I said, showing him the cordite.

"I'll be with you in a minute," he responded, hastily putting his shirt back on.

The first mound we came to had six entrances. J.C. plugged all the holes except one, into which I shoved a handful of cordite, leaving one stick out far enough to light. I covered the hole and applied a match, while J.C. and Ted stood in readiness with clubs. There was a muffled explosion, followed by a shower of earth, sparks and rats. Ted and J.C. were running everywhere at once, killing the half-burnt, squealing rats.

"Say, that's great stuff!" cried Ted gleefully when there were no more rats in sight.

"Look here, Ted," called J.C., point to a large and plump rat. "This must be the one that was bothering you last night."

"Well, if it is, I hope it got burnt good and plenty," replied Ted, wiping his face.

"Don't be too hard on the poor creatures," said J.C. suddenly magnanimous; "they are only trying to make a living, same as any other creature. Why, Ted how should you like to be a rat?"

"If I were a rat," said Ted, "I shouldn't stick around here very long."

"What should you do?"

"I'd dig my way down, under the ocean, clean back to Canada."

J.C. thought for a moment, and then burst out laughing.

"Tell us the joke J.C." I begged.

Finally he cooled down. "I was just thinking of Ted's predicament, if when he got back home, he couldn't change back from a rat to a human being. Just think of the school ma'am's surprise on seeing a rat poking its nose into her schoolroom. But, of course, she'd recognize Ted immediately. She'd probably say – 'Why Teddy, my darling, I'm so glad to have you back again! And you haven't changed much at all dear!' Then, since she couldn't have him any other way, she'd probably tie a blue ribbon around his neck and keep him as a pet.

J.C. jumped nimbly aside to dodge a dead rat that was flying through the air.

"J.C." said Ted, disgusted after having missed, "you are an ass."

"Well," returned J.C., "if you must class me in your animal world, then I'd like to have my own choice. Now, for instance, I shouldn't mind being a cow."

"A cow?" I echoed, laughing.

"Sure, a cow, a real old brindle, with a crooked horn to boot. Just to think, fellows, of the nice little milk maids that would come out to visit me every morning and night, and all the petting –"

"Don't forget, J.C.," Ted broke in triumphantly, "that you would only be a cow!"

"You win, Ted," said J.C. "The next bottle of champagne is on me, and I hope we don't have to wait very long to get some place where I can buy it."

Blowing up rats was great sport, and we kept it up until our supply of cordite was used up. Our efforts to exterminate them seemed in vain, however; on the following night we were tormented as badly as ever, and had to sleep with our faces covered.

One afternoon, as we were sitting in front of our dugout, "reading our shirts", there was a sudden explosion behind us, and shrapnel whistled over our heads. We jumped up quickly to see what had happened. Three of our new men lay on the ground, one of them was shouting for stretcher-bearers – one was dead, and the other two severely wounded. They had found a "pineapple" and while they had been trying to remove the nose cap, the shell had exploded. The dead man was buried and the two wounded carried out to the dressing station.

"That's what happens when a fellow tries to be too inquisitive," said J.C. "My motto is not to tamper with the tricky devices that come from Germany. After all, curiosity killed the cat, you know."

"Cat be damned!" said Ted. "It killed one good soldier and wounded two others."

We were ordered out for divisional rest. Happily, we turned from the front, anxious to get away before disaster broke loose.

Our life of ease was shortly terminated, however, as on the second day out we were ordered to go back to the line. Disappointed and dismayed, we marched back, arriving at a small village, shot down and in ruin, behind Hill 70.

That night we moved to the front and relieved a battalion in some chalk pits and mine craters. A and D companies went into the front line trench; B and C companies stayed in immediate support.

The trench we were in was all chalk and very shallow. Fortunately, however, we had an excellent German dugout for shelter about twenty-five feet underground, large and roomy, with two entrances.

"This is a real place," remarked J.C., as he gazed around. "I hope they keep us here all summer."

"One thing about it," said I, "We ought to be safe from shells in here."

"Don't worry," muttered Ted, "things won't be so quiet for us. There must be some dirty work afoot, or they wouldn't have shot us here in a hurry."

We were scarcely settled, when the sergeant appeared and detailed Ted and I on a ration party. We took our gas masks and followed the sergeant out of the dugout. On top we found several men waiting, and started off down a communication trench. The ration dump was situated at the end of a narrow gauge railway, and we had to wait for a gas train which was bringing up the supplies.

We had been at the dump but a few minutes, when a salvo of whiz-bangs came over, exploding near us. We scattered, and had scarcely flopped when another five shells burst around us, wounding two men.

We were told by an engineer who had come up from the ration train that a rail was blown out about three hundred yards down the track. In single file we followed him to the ration train. We were each loaded down with two bags, and then we started back. Fritz started shelling heavily and made several direct hits on the railway, blowing the track to pieces. Dodging from one shell hole to another, we finally reached our trench without any further casualties.

Ted and I were ordered on trench duty. J.C. went out with some others, on a working party to repair the railway.

The night was quiet for a while. Then whiz-bangs came over, at odd intervals, landing around our dugout. I crouched lower, expecting a direct hit any minute. Ted came up from the dugout to relieve me on guard.

"Watch out, Ted; some of them are coming pretty close," I warned him.

"So I noticed," he grinned. Every time I lit a candle down there the concussion of a shell blew it out."

I was back on guard when the work party returned. The fellows were nervous and exhausted.

"How was the work party?" I asked J.C.

"The worst I have ever been on. Every time we got the track fixed, a shower of whiz-bangs came over and blew it to pieces."

Towards morning the shelling increased. A heavy barrage was falling on our front line. Gas shells were coming over along with the high explosives. We donned our masks and stood to, gasping for breath. Three stretcher cases, badly gassed, came down our trench. They were new men who had not donned their masks in time. One of them, a very young chap, was dying. In his last moments he whispered faintly: "Mother, O Mother!" It is heart-rending to see a man die with the word "Mother" on his lips.

There was a rattle of machine guns on our right. The Germans attacked our D company, but were repulsed. The gas slowly drifted away, though the heavy shelling continued on our front. The heavy barrage of shells, bursting and thundering, foundations of earth shooting up, formed a dense wall, beyond which it was impossible to see.

All day long, through the intense heat and the fumes of bursting shells, we stood to, pale and terror-stricken; while death, horrible and menacing, lurked in our midst, picking a few here and there from our ranks. Any moment might be our last.

Towards evening, the shelling died down. Weary and exhausted, we returned to our dugouts. We had suffered heavy casualties: A and D companies in the front line had been all cut to pieces. We were relieved that night and went back to a little village for a rest.

On the evening of the fourth day of our stay in the blown-in collars of the village, the sergeant appeared and asked for Ted.

"Here I am. What do you want me for?" Ted spoke up.

"Report at headquarters in full marching order."

"Where am I going?" asked Ted, greatly surprised.

"I don't know. You will find out at headquarters. Hurry up and you will be able to go out with the ration limbers." With these words the sergeant strode off.

"Going on leave?" I asked Ted.

"No such luck," he snapped back. "I suppose they want to stick a stripe on me and send me out to the training school at Ferfay. But don't you fellows worry about this kid: they shall never stick any stripes on me."

Ted packed his things and with a soldier's farewell, left us. My heart ached to see him go. He was the best friend I had; and I needed his presence. I know that I should miss him terribly.

Next morning, early, we packed our things and moved further back from the front. After a hard day's march, we landed at a small mining town near Bruay, where, its was rumored, we should stay in reserve.

Chapter 13

Paris in World War 1

I was sitting in the barn, polishing my buttons, when a runner appeared, requesting me to report to headquarters. Wondering why I was wanted, I got up and walked over.

When I entered, the orderly room sergeant looked up and smiled. "You have been granted ten days leave of absence, Miller. Where do you wish to go, Paris or London?"

I could scarcely believe my ears. "Paris!" I shouted excitedly, although I had no idea where to go.

He gave me an order for a bath and a change of clothes and told me to come back when I was ready. I received a new uniform, boots and underwear. After a bath, I dressed up in my new outfit and reported back to the orderly room. The sergeant handed me a pass to Paris. I went over to the paymaster and received five hundred francs. Then to the M.O., but he merely wished me good luck.[4]

That evening, after a tiresome journey, I landed in Paris. Having no idea where to go from the station, I asked two Americans in khaki to show me a good hotel.

[4] According to his active service records, Jacob was granted leave for 10 days in Paris, August 4, 1917

"Come along with us," one of them invited. "We are going to a hotel right now."

I followed them to a car. After driving through the streets for a while, we stopped in front of the Hotel de Bretagne. I thanked them and entered the hotel. There was a young lady in charge. I addressed her in English –

"Good evening, Mademoiselle."

"Good evening," she returned in perfect English. "Do you wish to have a room for the night?"

"I should like to have one for about ten nights."

"Oh, you are on leave from the front!"

She showed me a fine bedroom with bath and sitting room.

"Eight francs per day – but we do not allow you to bring women up here."

I smiled at her knowingly and handed her forty francs for the first five days.

What a contrast to life at the front! Here everything was so nicely furnished, so spotlessly clean and so soft. The very air seemed to hold some charming, exotic perfume. I gazed out of the window, down upon the street. Low powered electric lights diffused a pallid glow over the crowded thoroughfare. Small groups of people, conversing by speech and gesture, and laughing gaily, strolled leisurely along the sidewalk. I was enthralled by it all. It was hard to believe that I was amidst civilization again. After enjoying a hot bath, I went to bed, feeling almost certain that I should wake up to find myself back in a filthy, malodorous trench at the front.

Next morning I awoke, much refreshed. After shaving and dressing, I went down for breakfast. Buns, marmalade and coffee – it was delectable food after the invariable army rations.

Two American soldiers entered and sat down. On of them ordered Scotch whisky. The waitress brought them a bottle and glasses.

"What part of Canada do you hail from Buddy? "asked one of them.

"From Saskatchewan," I responded. "And where do you fellows come from?"

"We come from Tennessee," he replied.

"Have a drink with us," the other invited.

I moved over to their table. We sat there for an hour or so, drinking lightly and talking. They were very likeable chaps, and we spoke freely, as if we had known each other for a long time. They told me many things about their homes in Tennessee; and I in turn told them about my own. When they rose to go, we shook hands and expressed hopes of meeting again.

In the afternoon I took a walk. After strolling along the streets of Paris for some time, I came to a beautiful park on the bank of the Oise River. Here I sat down on a bench to listen for a while to a string band. A grove of stately trees, with their dense foliage, formed an arch overhead and shaded us from the hot sun. The place was quite crowded. I watched the people around me with curiosity. Some were talking and laughing; others were silent, smiling and listening to the soft strains of music. Near me an old lady was reading a letter to a young girl. Tears were running down the cheeks of the old lady, and the young girl was wiping them away with a silk handkerchief. A letter from the front, I thought. A lonely French officer came hobbling by on crutches. He wore the Croix de Guerre and another medal, yet his face was lividly pale and held a hopeless expression. Two nurses passed by, pushing a wheel chair. In it was strapped an old man. He wore the uniform of a French officer and had three medals on his breast. My heart ached at his helpless condition, for I saw that both of his legs were amputated. Even here I could not get away from the terrible evidence of war!

On returning to my hotel, I went though the arch to the glass enclosed recreation room. There was a large sitting room, elegantly furnished with divans, writing tables, books and a piano. Seeing no one around, I sat down to write letters home.

I wrote a letter to my mother, telling her that I was on leave in Paris and having a great time. I described my surroundings and some of the things I had seen on my stroll through the city. In regards to Anne, I wrote, she should not misjudge the poor girl. Likely Anne was lonely, and there was no harm in taking an occasional car ride. And yet as I wrote this, I felt that my mother had reason to warn me. I finished my letter by telling her that I was getting a bombproof job, away from the line – she was not to worry any more about my safety. This was not true, but I thought it best to relieve her of the anxiety and worry she was suffering on my account.

A letter to Anne followed. In it I expressed disappointment at not having heard more often from her. But in all, it was a letter filled with tenderness and love, written in the flourishing style, which every soldier uses when he writes to his sweetheart.

On entering the lobby of the hotel, I found an old man waiting for me. He introduced himself in good English and asked if I cared to go sightseeing next morning at nine o'clock. He told me he was organizing a party and already had sixteen men; the price was five francs per day, including expenses. Should I care to come? I told him I should be pleased to go and should be waiting for him next morning.

I enjoyed a good night's rest and awoke feeling fine. After a light breakfast, I went outside to wait for the party. I had waited but a few minutes when a party of seventeen men came up. After paying five francs each, we all boarded a bus and started off.

Our first stop was the Eiffel Tower. What a gigantic structure! We were filled with admiration at the wonderful architecture. The tower was constructed of steel trestlework, being founded on four great steel arches. It reached such a dizzy height, that I had to crane my neck to gaze up at the peak. It seemed over a mile high, although our guide told us it was only nine hundred and eighty-four feet. There were two platforms built in the trestlework, quite high up. Our guide told us that in peace time the first had served as a dancing pavilion and on the second there had been a restaurant. A park of lovely trees, lawns, walks and flowerbeds surrounded the tower. After wandering around for some time, we again started off.

We drove to the outskirts of the city. The guide showed us where the German Uhlans had landed in 1914, but had been driven back by the two hundred thousand Frenchmen who had been organized during a single night.

We came to a square wherein some captured guns were on display. There were about a hundred German field guns and trench mortars of various calibers, all lined up. There was also a captured aeroplane.

We visited the Hotel des Invalides, where Napoleon was buried. On entering the chapel I was overcome with awe and reverence. The many varicolored flags, which Napoleon had won in his battles, drooped majestically down from the high arched vault of marble, surrounded by a balustrade. This was Napoleon's tomb. His last remains lay in a casket of red, inlaid granite, resting on a marble block in the centre of the vault. All around the circular wall were many statues and carvings representing Napoleon's victories.

It was quite late when we emerged from Les Invalides, so we decided to call it a day and returned to our respective hotels. I felt tired and went to bed early.

I went sightseeing almost every day following and visited many historical places, public buildings and parks. I saw the Place de la Concorde, which was the most beautiful square in Paris. In the centre stood an Egyptian obelisk with two water fountains playing on opposite sides of it. I went through the Chambre de Deputes and walked over a piece of carpet, which our guide said, had cost a million and a half francs.

One afternoon, during the latter part of my leave in Paris, I went for a stroll. After sauntering idly about for some time, I stopped in front of a saloon, inside of which were many soldiers leaning against the bar. Deciding to have a drink of cold beer, I entered and received a shock, which almost knocked me over. Whom should I see but good, old Ted, coming toward me with a cigar shoved half way down his throat. Resplendent in a new uniform which, however, had not been made for Ted, for the pants were too small, the sleeves reaching only a little below his elbows – he strutted about like a bantam rooster.

"Hello, Miller!" he roared when he saw me.

Everyone stared and turned.

"Hello, yourself," I greeted in response. "What are you doing here? I thought you would be at Ferfay by this time."

"That's what I expected," he replied. "But when I got to headquarters they sent me out on leave – so here I am kid! And where are you off to?"

"On leave, same as you."

"That's fine Miller. This is my last day, but we can still have a few drinks together, anyway." He led the way to the bar.

"What'll you have, Ted?" I asked, pulling out some money.

"Mulliga. It's the best drink in Paris, and I've tried them all."

"Mulligan?"

"No, not stew, you darn nut," he laughed. "Mulliga, or in other words, gin."

"All right, Ted, I'll try it myself." And I ordered two mulligas. We finished the drinks and Ted ordered another round.

"Well, Miller, how do you like Paris? You know, I've been living here like a king. Real hair cuts, shaves and everything. I even had my picture taken."

"Not in that uniform, surely?" I laughed, sizing him up.

"Never mind, Miller. I know it looks funny, but what can I do if the dumb saps haven't got a man sized outfit in the quartermaster's store? Anyway, Betty won't mind. It's not the uniform she cares for; it's the man that in it."

"Yes, but you might have had it altered a bit. The way it fits you now, it is a sure remedy for sore eyes."

"But how could I? I've only got this one pair of pants and tunic. And if I took them to a tailor, what should I wear? Besides these French guys might misunderstand a fellow and make them worse. I shouldn't like to trust them."

"Even a poor tailor couldn't make it much worse," I laughed. "I'll bet its some picture."

The door of an adjoining room opened and we had a glimpse of soldiers sitting at tables, each with a woman on his knee, drinking a laughing merrily. Two women came through into the saloon and walked unsteadily to the bar. One was short and plump, the other taller and more slender; both were half stewed.

Seeing Ted and me, they edged closer, intending to victimize us. The slender one, giggling spasmodically, slipped her arm through mine and spoke brokenly and inarticulately in French. I was not interested and modestly withdrew from her.

She produced a card and held it up. "Tres bien, Monsieur." I said, rather rudely: "No thanks!"

At that she gave up and regarded me with venomous eyes because I had not turned out to be a compliant victim.

Ted, however, was having a more difficult time. The plump young lady was determined to have his company. She held his arm tightly, declining to relinquish her hold even after his abrupt refusal. He made innumerable excuses, all of which were incomprehensible to the ambitious coquette. She harassed him more, caressing his arm softly and making gesticulatory appeals that he should come with her into the adjoining room. Ted was nonplussed. Seeing that I had successfully dismissed the slender one, he turned to me in his plight –

"Miller, for goodness sake help me shake off this wild cat!"

"What can I do?" I asked, wondering what recourse was necessary under such peculiar circumstances.

"Tell me what to say to her," he pleaded.

I had to laugh. "Well Ted, about all you can say to her is – 'Get thee behind me, Satan'. Maybe she'll understand."

"She understands nothing. She's too dumb. No matter what I say, she keeps whining and grinning at me just like a cat."

"Then you'll have to go ahead and play with her, Ted. It's all you can do."

"No by a damned sight! What would Betty think of me?"

The recollection of that fair one gave him new confidence and determination to throw off his tormentor. Turning to her, he said with great vehemence: "Say sister, you get away from me! I've got a decent girl, and I think too much of her to stand for your fooling. Now get!"

But the object of his wrath stood immobile, smiling sweetly, as persistent as ever. Ted, with a distressed look on his face, stood helplessly by.

"She'll get the best of you, Ted." I grinned at him.

"Miller," he blurted out, "in a case of this kind, you're as useless as the nipples on a boar. This is once in my life that I wish I had J.C. beside me, instead of you; he sure knows how to make these French dames understand."

"Buy her a drink," I suggested.

He ordered a drink of Mulliga. The slender one who had accosted me, and who in the meantime had been abetting and advising her companion, seeing that no response was forthcoming, began to coax her away. After having the drink, the plump one released Ted – much to his great relief – realizing at last that he was not susceptible to her charms. The two of them then played up to two other soldiers, whom they succeeded in abducing into the adjoining room.

Ted and I quietly enjoyed a few more drinks. I saw that Ted was keeping his eye on the clock, and that he was growing restless.

"What's on your mind, Ted? Running short of time?"

"Yes. In a little less than two hours I'll be hitting back for the front. I just hate the idea of leaving Paris."

"Cheer up, old boy," I said, "in two days I'll have to go back too. We'll be together again, anyway. You know, when you left I thought we should be parted for good."

"So did I, said he. "It is one good thing that it turned out this way."

We went out and strolled around till it was time for Ted to go. We shook hands and parted. It was not until I got back to my battalion that I remembered I had not told Ted the battalion had moved since he had gone on leave.

The time passed very quickly and soon I realized that my leave was almost over. On the morrow I should have to leave Paris and go back to the front to face suffering and death once more. I dreaded the thought of going back and wondered if, ever again, I should see Paris. I had been through so many close calls that I could not last much longer.

After supper I strolled down to the park by the river and sat down on an empty bench to listen to the string band for a while. The place was filled with people, as before. My heart ached as I realized that in less than twenty-four hours I should have to say goodbye to all this and go back. My body, after having been soothed by this life of ease in Paris, would again have to undergo the abominable indurations of the front line. It was a gloomy outlook.

A soldier approached and sat down beside me. By his badges I saw that he belonged to the Canadian Engineers.

"Say, mate," he began, "how about a little touch for five francs or so? I am six day over leave already and am flat broke."

"Well, you had better go back to your battalion, or there will be the dickens to pay for you," I advised him, handing him five francs. He accepted the money with profuse thanks.

"Where are you staying? I asked, feeling sorry for him.

"With a woman," he answered nonchalantly.

"Another man's wife?"

"Yes, you see her husband is at the front, at Verdun."

"How can you pull off a stunt like that?"

"Well," he began, "I used to knock around with her; and when I was tight she would take me home. I never stayed with her while I had money; but now I am broke and have no other place to go."

"How come?"

"I used to buy cigarettes from the Y.M.C.A. for half a franc per packet and sell them to the French tobacco stores at a nice little profit. But they got on to me and I had to cut it out."

I felt sorry for him and decided to help him. Laying my hand upon his shoulder I said kindly: "Better quit this nonsense and go back to your outfit. Come back with me, my time is up tomorrow."

He seemed very grateful. Promising to meet me next afternoon at the station he got up and left. I never saw him again.

I went to bed, but could not sleep for a long time. I kept on worrying about going back, and desperately hoped that the war would end soon, so that I should not have to stand it much longer.

Next morning, I walked until I became tired. I had a last good meal in the afternoon, and then started off for the station.

The train was packed with French soldiers going back to their units. A French officer joined me and, in English, asked where I was going.

"To Vimy," I responded.

"I am going to Verdun and it is a bad place," he informed me.

We had a long conversation. He told me about the terrors of the French people during the first great German drive – it had seemed that the very devil had been after them; and how, by the intervention of the Allies, France had been saved from conquest by the Germans. The war was costing his dear country more than she could stand. He felt certain, however, that now the tide was turning. Now that we had that powerful Ally, the United States, we were certain of victory. The German morale was weakening, and it would not be long until they would be forced to ask for peace.

The railway junction, at which the French soldiers changed trains, was reached, and the friendly officer rose to go. We shook hands as we parted. He smiled at me encouragingly. "It will soon be over, my friend. Courage, le diable est mort!"

It was daylight when I arrived at my destination. I hastened to enquire about my battalion and found that they were still quartered here. The adjutant informed me that I was just in time – the battalion would leave in the afternoon for the front. I entered the old barn and found J.C. and Skinny packing their kits.

"Hello Miller," they greeted, smiling.

"Hello fellows," I returned, glad to see them again.

"You are just in time," said J.C. "We are leaving for the front this afternoon.

"Just my luck," I grumbled. "I couldn't miss a trip in the line if I tried."

"Hello Miller," a familiar voice cried behind me.

I turned to see Sneezigs entering the barn.

"Hello Sneezigs! You back so soon? You could not have been hit so badly to get out in such a short time."

"Yust through the shoulder," he answered modestly. "It was a Luger bullet, bullet didn't do much damage."

"Isn't Ted back yet?" I asked.

"Is he coming back? asked J.C. surprised. "I thought he went to Ferfay."

"No. He was on leave in Paris. I met him there. But he left two days ago." Then I remembered – "Oh, I forgot to tell him that we moved since he left. Now, I suppose, he will be marching all around Lens, looking for the battalion."

The boys burst out laughing.

"It won't hurt him," said J.C. "He has long legs, so it won't take him quite as long to catch up with the battalion it would take me, for instance. I expect that in about a week he'll come trailing around."

That afternoon we were ordered to fall in. We lined up in full marching order; and with our pipe band in the lead, we started our march back to the front.

Chapter 14

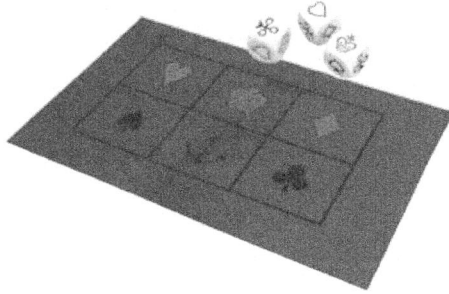

A game of Crown and Anchor

Late next afternoon we arrived at a small village near the La Bassee Canal. We were billeted in barns and told that we should stay here in reserve.

After we had been settled and divested of our equipment, Skinny and I went for a stroll. The small village was well shaded by tall poplar trees. In one grove, near our billet, stood a long-range naval gun, its long, grey barrel pointing sinisterly toward the enemy line. After going down the road a little way, we came to the canal. The water, clear and cool, rushed swiftly past. Ahead of us was a bridge, blown up in the middle by a direct hit. We wandered along the bank for a while before returning to our quarters.

After supper, J.C. approached me. "Miller, how much money do you have?"

"About sixty-five francs," I informed him.

"That's fine. I have seventy-five francs – let's put it together and start a game of Crown and Anchor. We ought to clean up a nice little pile.

This proposition seemed quite profitable to me. I had seen some of the fellows operating a game and winning from two hundred to a thousand francs in a single day.

"Who has a board?" I asked.

"I have," he responded; "just received one from my sister in England."

"Jakaloo with me. Let's get going."

J.C. pulled out his money. "Here, Miller, put the cash in your cap. You can be paymaster and I'll do the shaking."

We selected a nice, green patch beside the road and spread the canvas. J.C. rattled the dice in a can and called out: "Come on boys. Give us a bid. Try your luck on the old sergeant-major." He dumped the dice on the board. "See, what did I tell you? Two crowns and a spade. The old sergeant major wins the bacon. Two crowns and a spade. Come on boys, try your luck."

Two fellows from another company sauntered over and dropped a few coppers on the board. J.C. turned up the dice. We won and I raked in the money.

"Come on fellows," J.C. called to a group standing nearby, "try your luck on the old board. What you win is what you get."

They all came over and covered the board with francs, half francs and pennies.

"That's the spirit. Put some more on the old hook. And what about the sergeant-major?" J.C. gave the dice a good shake and turned them up. They were in our favour and I raked in the money. After paying out, I figured we had made about five francs.

More men crowded around, placing five-franc notes on the sergeant major, as it had not turned up last time. J.C. tuned up the dice. Two hooks and a crown – not so good: I had to pay out a little more this time.

"All right fellows" cried J.C. "Try the old sergeant-major once more. That's the stuff boys; place your bets. Anymore for anymore? All right then; if you are all satisfied, up she comes."

Everyone had the crown covered. I noticed three five-franc notes along with a great deal of silver. The rest of the board was almost empty. Three crowns! Holy smoke! Surely we were broke now! After paying out, I counted all the money and found that we still had forty francs left.

"That's not so good," J.C. whispered to me excitedly. "I hope we don't go broke. What do you think about it, shall we quit or go on?"

"Shoot the works," I told him. "We might make something the next throw."

"All right, fellows," J.C. piped up, "cover the old sergeant-major once more. Place your money on the board and sleep in the street".

Most of the money was on the diamond this time. However the betting was not heavy. J.C. raised the can and to my surprise two diamonds and a spade. Lost again. After everyone had been paid off we had ten francs left.

"I guess we can sleep in the street," I said, handing J.C. five francs.

"Yes, that finishes us with Crown and Anchor," he replied wistfully as he rolled up the canvas.

After the crowd had scattered we went to the estaminet. We spent the last of our money on beer and returned to our billet, penniless but satisfied.

During the night we were awakened by the loud reports of the naval gun in front of our billet. Our barn nearly collapsed from the reverberations of the heavy discharges. After the fourth shot, the firing ceased and we went back to sleep.

Next day was Sunday. In the afternoon we strolled down to the canal for a swim. There were many fellows already there, swimming about or sunning their naked bodies on the other bank. The water seemed fresh and cold to our nude warm bodies. It was great sport, though, after we were in, to swim about or splash water at one another. Our only worry was the French civilians passing by along the bank. Every time a group of women or girls approached, there was a mad scramble to get to the other side and conceal ourselves in the high grass. The passersby, however, did not seem to mind our appearances and only smiled at our hasty embarrassed retreat.

Sitting on the bank, gazing into the water, I saw small fish swimming about. They reminded me of the alluring odor of frying fish and I tried to conceive a plan to snare a few. Suddenly I remembered the bombs back in our billet and called over to Skinny and J.C., who were on the opposite side.

"Hey, fellows, come over. I have an idea."

They both dived in and were soon puffing and dripping beside me.

"What's up?" Skinny inquired.

"See those fish there? How about fried fish for supper?"

"Yes, but how are we going to get them?" J.C. broke in. "I tried to coax out a few already, but they won't pay any attention to me."

"There are about a dozen Mills bombs in our barn," I explained. "We'll throw in a bomb here and there along the bank and when they come up, one of us will be ready with a stick to fish them out."

"Sounds kind of fishy, but we can try it anyway," said Skinny.

We dressed hurriedly and went to our billet. Taking two bombs each, we returned to the canal. Skinny found a long stick, to which we attached a sandbag to serve as a net. We wandered down the bank, away from the swimmers, to try our experiment.

Pulling the pin, I tossed a bomb in the water. There was a muffled explosion; the water heaved, bringing up a small fish. Skinny put in the net, and, after careful manipulation, pulled out our prize.

"Sardines for supper," laughed J.C., as we examined our first catch, about four inches long.

"Quite expensive ones, too – two shillings and sixpence each," said I, tossing in another bomb.

This time two came up, each about six inches long.

"That's better," cried Skinny. "We'll get enough for supper yet."

After all our bombs had been used up, we started back with seven fish, varying in length from two to seven inches.

We borrowed some bacon grease from Scotty and had fish and chips for supper. The poignant odor of frying fish attracted many inquisitive noses to our billet. "Where did you get the fish?" was the general inquiry. We told them and explained our method of fishing. That night we could smell fish throughout the entire village. Next day we were going to repeat our successful experiment, but the officers put a stop to it. Too many bombs were being wasted; they had been made to serve another purpose, not to kill fish.

That afternoon, J.C. and I sat against the shaded side of the barn, smoking and talking idly. The conversation drifted to Ted's misfortune of missing the battalion. We wondered where he was and what sort of time he was having in tracing our moves. J.C. looked down the road, which led to the village, and started to laugh –

"Talk of the devil and he is sure to appear. Look, Miller, if that isn't Ted Davies coming back from leave, I'll eat my shirt."

"It's the old warrior himself," I said. "Let's go up to meet him."

We met him on the outskirts of the village. Poor Ted – he certainly looked tired. He was covered with dust from head to foot. His face was dirty and, according to the scraggy beard, had not been shaved since leaving Paris. Perspiration was running down his face and converging into large drops at the end of his nose. He stopped and regarded us with a weary expression.

"Where have you been all week?" I asked.

"How can I tell?" said he wearily. "I don't know the names of all the villages and towns in France."

"Welcome back to the battalion old boy," said J.C. "The long lost son has returned at last. Here, let me carry your pack for you, because I am sure you have brought some wine back for Miller and me."

"Miller," said Ted quietly, "why didn't you tell me that the battalion moved from Hill 70?"

"I forgot all about it, old man, and didn't think of it until I was back. Surely, though, you didn't go all the way back to the cellars?"

"I sure did; and when I got there, I couldn't find out where the C.M.R.'s had gone. All those fellows could tell me was that they hadn't seen any Canadian blokes around."

"Where did you go from there?"

"I trailed through every village from Lens to Aubigny. No one knew anything about Canadian Soldiers. When I got to Aubigny, a few old froggies told me about the *Canadian Soldats partee*, pointing to the front. So I started back for the front, without the slightest idea where to go. Finally I met a Third Divisional dispatch rider and learned from him that you were here."

"Well, you've done some traveling," I comforted him. "I supposed your old dongs are pretty tired."

"Not tired," he laughed; "they are completely worn out."

"Too bad you didn't get here last night," said J.C. "We had a nice feed of fresh fish."

"I had all the fish I want in Paris," Ted replied. "What I want is a good bed where I can sleep for about a day."

We had hardly rolled into our blankets that evening when the rubber gun opened up again. It fired several shots, then ceased.

Ted looked up at me nervously. "Where is that gun?"

"In front of our billet," I answered.

"That's done it!" he cried moodily. "Now I won't be able to sleep all night."

"Why not? There won't be any more firing tonight."

"Maybe not, but don't you suppose the Germans know the gun is here and will retaliate?"

"They haven't done it so far and we've been here two nights," I stated.

"That may be so, but I am not staying in this death trap." He took up his blankets and greatcoat and went out to sleep in the open.

Next day we were lying in the barn, smoking and talking. Ted was busy in one corner, concentrating his thoughts on a letter he was writing. After a great deal of effort, he leaned back and heaved a sigh of satisfaction. Reaching into his pack, he pulled out a small photograph and gazed at it intently.

"Picture of Betty?" inquired J.C.

"Not of Betty," Ted grinned; "to Betty. It's a photo I had taken in Paris."

"Let's have a look at your miniature self," Skinny requested.

Ted proudly exhibited the photograph. It was a full size picture of him standing beside an arm chair; he was staring blankly ahead, with gaping mouth.

"Were they any flies in the studio?" J.C. asked innocently.

"No. Why?"

"Because I see you had your mouth wide open when it was taken."

"That's a poor picture to send to a girl," said Sneezigs. "She will throw you over as sure as anything. But if you'd send her a picture of me, she'll wait for you forever."

"Aw dry up, you jam-face," Ted growled, snatching away the photo. "If I wanted to send her a picture of you, all I'd have to do is send her a tin of apple and plum jam."

There was a sudden deafening crash outside. Our barn almost shook to pieces; tiles from the roof fell all around us. We jumped up quickly and rushed outside.

"Where did the shell land?" I asked.

"Over there, in the garden. Can't you see the hole still smoking?" Ted pointed.

The shell had landed about twenty feet from the barn.

"I told you fellows it was coming," Ted continued. "Let's get out of here before the next one comes."

We ran to the right and sought shelter behind a railway embankment. Another shell came down near the gun. We saw the gunners scramble in all directions like scared rabbits.

"I don't wish those fellows any bad luck," muttered Ted, "but I hope they get blown sky high for starting trouble. The darn fools can't bear to see a poor infantryman at rest, without shooting off that damned rubber thing over there."

He expressed not only his own opinion.

After the fourth shell, all was quiet again. We were ordered to fall in, and started off to the right along the railroad track. In many places is had been blown up by mines, and we had to pick our way carefully.

In the late afternoon we arrived at a fairly large town, and prepared to stay. The place was entirely deserted; not a soul to be found anywhere. They had all fled during the drive, leaving everything in the houses: furniture, stoves and dishes – all were in place as if the occupants had stepped out only a few minutes before. Ted Sneezigs, J.C., three new men and I were billeted in a large house on the outskirts of the town.

After we had been settled, J.C. and I went out to get something to eat and to look for souvenirs. We made our way to a large building which stood a little way back from the street. J.C., recognizing it as a brewery, immediately made a bee line for it. On entering we found the place empty. We searched high and low but could not find any beer. J.C. was greatly disappointed.

"The doggone Germans must have cleaned this place out before they left," he said regretfully.

"Let's look around some more," I encouraged. "They might have left an odd keg around here somewhere."

We came to a vault-like chamber, built with bricks. It was too dark to see clearly inside, so I lit a match. In one corner stood a demi-john, about a five gallon size, encased in wicker basket. J.C. performed a little step dance and sang out: "Glory halovalarium, Old Roger Rum!"

We dragged the jar out into the light and examined it. It was full of pale, transparent liquid. J.C. pulled the cork and took a smell. "It seems familiar but I can't place it."

He poured a little over his finger and tasted it. "There is alcohol in it all right, but it tastes kind of funny."

"I think we had better leave it alone," I advised. "The darned stuff may be poisoned for all we know."

"Nothing doing," said J.C. determinedly. "I won't leave it until I am absolutely sure that it is no good. I shall get the M.O.'s orderly to test it – he's a graduate from medical college."

J.C. went out. It was getting late, so I started back to my billet. As I drew near, I saw some fellows carrying bedding from another house toward the one in which we were billeted. One of them was Sneezigs, laboring under a heavy feather tick. When he saw me he started to laugh –

"I am going to sleep on a real feather bed tonight."

"Maybe there is enough room for two to lie on? I suggested.

"Nothing doing. You get your own bedding." He answered greedily.

I opened the door for Sneezigs and we both entered our house. Ted was busy in the kitchen, preparing supper. He had baked potatoes and stewed carrots, vegetables he had procured from the garden back of the house.

"Say you fellows, get busy and find some firewood if you want any supper," he ordered.

I went out to look for some wood but couldn't find a stick anywhere. I returned to the house.

"Where did you find the wood, Ted?"

Ted looked at me for a moment, then burst out – "Miller, you give me a pain in the neck! It's too bad that you have been in the line eighteen months and still can't find firewood." Whereupon he pulled the entrenching tool out of his equipment and began to smash of an expensive, hand-carved chair.

The door opened and in stumbled J.C., his eyes shining. "Hello Gang!" he shouted happily.

Ted looked up in surprise. "Well, look at that mug. Tight again."

"Where did you get it?" I asked J.C.

He grinned at me. "Down at the brewery – the big bottle you and I were looking at."

"Are you sure that stuff is all right?"

"Sure I'm sure. I had the M.O.'s orderly there to test it. He said it was absinthe, liquor that isn't sold anymore. I brought some home for you guys too."

Sneezigs suggested that we move the table down to the basement because we could not risk lighting candles up here. We thought it a good idea and proceeded to move the furniture. There was plenty of room, so we brought down beds and all.

"That's better," Sneezigs grunted. "Now we are more bombproof."

We decked the table in gay style. J.C. and I brought down the dishes, beautifully cut glass and Old Dutch hand-painted china, and arranged them as we thought befitting. We even had costly crystal goblets for drinking the absinthe which J.C. had brought from the brewery. Sneezigs discovered a chest of silverware, the entire contents of which he distributed around the board. Our large, underground room was brightly lit up by many candles placed around the walls in heavy brass candelabra which the new fellows had gathered from other houses. When all was in readiness, we sat down around the glittering array. Ted presided as host at the head of the table, looking very distinguished and formal.

"How about a speech from the president?" suggested one of the new fellows.

"Hear, hear!" shouted J.C., who had taken a few more drinks.

Ted rose up very ceremoniously. After screwing his moustache gravely and coughing several times, he began: "Gentlemen of the Jury, it is ---"

"You mean me," interrupted J.C., "I'm the Gent from the Brewery" and he held up his bottle of absinthe to vindicate the statement.

"Order in the courthouse!" Sneezigs shouted sternly and pounded on the table.

After roaring had died down, Ted continued –

"I'm no speecher, but I'm glad to see you all gathered here before me tonight anyway. And – and – I – I welcome you to – to this here feed. Eat, drink and be merry. Shove down all the carrots you can, so that if you die on the morrow, you will have a full stomach to last you through eternity." He sat down, grinning with satisfaction at his elocutionary effort; while the rest of us held our sides, almost bursting with roars of laughter.

We set to, eating and drinking merrily. What a time we had! Never was a King's banquet enjoyed more!

We were not yet through the feast when the sergeant intruded and ordered Sneezigs and the three new fellows to get ready to go on outpost duty at the Front.

Sneezigs was crestfallen. "What do you mean outpost duty? Are there no trenches there?"

"No," answered the sergeant. "The Germans have flooded the whole country and we can't get across the water."

"That's a new stunt," remarked Ted, after the sergeant had gone.

"Yes," said J.C. "I suppose they will supply each man with a canoe to paddle up and down No Man's Land."

After supper, Ted and I washed the dishes, while the boys got ready to go on night duty. J.C. sat back, happy and content, looking on.

"Say you fellows, how about a little music?" he suggested.

"Fine," I agreed. "Better ask the pipe band down here, - Ted is very fond of Scottish music."

"No kidding, though," said J.C. "I know a house where there is a nice gramophone."

"Well then, go fetch it, before somebody else gets it," said Ted.

J.C. left the house along with Sneezigs and the rest. We were just finishing the dishes when there was a loud rap at the door. Ted opened it to see who was there.

"Well, I'll be!" he gasped.

I turned to see a large tin horn coming through the door, followed by J.C. carrying the music box.

"And you call that contraption a gramophone," laughed Ted.

"Sure, and I tried it out. It works fine." He set the instrument on a table and wound it up.

Ted and I could not help laughing. The horn was at least five times as large as the rest of the gramophone, and I was constantly worrying lest the horn overbalance the small music box and crash down upon the stone floor.

Ted went upstairs and brought down a large arm chair. "All right J.C.," he ordered, sitting down with a bored air, "you might give us a little number now."

J.C. got the machine working at last. We sat back, recumbent and at ease, listening to the music. When the first piece was ended, Ted stretched his long legs languidly and yawned. "That was fine," he said, fastidiously flicking the ashes from his cigarette. "And now you might pour us another drink James."

J.C. took three goblets, poured them half full of absinthe, and then filled them with water.

"Anything else you two lords wish?" he said, handing us the drinks in an obsequious manner. The liquor turned as white as milk for a few seconds, and then returned to its natural transparency.

I complimented J.C. on his ability to mix drinks. "The captain certainly gave you good training. After the war is over, you will almost be able to qualify as a butler."

"Yes, but he won't have to worry about a job," Ted broke in pretentiously, "when I become general, I shall have J.C. attached to my personal staff. He makes a real good flunk, you know."

We sat around drinking and smoking, while J.C. kept winding the gramophone. A sensation of warmth and pleasure surged through our veins. The room was filled with the magic influence of the music.

Bodies, relaxed and soothed, swayed unconsciously in the unison with the rhythmic impulses. Blood tingling, minds imbued with romantic fancies and imaginations, visions floated again before our eyes. Life and love were born anew, blending in our hearts, while the lazy cigarette smoke curled steadily up to the ceiling.

At midnight we broke up and retired. I rolled into Sneezigs' feather tick and was soon fast asleep. It was early morning when I was aroused by Sneezigs and chased out of my soft warm bed.

"What is the front line like?" I asked.

"No front line; it's all patrol and outpost duty," he answered. "The Yermans have flooded the country, and all you can see for miles is bush and water. I saw a Yerman paddling a boat, but yust when I started to snipe at him; he pulled in behind a clump of trees."

After breakfast the boys went for a stroll around town. I settled down to write a letter, but Sneezigs was still sleeping and snoring so loudly that I was compelled to go upstairs into the sitting room. I concluded my letter and looked out through the window. Of all things imaginable! There were four men carrying a piano toward our house. I recognized Ted and J.C. in the lead, and two other fellows in the rear. Apparently it was too heavy for them, so J.C. called two more men to give them a hand. I went outside and helped them bring it to the front door. After much banging around, we finally managed to get it down into our cellar.

Sneezigs awoke and rolled over. "Say, what's going on here?" He saw the piano and burst out laughing. "Of all the childish tricks, you fellows take the cake."

"Why, what's the matter with us having a piano in our home?" said J.C., wiping the perspiration from his face.

"Nothing wrong at all," Sneezigs laughed. "But who will play it?"

We gazed at one another for a moment, and then burst out laughing. No one had thought of that. Ted dragged a chair over to the piano and sat down. "I can play a little, but only with one finger," he grinned.

"Go ahead," said J.C. "See what you know."

"Well it goes like this." Ted started to plunk away at the keys.

"That's fine!" cried J.C. "That's real music, and I know the words to that piece."

He made a very formal bow to the rest of us and spoke with a dramatic gesture: "Ladies and Gentlemen, Horses and Mules. My friend here, who is the greatest pianist in the army since all the others were killed, and I will render to your pleasure the musical selection entitled....oh I forget the name of it, but go ahead, Ted. Shoot."

Ted started to play with one finger. J.C. sang fervently and intensely, his face distorted in sadness and with arms outstretched appealingly to Ted –

"The lights will burn, and a heart will yearn

And it always will till you return – "

We almost brought the roof down with our roars of laughter.

"By gosh!" said Sneezigs, wiping the tears from his eyes, "I would carry that piano over here myself rather than miss such a show."

We went upstairs to prepare our dinner. One of the new fellows and I went out to the garden to get some more potatoes and carrots.

"There are a couple of rabbits in a backyard down the street," he told me.

"You go down and get them and we shall have rabbit stew for dinner."

He went for the rabbits, while I prepared the vegetables. In a few minutes he returned, dragging two rabbits by the ears. In no time we had them killed and skinned. I cut them up into small pieces and put them on the stove to cook. Ted supplied the firewood by hacking up some more furniture.

While our dinner was cooking I sat down by the open window to have a smoke. A shell came screeching over. Like a flash we dropped to the floor. The shell landed about a hundred yards up the street, exploding with a terrific roar. I dashed outside and lay flat on the ground. Three more shells came over and struck a row of houses with a deafening crash. Bricks flew in all directions. Men were running everywhere at once.

I remained in prone position until all was quiet. On returning to the kitchen I grabbed the utensils containing our dinner and made a hasty retreat down the cellar. In silence we ate our dinner, which was only about half cooked.

I saw that Ted was not eating any of the rabbit stew.

"Have some rabbit, Ted," I offered.

"No thanks," he declined. "It reminds me too much of the Australian cats we used to get, coming over on the boat."

"Yes, that's true, Ted" said J.C. slowly. "And remember the strings of beads in them."

Ted turned away from the table.

That night the Germans shelled us. Two of us had to stand watch all night, because there were a few gas shells dropping in the town. Towards morning the shelling ceased and we were able to turn in for some sleep.

After breakfast, the order came to move on. J.C. started to curse. "Darn the luck anyway! Just when we begin to live again along comes the order to move."

"Yes, I suppose they have some dirty work for us at the crossroads." Ted grumbled bitterly.

"I wish I could take my little gramophone along," said J.C. wistfully gazing at his treasured music box.

"You'll have to leave it for the owner of this house," I said. "When he comes back he'll find a few musical instruments he did not have before."

"Well, that ought to compensate for the chairs I smashed," laughed Ted.

We started off to the right, landing near Avion. Here we stayed in supports, lying around in dugouts on an open field. Behind us were thousands of transports, on whom the enemy made nightly bombing raids. All night long the big German bombers flew to and fro, dropping their deadly charges on everything in sight. After each raid, we heard the blood-curdling squeals of wounded horses in terrible agony; and later, the cracks of rifles as the wounded animals were put out of their misery.

Some nights we were billeted in huts. This was worse than the front line. It was agony to remain there at the mercy of the German airmen who dropped their bombs – by the shovelful, it seemed – and went back for fresh loads to repeat the performance. All night long we lay frightened and tense, until the bombing raids were over or daylight came.

One day we moved into an old trench ahead. On our left were five observation balloons in a row, the nearest one about two hundred yards away. At sundown, we heard the drone of an airplane and saw a German plane swoop down on the farthest balloon. There was a bust of machine gun fire and a faint white wisp of smoke rose from the top of the balloon. Suddenly the smoke turned black and the balloon burst into flames. There was another burst of a machine gun, and the second balloon went up in flames. In this way, the plane swooped from one balloon to another until all five were shot down. Our anti-aircraft guns were bursting forth at the plane from all sides, but as usual, they were shooting wild. Then some of our planes came over. The German tried desperately to zigzag his way back to his own line, but it was too late for him. One of our fellows got directly above him and shot him down.

Next afternoon Skinny and I took a walk. We came upon the motor of a German plane, buried deeply in the ground. Farther on we found the aviator, his head and shoulders sticking in the ground. He must have landed headfirst with a terrific force.

On our right was another observation balloon. The Germans made many attempts to bring it down, but the balloon had always been hauled down in time to avoid that fate. One day the balloon went up higher than usual. We were told that it was loaded with explosives. This time it would not be hauled down; it would explode at the first bullet, the concussion bringing down the plane.

Anxiously we watched. It was not long until a German plane came straight for the balloon. With a burst of machine gun fire there was a terrific explosion. But the plane was too far away to suffer from the force of the explosion; and in a sharp bank, it turned and retreated to the German lines.

That night we could not sleep anywhere. We were bombed from dusk until daylight. There was much machine gun fire above us. I saw two planes come down in flames, the long streaks of fire spiraling slowly down to earth like huge comets.

We moved into the front line. Here we had little shelter and were shelled a few times. However, I felt safer than in supports. The bombs were worse than the shells.

We did not know the location of the German trenches and every night a patrol of six men and an officer was detailed to go out into No Man's Land to scout around. One night the party went out and never returned. Three weeks later we received word from the officer: they were prisoners in Germany! Evidently, they had wandered too far and had been captured.

About the middle of October, we were relieved and went back to a small village for a rest. There were rumors about that we should be sent up to the Passchendaele front.

A few days later we marched to a nearby railhead and entrained.

Chapter 15

A shell hole at Passchendaele.

After weary hours of travel, we arrived at Hazebrouch on the Belgian front. We alighted from the train and were divided up into small parties. Our party, consisting of eleven men, was billeted in a comfortably large house on the outskirts of town.

On entering the house, our host directed at me a question in Flemish, I did not comprehend his meaning, so he tried me in French. Although I had a slight knowledge in that language, it was too inadequate to understand him. I shook my head. "I can speak only English."

His wife, an elderly woman of about fifty years, seemed to be enjoying our inability to comprehend each other and laughingly addressed her husband in Low German: "Los ihn Geh. Er versteht ja doch nichts." (Leave him alone. He understands nothing anyway.)

At this remark, I could not refrain from laughing and quickly turned away, lest she might know that I understood her.

The next day we moved on; and arrived late in the evening at a camp situated a few miles north of Ypres. The shelter I was in contained nine men, including Skinny and J.C. We felt quite fatigued after our last move and decided to get a good night's rest in store for the early activities sure to follow the next morning.

We had scarcely begun to make preparations for sleep, when we heard the drone of approaching airplanes. I immediately guessed that it was the enemy and intimated to Skinny and J.C. that it would be wise to gather our kits and seek some shelter that was more bombproof. J.C. argued against my suggestion, pointing out that we were as safe here as anywhere and could be injured only by a direct hit. Our argument was stopped when hell broke loose on all sides.

The roars of the motors were completely drowned by the ear-splitting reports of exploding bombs. Shrapnel was flying all around, tearing large holes in our canvas roof. The bursting yellow flashes seemed everywhere at once; and the air was filled with sulpher from the exploding bombs, so heavy that it congested our lungs. The sudden inferno, lasting but a few seconds, seemed an infinite period.

At last the intense racket subsided and we again heard the drone of motors, diminishing as the planes drew away from us. My ears were ringing; faintly I heard Skinny's voice, asking if anyone was hurt. I looked around for J.C. and saw that he was very pale. He did not speak for a moment and then he said:

"No one hurt. But it would be better to be either killed or wounded; then we could get away from it all. But now we shall just have to wait until he makes the next call and go through it all again."

We soon found out that J.C.'s prophecy was correct, and again we heard the drone of approaching airplanes. Knowing that there were a large number of divisional transports' horses and mules station to our right, we concluded this to be the object of the German Gothas, and made a hasty retreat to our extreme left. We had gone about a hundred yards, when the terrific din of exploding bombs again rent the air. After the explosions ceased and as the sound of the planes' motors died away, there was an awful squealing of horses and mules in extreme anguish. We heard someone firing shots and in a few minutes the wounded animals were silenced.

Fortunately, everything was quiet for the remainder of the night and we were able to get some sleep. We remained in our shelters throughout the following day.

In the evening the order came to move on. After going for some time, we arrived at an old, deserted trench, which had been the German front line before the Third Battle of Ypres; and orders came to halt. On exploring the trench, we found it well equipped with deep dugouts, which we considered quite bombproof and we soon settled ourselves in the temporary quarters. The sergeant major came around and revived our spirits with a stiff drink of rum. He explained to us that we were within four miles of the line which was now in front of Paaschendaele. On the following night the battalion would move into supports and occupy some captured German pill boxes.

After the sergeant major had left, we rolled into blankets and greatcoats and were soon asleep. Several times during the night we were awakened by the loud reports of bombs exploding near at hand. I did not understand the motive of the enemy as usually their nightly raids occurred farther in the rear.

Next morning I went out, intent upon learning the result of last night's bombardment and I learned that the enemy had been trying to prevent a working party from repairing a railway which had been blown out previously, and that they had also been bombing another party engaged in laying a plank road near our entrenchment. Thinking that we were comparatively safe in our present position four miles behind the front, I decided to go over and examine the plank road. At that moment Skinny came up.

"Come, Skinny, let's go and see what damage they did to the plank road last night," I invited.

"Miller, for goodness sakes, stay away from there! I heard one of the engineers say that the plank road is kept under continual shell fire to prevent transportation.

J.C. came up, and I asked him to accompany me. He assented quite readily. "Where you go Miller, I feel safe."

We took our gas masks and set out. After proceeding a few hundred yards to the right we came upon a long windy row of debris: wagons, smashed beyond repair, dead horses and mules, bits of harness, tin and every other conceivable rubbish, piled three and four feet high. We climbed over it all and found ourselves on the plank road. It was evident that more then one scene of horror had been enacted along this road.

We turned toward the front and followed the plank road which wound here and there, around stagnant water holes, through the shell torn country. Everywhere there was the awful evidence of death, seemingly to hover about us and all over the landscapes. Occasionally we stopped to examine a dismantled field gun or a derelict tank lying in the mud and water at the side of the road.

We had advance about a mile, when a shell exploded ahead of us, hurling two large planks and other objects about a hundred feet in the air.

J.C turned to me. "I don't think it safe to go any farther. Let's go back. This is no place for a preacher's son."

On turning, we came upon a German Officer's high top boot lying at the side of the road. Evidently, he had lost his leg for the bone from the knee down was still protruding from the boot. I looked away in disgust. J.C. turned to me with a grimace.

"Miller, is that what we are fighting for?"

"It is not for us to decide," I answered.

"Then who is to decide it? He cried. "Oh, I wish I were back home. I would be content to clean out stables for the rest of my life, if I could only get away from this."

I remained silent on our way back to our underground quarters. On arriving there, Skinny told us that we should move up into supports in the afternoon. He had spoken to a runner who had been sent down to guide us. The quarters were very good up there, but there were not enough pill boxes to accommodate the entire battalion.

"I suppose we shall be the unlucky ones," J.C. remarked.

"I don't mind staying outside," I said, "as long as we are not shelled or bombed."

I looked around for Ted and found him sitting in a small funk-hole, with despair written all over his face. I tried to cheer him, but he stared gloomily ahead in a hopeless manner. The war depression was on him, too. Feeling sorry, I let him to his own thoughts and went back to Skinny and J.C.

At four o'clock that afternoon we started off for supports. We followed a duck walk for about two miles, and everything went fine. I suspected, however, from my many experiences in the front line that the enemy would not allow our whole battalion to proceed quietly in broad daylight without peppering us with whiz bangs. A German observation balloon was up ahead and I told Skinny and J.C. to watch out – something was sure to happen.

I was not wrong. A moment later there was a faint report; at that same time five shells dropped around us, fortunately doing no damage other than throwing up a great deal of mud and water. Had we kept moving, we should have been safe, for I knew the enemy would have difficulty in locating our exact range. But the order came down the column to scatter. I told skinny and J.C. to follow me and be quick about it, because another salvo would soon follow the first. We ran as fast as we could for about a hundred yards and then flopped. Another five shells came over, landing in a diamond shape and exploding. The call for stretcher bearers rang out, and men ran about in every direction. After the smoke cleared away we learned that one man had been killed and several wounded.

Volunteers were called to bury the dead man. I asked Skinny and J.C. to come with me, but they were not in the mood and tried to dissuade me. I went, however, and found two men already digging the shell hole a little longer, while the battalion chaplain was going through the dead man's pockets in search of his pay book and personal effects.

When the hole was long enough, we rolled our unfortunate comrade in and commenced to cover him up, while the chaplain read the Lord's Prayer out of a small bible. He had just begun, "Our Father, Who art in..." when bang! Another salvo of shells exploded near us. We all ducked. When everything was quiet, we again started to roll in the earth, while the Padre continued his prayer. He got as far as "Thy Kingdom come..." when bang! More whiz bangs. The Padre was feeling pretty shaky by this time but he was determined to finish what he had started and we began shoveling once more. He got all the way through the Prayer without any further interruptions and immediately left for the nearest shell hole.

Orders were to stay concealed until dark. My grave-digging companions and I retired to a nearby shell hole and crouched down. A drizzling rain descended upon us and soon we were soaking wet and miserable.

At dusk I arose and went to the back of the platoon to locate Skinny and J.C. I found them crouching in a small shell hole and asked them how they were feeling. Skinny answered me by bawling me out for having undertaken the unnecessary risk –

"What did you expect to get out of it?" he asked.

"Well, I thought I might get the D.C.M. or the Victoria Cross." I answered facetiously.

"You are more likely to get a little white cross with R.I.P. on it," he muttered.

Orders came to move on. After following the walk for another mile in the dismal rain, I saw, silhouetted against the sky, a box-like structure which proved to be a pill box. Our platoon was to occupy the pill box. The sergeant ordered the first fifteen men inside, leaving Sneezigs, Skinny, J.C. and me, along with about a dozen others, outside to seek whatever shelter possible.

About a hundred paces to the left we found a suitable shell hole. After digging it considerably larger with our entrenching tolls, to suit our purpose we fastened four rubber sheets together and stretched them over the top to keep off the rain. Sneezigs scouted around for a few moments and returned with some sand bags for seats. Then we crawled in.

As it was still raining heavily, I was soaking wet and covered with mud. There was no chance to dry myself, so I leaned on my pack and lit a cigarette. All was still, except for the incessant patter of the rain. I felt cold and miserable and knew from the expressions on the various faces around me, that the rest of the boys felt likewise.

I was sick of war. This was some life! Mud and water and shivers – how much longer would it last? This was one of my moments of deepest depression. I longingly thought of home and a nice, cozy fire to warm myself. I was at home again, sitting beside the stove, while my mother was bustling about making dinner. I could almost smell the appetizing odor that permeated the kitchen. Then I was outside with my sisters, sliding down the snow bank back of our house. I could hear their joyful laughter and could see the white, misty snow flying before my eyes – I began to feel cold and heard someone shout – "The water is coming in!"

I awoke with a start and found myself sitting in pool of cold water. A voice beside me cried. "Let's get out of here, Miller."

"Where do you fellows want to go?" I asked.

Sneezigs suggested that we dig a trench beside the pill box and stretch our rubber sheets from the roof down, to keep off the rain. Skinny, J.C. and I thought this a good plan and followed Sneezigs; the rest of the boys stayed in the shell hole. We soon had a better shelter fixed up and lay down inside.

The rain slowly subsided. The moon came out from behind the clouds and lit up the muddy landscape. I arose and went out to have a look around. Strings of pack-mules, heavily laden with shells were slowly making their way around the water-filled shell holes, sinking deeply in the mud at every step. Some of the mules became stranded in the mud, belly deep, and had to be shot by the drive.

My attention was drawn back by the report of a gun in the distance and the sound of a shell coming towards me. Instinctively I flopped. A terrific explosion shook the ground. On arising I saw that the shell had almost made a direct hit on the shell hole we had previously occupied. I ran over and found that two men had been killed, three badly wounded and several others severely shell-shocked. Surely it had been God's hand which had guided the four of us to a different shelter!

We remained at the pill box for several days. The rain continued in periodic outbursts. Scarcely would we be dry after a previous shower, when another torrent would descend and again drench us to the skin. The enemy observation balloon was up every day and we had to remain in seclusion for fear of drawing their fire.

On the evening of the fourth day, we were ordered to the front. We all felt indifferent to the order; one might as well lie in the mud up there as here.

We had proceeded by a short distance, when a salvo of shells burst around us, but strangely fortunate, did not damage. The order came to scatter. Another salvo came screeching over, this time carrying disaster with it. The call for stretcher bearers rang out, and I learned that five men had been wounded.

Soon we were moving forward again. By the flares ahead, I knew that we were almost upon the front line. Two companies moved to the left, we continued ahead. I learned that the first two companies were going into the front line, and that we were going up into immediate supports. After a few hundred yards more, we came upon our captain standing on the bank of an old trench, the bottom of which was covered with water. We were ordered into the trench, with instructions to keep our equipment on and be ready at a moment's notice, because it was expected that Fritz would make a counterattack in the morning.

I looked around for my close mates, not having seen any of them since the last shells came over and finally found Sneezigs who told me that Ted was still around, but that Skinny and J.C. had been sent back shell-shocked.

The moon appeared from behind a bank of clouds and lit up the surroundings. Sneezigs, who was having a look around, turned to me, "Look Miller, this looks yust like the Ypres Salient! We are hemmed in on three sides!"

I climbed out of the trench to have a look also. In the moonlight, every feature of that desolate area was easily discernible. The front line was ahead and on both sides, winding around us like a horseshoe; the right flank curved in almost directly behind us before straightening out to the south. We were exposed to the enemy on three sides. It certainly looked at if we were in a precarious position.

I crawled back into the trench, dug a funk-hole in the side, and sat down. All was unnaturally still. Occasionally there was a short burst of a machine gun. Then all was quite again.

I was half dozing when a lieutenant came down the trench, asking for volunteers to go with him into No Man's Land to bring back a wounded man. He explained that the man had been lying out there for forty-eight hours, and was being heard from time to time, calling for help. A search party had been out all night, but had been unable to find him; so there would be another out tonight – would we go? Sneezings and I volunteered immediately. We were told to leave our equipment, with the exception of gas masks, and to follow him. We picked up two men and a stretcher bearer from D Company farther on down the trench, and started off across the muddy field.

The moon had hidden itself behind a large cloud, which gave us a greater sense of security. It was hard going. Our feet were soaking wet and sank in the soft mud ankle deep at every step. The stretcher bearer had the greatest difficulty of all. Every little while he fell headlong into a shell hole and had a hard time extricating himself and the stretcher.

We reached the front line and halted while our officer made inquiry as to the direction of the call for help. Then we resumed our advance, in extend order about twenty yards apart, proceeding very slowly and listening intently for any sound or moan that might lead us to our wounded comrade. We had gone a considerable distance and were beginning to feel doubtful of our position, when flares started to go up on all sides. Our officer came up, saying excitedly: "I think we'd better go back before the fun begins."

At that moment, we heard a deep moan. The officer flashed his light in the direction of the sound. I expected to see a German, but to my surprise it was a wounded Canadian Indian, lying in a shell hole with one leg doubled up behind him. On approaching him I noticed that his thigh was smashed right through; and on close inspection, to my great horror, I saw that the flesh had burned back from the effect of the sun, and that there were maggots crawling around in the mutilated stump.

The poor fellow silently regarded us with glazed eyes, not knowing if we were friends or foes. Our officer asked him how he was.

"Cig – a – rette," he gasped weakly, the last part of the word trailing off in an anguished whisper.

We promised to give him one as soon as we got him back in our own lines, as we could not risk lighting one now. Gently we lifted him and placed him on the stretcher. As careful as we tried to be in carrying him back we could not help stumbling occasionally, each sudden jar drawing from him a suppressed groan of unendurable anguish which pierced me like a knife. I knew there was little hope for him.

After some hard work, we landed in our front line and there lit a cigarette for him. He inhaled a few times then closed his eyes. We left him in other hands and went back to our own trench in the support line.

A faint red showing in the eastern sky and although I was dead tired, I knew that we should have to stand to, in case that Fritz should make his counter-attack. At about five-thirty it started to rain again. The captain and the sergeant major came around with the rum issue. After we had a drink, the captain told us that if the Germans attacked, we should go up and meet them with our bayonets. I hoped that it would not come off, for the one reason that I was tired and craved sleep badly.

At six o'clock, or a little later, a red flare went up, followed by a green one. My hopes were ended. I knew from experience that hell would break loose at any moment.

Chapter 16

An opening morning artillery barrage

Like a shot from a pistol, the whole German Artillery opened up simultaneously. Shells burst everywhere on our front and support lines, but as the ground was soft, they buried themselves deeply before exploding and did little damage.

A sniper's rifle cracked faintly, close at hand, to our right, and the man second from me fell dead, with blood oozing from his temples. There was a little wood between our support line and the front, though only the stumps were now standing; and a German sniper, evidently, had crossed the front and lay concealed behind the stumps. My eyes were trained on the spot where the report had come from and I held my rifle ready to retaliate.

Germans were coming over the ridge on our right. The drive was on.

Sneezigs shouted in my ear "Miller, I think we are surrounded! I am going to see the captain!" And he went on down the trench.

A moment later he returned, "I don't know what's wrong with the captain. I told him about our position, but he yust looked at me without saying a word.

"Never mind, Sneezigs. We shall stay here until we are ordered to move. Keep your eye on that bunch of stumps; there is a sniper in there"

A moment later he raised his rifle to fire, but withdrew it.

"What did you see?" I asked.

"Someone behind that stump," he pointed.

I looked closely and saw a man tumbling from behind a stump into a shell hole, but I could not distinguish if he were a German or one of our fellows. The heavy firing died down. We could hear only the rattle of machine guns beyond the woods. At last the firing ceased entirely. The rain increased and was soon coming down in heavy torrents.

The sergeant-major came around with another issue of rum. He told us that the Germans had driven our right flank and were now directly behind us; they were in possession of the woods, thus cutting us off from A and B Companies.

"What are we going to do?" I asked.

"Counter-attack, I think," he responded. "You fellows better have something to eat; it may be the last meal for some of you."

I had two tins of pork and beans and some hard-tack. There was no more gas in our Primus, although I would have given anything to have something warm to eat. Sneezings had his beans in his mess tin and was burning his love letters, and everything available from his pockets that was not too damp, in trying to heat his grub.

After our cold meal, Sneezigs said to me, "Miller, you look all in. You better get a little shut-eye. I shall keep watch and wake you if anything turns up."

I was awakened by Sneezigs shaking me and saying excitedly: "Miller, wake up! The captain wants to see you at headquarters."

I quickly aroused myself and went down. The captain was in his quarters, with two runners waiting.

"Miller," he said. "I want you to deliver a message to headquarters at the front. These two men will accompany you. You must be very careful and use every precaution, because there are German snipers in the woods on our right, close to where you fellows have to pass.

This was staggering news to me – I felt that it would mean the end. Yet I experienced a great sensation of pride at being the picked man for the job. If ever there was any glory to be gained in the war, now was that opportunity; and I was determined to do my faithful best.

"You will go over one at a time and about thirty paces apart, so that you will not all be hit at once. Follow to the end of this trench, where you will run into an old German communications trench leading to the front. Follow it to the end, and then you will have to go overland about three or four hundred yards to the front. Best of luck to you boys!" With these words, our captain saluted. We returned the salute and left him.

One of my companions, a small chap named Hubbert, seemed quite unconcerned at the time; but he was very young; and I gathered that he knew not what was in store for us. The other, a tall fellow by the name of Roberts, was a very happy-go-lucky type; he wore a constant smile and seemed to carry a great deal of hope around his person.

We started down our trench, Roberts leading, then I, and Hubbert following. When we reached the end, we came to the communication trench. Roberts stopped.

"I wonder if this is the right trench."

Hubbert looked over the top; "Yes, I can see a pill box ahead."

We turned and continued along the old German communication trench toward the front. The rain had stopped, and the sun was breaking through. We were feeling better now, as things were warming and brightening up.

I saw Roberts stoop down, then hold up a sand bag and shake it. I thought it was a bag of rations and was glad because I had run out. It turned out to be a gallon jug.

"Rum," said Hubbert joyfully smacking his lips.

"No such luck," said I.

Roberts, with a wide grin on his face, was pointing to the seal on the jug. "There she is, boys, S.R.D. – Seldom Reaches Destination, but it sure reached its destination this time." He began to pull the cork.

"Rum she is," laughed Hubbert, happily and slapped my back.

"Who has a knife?" asked Roberts. "This cork is in tight."

I pulled out my army issue jack-knife and began to pry out the cork. At last it came, and the strong odor of rum assailed our nostrils. I lifted the jug and took a small drink. It was the real stuff, so I took a lengthy draw and passed the jug to Hubbert.

"I suppose our fellows were forced to abandon this in a hasty retreat," said Roberts, as he took the jug from Hubbert and put it to his lips.

I began to empty my water bottle; and when my turn came again, I filled it to the brim with rum. Hubbert did the same, and Roberts was about to follow suit, but I restrained him –

"Save your water. Two bottle of rum is plenty for us and you may need your water worse than rum."

"Well, we can hide it and pick it up when we get back," he said rather regretfully, as he replaced his water bottle.

We sat down for a while and each had two more drinks from the jug. Then we had a smoke. While we were thus occupied, I took out the Captain's message and read it aloud to the other two. It read: We are cut off by the enemy. It would be suicide for us to attempt to move to the front line." At the bottom it bore the signature of our captain. I made Hubbert and Roberts repeat it twice and then replaced it in my breast pocket.

"How in the world does he expect us to get through?" Hubbert asked nervously.

"I don't know, but let's get going anyway," I said, already feeling the effects of the heavy imbibing.

"One more drink, boys," said Roberts, as he again lifted the jug.

We each had another long snort; and after setting the jug down at the side of the trench and covering it up, we set out. I gave them orders to follow me in extended order, about twenty yards apart. We went over the top and separated.

We had scarcely gone fifty feet, when a sniper's rifle cracked on our near right; by the report, I knew that he was shooting at us, and quickly dropped into a shell hole.

After having remained still for about twenty minutes, I cautiously raised my head and peered over the edge to see if I could locate the others. Bang! My eyes were filled with mud, and small particles stung my face; the bullet had struck the ground right in front of my nose.

I dropped back into the hole and wiped my face. Then I took another stiff drink of rum and lay back, intending to stay here until dark if necessary. I was trying to conceive an idea to fool the Heinie marksman, when another shot rang out. On looking out I saw Roberts falling into a shell hole, clutching his right side, and Hubbert tumbling in after him.

Thinking that if Roberts were wounded, Hubbert would be able to attend to him; I made another dash and sprang up out of the shell hole. Three consecutive shots were fired at me – I felt the air pressure as a bullet whizzed past my face. After running about fifty yards, I dropped into another shell hole to catch my breath. A moment later, Hubbert, out of breath and very pale dived in after me.

"Roberts is dead!" he cried. "He got hit in the stomach and after taking a drink of water, he passed out. I have his paybook and watch and he told me to write to his mother."

I noticed that he was trembling. "How do you feel?" I asked, hoping to encourage him.

"Give me a drink of water," he said desperately.

"I have only rum."

"To hell with rum! I want water!"

He was almost hysterical and as pale as death. Then I saw that he was bleeding quite profusely, for on his tunic there was a deep red stain which was rapidly growing larger. I immediately unbuttoned his tunic and found that he had been shot in the neck, but fortunately it was only a flesh wound. Pulling out a tube of iodine, which I always carried, I painted the wound.

He began to tremble more. "For God's sake give me a drink of water!"

"I have no water," I replied. "I have only rum in my bottle, same as in yours."

"To hell with rum!" he cried again.

I gave him a smoke and he leaned back with closed eyes. The colour slowly returned to his face – I realized that he was more frightened than hurt.

When he seemed calmer, I said: "Well, let's try again for the pill box."

"Give me a little more time," he begged.

I could feel the effects of the rum more than ever and was becoming drowsy. This was no time for sleep, though, so after taking another drink, I roused Hubbert. "Let's go. If I get killed, you will find the message for headquarters in this breast pocket. In the other is my paybook with my home address. Write to my mother and explain how it happened. I would do the same for you."

He nodded his head, but was too overcome to speak.

With a leap I started off. Bullets whizzed past me and struck all around. A sudden burning pain stung my right shoulder. But I did not stop until I was out of breath, and then flopped into another shell hole. After my wind returned, I raised my head to look for Hubbert, but could not see him. I had a drink of rum, and then looked again. This time I saw Hubbert running like a deer toward me. Several shots were fired at him, and his helmet flew from his head, but he did not stop. I held up my helmet, so that he might see where I was and a moment later he dropped into the hole beside me, completely out of breath.

"Are you hit?" I asked.

"Up here!" He pointed to his head.

I looked at it, but found that there was no blood, only a bunch of hair missing in one place.

"No blood, so don't worry, Hubbert."

As I raised my arm, I felt a sharp pain down my side. "I believe I am hit somewhere," I said, "but I don't know where."

Something warm and wet was creeping down my back. I thrust my left hand inside my trousers and reached back under my tunic as far as I could. When I withdrew my hand, it was covered with blood. I began to shake then, and had many queer sensations.

Hubbert, who was watching me, burst out: "My God, you are cracked up badly!"

This, I believe, frightened me more than anything. I pulled out my bottle, drank greedily, and cried: "Come on, let's get going!"

Away I went. A number of shots went flying around me, but I did not stop until I reached the front line trench, tumbling in head first.

On rising, I asked for the major of the company and was told to follow the trench up to the pill box, where I should find the major in the first partition. I followed these directions and soon found myself outside the pill box.

There was a German officer lying on a stretcher. There being no one else around, I asked him in German: "Are you wounded badly?"

He looked at me closely, somewhat started. Then, after a moment he said: "It's bad. My legs are broken."

"Should you like a drink of rum?"

"Yes, I should like to have a little please."

I put my bottle to his lips and let him take as much as he wished. The sun was sinking in the west and I figured that it must have taken me about three or four hours to get across.

I entered the pill box, saluted the major, and handed him my message.

After reading it, he asked: "How was it coming over?"

I gave him all the details of our mad scramble from shell hole to shell hole; and told him that Roberts had been killed, that Hubbert had been wounded and had not yet arrived, and that I had been hit also; but I withheld from him our incident of finding the rum.

When I had finished, he said: "Well, Miller, you look all in. Would you like a good, stiff drink of rum?"

Although I was already full of it, I said: "Sure, Sir," and swallowed another large mouthful of the fiery liquor.

"You had better take a good sleep," the major said kindly. I shall call you if I need you."

I lay down on the floor and was soon fast asleep.

It was broad daylight when I awoke. My head ached badly and the pain in my shoulder was so intense that I could not move my arm. There were only strange faces about; by their badges I knew they were from a different brigade. I asked one of the fellows about my battalion.

"They were relieved at ten o'clock last night."

"What time is it now?"

He looked at his wrist watch. "It is now eight o'clock. How come you missed your battalion?"

I explained that I had fallen asleep and had not been called. He offered me a drink of water. After taking a good drink, I felt better and went outside.

The day was beautiful. Everything was calm and the sun was shining brightly. I began to feel warm and my spirits rallied.

The German officer was stilling lying in the same position as before; but I noticed that he was much paler – his face was ashen. I approached and offered him another drink of rum, which he accepted greedily. Then he told me that a shell had landed near the pill box during the night and a sliver had struck his chest. I opened his tunic and saw a very ugly wound. I had great difficulty on account of my wounded shoulder, but I put some iodine in the gash; and with my own dressing, I put on a rough bandage. He thanked me very profusely, saying he hoped he would be able to do something for me some day.

Even though I had been wounded by one of his comrades on the previous day, and even though I was living in constant dread of death by a German hand, yet I felt sorry for him. Here was a man for the other side of the fence; and as I regarded him, I realized that there was no animosity between us – only a mutual sympathy. These Germans were being impelled to kill and destroy, not to suit their own purposes any more than it suited our own. My heart rebelled against the cold-blooded executions of war; and when I thought of the trivial reasons a few statesmen had for declaring war, I was filled with repugnance; all this unnecessary bloodshed, millions of men suffering needlessly and living in dire torment – all because someone said: "Let's declare war."

I asked him for his shoulder strap, a silver-edged strap with the gilt figures "22" on it, as a souvenir. He said I was welcome to anything he possessed, so I cut it off. (It is one souvenir I prize very highly and shall not willingly part from.) I bade him farewell with words: "Auf Wiedersehen" and left him.

A group of stretcher bearers approached and asked me where the wounded German officer was. I showed them and watched as they lifted him up and started back way I had come the day before. They were carrying the Red Cross, and I decided to follow them, if they got over unmolested.

An officer of the Second Battalion came up and asked what I was doing here. I explained my predicament and inquired where my battalion had gone.

"They went back to the railhead," he responded. "I shouldn't try to get back now if I were you. Better wait until the next stretcher party goes over and go along.

"I think I shall try it if that party gets over," I said, pointing to the stretcher bearers, who were about fifty yards away by this time.

I watched them closely. Suddenly two shots rang out, and one of the stretcher bearers fell. The rest set down their burden and disappeared into shell holes. I realized that my chances of getting through were pretty slim, and decided to stay here a while longer.

A dead man lay in the shell hole about six yards away. By his sleeve colours, I saw that he had belonged to my own battalion; and I quickly went over to ascertain who it might be. On turning him over, I saw that it was Mooney, one of our machine gunners. He had been a real fellow, always smiling and optimistic. Many times he had said to me: "Cheer up Miller, it will soon be over." Then he would go on and repeat the same to everyone he met.

My heart was lonely at the loss of another friend. I began to miss the cheerful company of my mates and resolved to make a run for it in an endeavour to get back to my own battalion. My shoulder was becoming more painful, and my whole arm felt numb. After taking a drink of rum and smoking a cigarette, I got up and started to run.

I had proceeded but a short distance, when two shots cracked sharply; one bullet struck the ground a few feet ahead of me, the other passed through my left sleeve. More shots rang out, and bullets struck all around me, but I kept on. I was soon out of breath; my lungs seemed to be bursting; my shoulder ached and throbbed at every step, but I was determined to run until completely over the first ridge. I passed our support line and not seeing anyone around, continued on. The firing ceased, but I did not stop until I was safely on the other side of the ridge. Exhausted and unable to go another step, I dropped down.

After resting for about an hour, I moved on, following the old duck walk which wound here and there around the water-filled shell holes. I reached the old trench near the railhead and found my battalion there.

The first man I met was our company sergeant-major. He was surprised to see me, and exclaimed: "Miller! Where did you come from? We thought you had been killed or taken prisoner, and reported you missing."

I narrated my experiences to him.

"Better come into my dugout, I shall fix you up with a drink of rum," he invited.

After having a drink, I told him that I was wounded. He immediately took me down to the medical officer. After examining my wound, the M.O. informed me that fortunately it was only a flesh wound, but that irritation from my tunic had caused infection; and he ordered his staff to apply hot fomentations every ten minutes. After my wound was entirely cleansed, my shoulder was swathed with bandages and I was ordered to the Casualty Clearing Station for inoculation.

What a great relief! Now I could walk freely, without my blood-dried tunic rasping and cutting my shoulder at every stride.

I left the dressing station and went down to find some of my company. On entering the old dugout we had previously occupied, I received a surprise. There, in the corner, sat J.C. and Skinny, reading letters and eating chocolate bars. Two lovely cakes lay before them, and a parcel on the floor gave evidence of more groceries.

"Hello, fellow," I greeted.

"My God, it's Miller!" exclaimed J.C. "Where the devil have you been? You look just like a dead man!"

Skinny handed me a mirror, and when I gazed at the skeleton-like countenance which confronted me, I was truly astonished. My features were shrunken, my skin was white as a sheet, my hair was over half grey, I had a ten-day growth of beard, and my uniform was splotched and splattered with mud and blood. I could scarcely believe my eyes. But it was I, twenty-two years old – with the features of an old, old man. I burst out laughing.

"I'll fetch your pack from the quartermaster's," said Skinny. He went out and returned shortly with my pack.

I took out my razor, soap and towel, and soon had my face scraped and washed. After that I felt better. Not having eaten since the morning of the previous day, I asked for something to eat. Skinny lit the old primus and made tea, while J.C. dug into the parcel and brought out some canned pork sausages.

Knowing that the boys would not be so very angry if I gave them a drink, I asked casually, "how is the rum issue hanging out?"

"Rotten as ever!" said J.C. vehemently. "Casualties or no casualties, we get only that shaving soap holder half full. The sergeant-majors and officers keep the rest to get tight on, or else the quartermasters sell it to the estaminets; and we have to pay half a franc for a measly smell, and then it's diluted. If I ever become a quartermaster, I'll see that you fellows get a water bottle full every day."

He was heating the sausages, when I asked, "should you like a drink now?"

His eyes nearly popped out of his their sockets, as he whirled around and looked at me. "You don't mean to tell me that you have some with you, do you?"

I pulled out my bottle and handed it over to him.

"Good old Miller!" he cried, bringing his hand down on my injured shoulder. I nearly jumped to the roof.

"Eat all the doggone cake and sausages," he laughed joyfully and tossed me a packet of Players cigarettes as well.

J.C. took a healthy snort and passed the bottle to Skinny, who did likewise. I sat down and devoured the food that was set before me as fast as I could. It seemed like the delectable Ambrosia of the Gods! At last my hunger was appeased and I lit a cigarette.

I told the boys of my experiences, and they, in turn, narrated their own; they had been sent back as shell-shocked, but had been on transport duty since.

J.C. was worried about the remainder of the jug of rum, which I had mentioned. "Let's go up now and get it. We have time till tonight to make it."

"Not for all of Belgium and France thrown in to boot, would I go," I said.

Skinny told me that the battalion had suffered heavy losses, and would be going out on rest the next morning. He did not know, however, what our destination would be.

At that moment, we were aware of a great commotion overhead followed by the explosion of bombs. We rushed out to see what was going on. Big German bombing planes, each accompanied by five or six smaller planes, or fighters, were bombing the railhead on our right. After unloading all their bombs, the formations turned and headed back to their own line. In an hour, they returned with fresh loads and continued the destruction.

I returned to the dugout for some sleep. When I awoke, it was evening and all was still. Skinny and J.C. were making supper. We finished the remainder of the food which the boys had received from home. Then J.C. turned to me –

"How is the bug juice coming?"

I pulled out my bottle, and we passed it around until it was empty. Then we rolled into our blankets and went to sleep.

Chapter 17

Canadian troops leaving the front

On leaving the Passchendaele sector, and after long marches and rough rides on motor lorries which bounced and skidded over the undulatory roads, controlled by relentless drivers whose main ambition it was to show off an adeptness they did not possess – movements that, as regular routines of our itinerant life, had long since become uninteresting – we arrived at Estree-Cauchy, as commonplace village, after the invariable style of villages of France, which was to be our next temporary resting place. We were billeted in barns, the usual procedure of that period humorously known as rest; and to add to our discomfort, the weather turned miserably cold, and it started to rain.

Cold and shivering, Skinny, Ted, J.C., Sneezigs and I huddled close together in the corner of the barn. We tried to resume our free and easy joking and chatter while on rest, but our efforts were fruitless; the last fourteen days at Passchendaele had sapped our spirits; we had grown old; no vestige remained of our former conviviality; and like lost children, nervous and trembling, we clung together. We were all the same. Each face lined with the irreparable expression of fear and worry, lean and pale, with haunted eyes staring gloomily ahead or casting furtive glances at one another. We were sick, mentally and physically. Even J.C., the laughing, talkative member of our group, was silent and glum. Only Skinny, the youngest of our five, still retained some of the old spirit. His eyes lit up occasionally as he watched the new men billeted with us enjoying themselves, laughing and joking and telling stirring tales of the new experiences. My heart went out to him as he gazed from us, silent and morose, to the new fellows, carefree and happy. This was no place for him. He was just a young kid. And even with us, his close pals, he was lost.

"Come on fellows," said J.C. rising, "let's go down to the estaminet and forget our troubles."

At this proposal, we arose and made our way to the nearest estaminet. On entering, we found the place almost filled with soldiers drinking vin blanc and French beer. We seated ourselves at a secluded table and ordered beer. Drinking slowly, we silently watched the new fellows around us, enjoying themselves.

"What about a dance?" one shouted hilariously.

"Fine, let's go," another returned.

One of the fellows went over to the hurdy-gurdy in the corner. "What will you have?"

"A waltz."

He dropped a penny into the slot, and the music box began to play a fast waltz. The young fellows coupled up and started to dance. Skinny's young blood stirred within him. He wanted to dance in the worst way, but none of us were in the mood. Finally, he spotted a young bugler and away they danced.

"I'd give anything to feel happy like those young fellows," said Ted sorrowfully.

"You talk as if you were old," I spoke up encouragingly. "Why Ted, we are just young fellows ourselves. I'll bet there are lots of them in this bunch that are at least ten years older than you."

"That's true," Sneezigs interposed. "I guess we are about the only old war horses left in this outfit."

"And yet," remarked J.C. "It's strange that we are still together. After all we've been through; the four of us have always come out. I wonder if we can last this way until the end of the war."

"We'll never see the end," said Ted gloomily. "I am sick of war and can't last much longer. The sooner something turns up, the better. Take Miller and me, for instance, we haven't missed a trip into the line yet."

"Not one," I asserted, "and I would rather walk into Death itself, than to keep on going into the line."

J.C. nodded. "I'll go crazy one of these days. My nerves are getting terrible. It's about time we got something else. What do you think fellows, about going to the doctor tomorrow to try and get a better job?"

"Suits me fine," I said hopefully.

Sneezigs was not very enthusiastic. It's no use. They would not give us older fellows a break anyway."

"Well fellows," commented Ted, "it may be all right for you, but for me, it's out of the questions. The M.O. knows me too well."

We ordered another drink. The French dame served us. I watched her as she toddled back and resumed conversation with an old French civilian. Apparently, their conversation concerned us, for the Frenchman leaned over and whispered in her ear; and she glanced over in our direction. She shook her head sadly. Her lips moved slowly, and I heard the words: "C'est la guerre".

Next morning, after breakfast, J.C. and I went to the doctor's office, which was established in the front room of a house. On entering, we were aware of the pervading odor of iodine and chloride of lime; one of our men, with a bad case of Impetigo, was sitting in a chair, having his legs bandaged. The M.O. was busily occupied marking the sick parade list and paid no attention to us.

At last our turn came. I saluted and told my story: I was nervous and weak from the terrible strain of front line life, and did not think I could stand another winter in the lines.

The M.O., a good natured fellow, was quite sympathetic.

"How long have you been with the battalion?"

"Eighteen months, and never missed a trip into the line."

"Have you ever been sick before?"

"Only once, last winter when I was laid up for eighteen days with Inflammatory Rheumatism."

"Well, Miller," he spoke kindly, "I don't know just what we can do for you; I shall speak to the colonel about it."

J.C. told practically the same story, with the exception that he had reported sick quite often. The M.O. cross-questioned him closely, and I suppose that he though J.C. was "swinging the lead". Finally, after a great deal of explanation, J.C. received the same assuring consideration.

Hopeful and light-hearted, we went back to our billet.

My joy was increased that night by a letter from Anne. Very concise as usual, yet the brief missive imparted a sweetness that made me fairly tremble. At the bottom, she had ended with love; that was all I needed to assure me of her steadfast devotion.

The following days were days of ease and rest. The sickly pallor began to fade away; eyes slowly lost the lifeless expressions and became rejuvenated almost to normal brightness. Every night the estaminets were brightly lit. Girls from neighbouring villages were attending dances, and our fellows were having a grand and glorious time.

One day I noticed Ted moping around with sorrowful mien. "What's the matter, Ted? Are you in mourning?"

"No," he answered gloomily. "They aren't worth mourning for."

"What's wrong?" I asked again, wondering what misfortune had befallen him.

"Oh, not much," he sighed. "Betty just got married to a lance corporal in Folkestone, that's all"

I felt sorry for him. "Never mind, Ted. She could not have loved you very much."

"Yes, she did," he defended her. "Only I believe that darn fool turned her head. Whatever you do, Miller, don't tell J.C. about it. He would roast me alive."

I promised to keep it a secret.

Christmas was approaching. Only three weeks remained, and we were still out on rest. But our protracted rest was not to be wondered about; naturally it would be our misfortune to be sent to the front for Christmas. I recalled our last dreary Christmas and wondered what was in store for us this time.

The boys were busy writing letters and buying trinkets to send home to their loved ones. I wrote long letters home and sent along a few souvenirs for Christmas. My heart was filled with longing. Oh, to be home with my dearly loved ones! What a Christmas it would be for me!

One morning a runner appeared, requesting J.C. and me to report to the battalion orderly room in full marching order. With strange misgivings, we packed up and went over.

When we entered, the adjutant handed us each a pass to Ferfay. "You," he addressed me, "will take up a short course in First Aid. And you," he turned to J.C., "will take up water resting."

This suited us fine. Happily, we set forth, assured that we were in line for bombproof jobs.

After a few days of training in Ferfay, during which time I acquired a light, rudimentary knowledge of First Aid work, we returned to our battalion.

That afternoon we started off towards the front. Everyone was feeling well after the long rest, and hope ran high that we should not have to go over the top.

We landed at a village that was partially destroyed, and were told that we should stay here in reserve for Christmas. This was good news; we were overjoyed at the thought of spending Christmas out of the line! A few estaminets were still operating and these were packed almost to the roof every night.

One morning, the M.O.'s orderly appeared, and asked J.C. and me to report to the M.O. immediately. We went over to his office, situated in a large house which was enclosed by an iron fence.

The M.O. received us with a smile. "I have jobs for you two fellows, if you think you can handle them. Corporal Miller, you will be attached to my staff and will remain here in the office as Medical Orderly. I have lost my sergeant and it put me out one man".

I was highly elated at this new undertaking, although I had some doubt about being able to handle the position. In any event I would endeavour to do my utmost.

To J.C. he said: "I am going to put you in charge of the battalion water wagons. Your duty will be to see that all water is tested and chlorinated. You will be attached to our staff, but will draw your rations with the headquarters staff."

J.C.'s eyes lit up. A smile played about his lips. The M.O. continued. "I have spoken to your major about this. Your can turn in your rifles and equipment to the quartermaster and begin your new duties immediately."

With light step, betokening lighter hearts, J.C. and I marched back to our billet. Ted and Sneezigs looked up, surprised.

"Why all the happy smiles?" inquired Sneezigs.

J.C. stuck his chest out proudly. "I am on the water wagon."

"It's about time you were," said Ted.

"No kidding," J.C. persisted. "I am in charge of the battalion water wagons, and Miller is Medical Orderly."

"Don't try to string that stuff J.C., I know you too well."

"It's true enough," I asserted happily.

At my words, they were convinced.

"That means," said Ted slowly, "that you will be leaving us."

I realized then how Ted felt, and my heart was heavy.

"Yes Ted. We have to report back for duty right away."

"I wish you fellows luck," said Sneezigs constrainedly.

"Thanks, old man," I returned, "but, we shall still be together on and off, you know."

"It will never be the same," Ted muttered sadly, "now that the old gang is split up."

J.C. and I gathered our things and prepared to leave. Ted came outside with me. We stood with hands gripped tightly, gazing at each other. My best friend in the outfit – for eighteen months we had eaten and slept together, confided our troubles and comforted each other, stood side by side and faced death together. Silently we faced each other. And invisible power held us together. I choked back a lump in my throat.

"Good luck, Ted."

"Good luck, Miller."

I turned in my rifle and equipment and reported for duty.

The new work was very interesting, and I soon learned the treatment for the various disorders and maladies that are brought on by army life. Allen and Ernie, the other two orderlies, were very likeable chaps and taught me many things about handling the sick and bandaging which rendered my duties easier.

One day, after watching me for a few minutes, the M.O. said: "Miller, you are doing good work. I like the way you handle the sick."

I was elated at these adulatory remarks and thanked him, at the same time assuring him that I should continue to do my best.

Christmas Eve, 1917, clear and frosty. I stood at the courtyard of our billet, thinking of our last Christmas Eve at the Etrun front. Should I see another at the front? Surely the war would end before another year! As I stood there, alone, I thanked God for having safely guided me thus far and prayed for His protection until the end.

The mail and rations arrived, and I received a parcel and letter from my mother. A strange feeling of excitement surged though me, and hastily I retuned to my billet to open the letter.

My mother was hopeful that this letter would reach me. They had seen my name in the paper, listed among the missing, and were almost worried to death. Also, there had been a rumor about that I had lost my legs in battle. But she could not believe it – God would protect her boy!

My heart stood still as I read further; "Your girl, Anne, got married to the returned solider with whom she had been driving around (as I wrote to you). Do not take this too hard, my boy – she never loved you as you believed, and you were both very young at the time. Pray to God for strength, and He will help you through ..."

My God! What strange tidings were these? It was incredible, utterly impossible! Anne Married? Why it was only three weeks since I had received a letter from her. But it was true! Had anyone else written me, I should not have believed it; but my mother was a woman of truth.

Weak and faint I staggered across the room and sat down on a chair. Despair clutched my heart. My sweetheart married to another – far easier it would have been to have borne news of her death! To her I had pledged myself and remained true; my faith in her had been my moral fortitude; she had been my shining star in every battle; but in vain – all my imaginations and my thoughts, filled with haunting sweetness, nourished by that beautiful memory, had been only vain illusions. Bereft of all my happy anticipations, deserted and forlorn, I felt like a condemned man.

The candle burned lower, spluttered for a few moments, and went out. I sat long in the dark, wrestling with the ponderous, enigmatical problem of how a woman could love one man, then turn suddenly, capriciously, and marry another. Bitterly I recalled the words of the general at the Somme. "You are fighting for your sweethearts..." My mind was whirling, becoming confused in a demoralizing turmoil. At last too weary to torment myself further, with my thoughts, I lapsed into a fitful slumber – that bewitching face hovers near me, encouragingly near. I strain with all my power; always beyond my grasp. I try again. Elusive and mocking, the tantalizing figure flutters away. It is no use; she is lost to me forever. I suffer in agony. Suddenly I am relieved. I feel strangely quieted and soothed. An angel is comforting me and stoking my hair. Very strange – it is the face of my mother!

I awoke with a feverish headache; my bereaved heart, heavy as lead, lay choking in my bosom. It was daylight. Voices came to me from the adjoining room. Dizzy and trembling, I went outside for a breath of fresh air. All was quiet and peaceful, not one shot was fired. It was Christmas morning, with a cold, wet mist hanging over the village. The crisp, moist air cooled my throbbing temples. In the broad daylight, sorrow is easier to bear.

Skinny came up to me grinning. "Merry Christmas, Miller."

"Thanks, Skinny, and the same to you," as we shook hands.

"I just came over to show you my new boots. How do you like them?" He had on a fine pair of brown leather trench boots.

"Very good," I offered. "Where did you get them?"

"From my dad, for Christmas. He was marked unfit for further service and is back in Canada now, you know."

"I am glad he got out of this mess."

"What's the matter, Miller? You look sick."

"Oh nothing, just a slight headache."

"Have a bad night?"

"No, not exactly."

"Come on, Miller, cheer up. This is Christmas, you know. I received a parcel and want you to try some of my Christmas cake." He encircled his arm about my waist and persuaded me to accompany him to his billet, where I enjoyed some of his sweets.

The sick parade came around, and I went back to the M.O.'s office. After my duties were over, I went out to find Ted. C Company's cook kitchen was in the backyard of our billet, and I watched the line up at the kitchen, hoping to see him.

Four Imperial soldiers were rolling a large barrel up the street. When they were opposite our billet, someone in our outfit shouted to them: "Watch out, you fellows; you are going to get pinched for stealing that barrel of wine."

The Imperials stopped short. "Strike me pink!" one of them muttered. After a short consultation, they turned and dashed off, leaving the barrel in front of our gate. Without hesitation, a number of our fellows, headed by J.C. went out and rolled the barrel into our yard. In no time the top was knocked in. There was a whole hogshead of French white wine.

Everyone crowded around, dancing and shouting: "Hurrah! Christmas wine for all!" Mess tins were dipped in again and again, and some of the fellows soon became tipsy.

I was filled with a sudden desire for drink. There was nothing else to hope for but to become intoxicated and drown my sorrows completely. I procured a mess-tin and joined in. Filling it, I gulped down the soothing contents. My veins re-acted warmly; new fire stirred my blood. This was real life. Ted was right – they were not worth worrying about.

I went into the house and called Allen and Ernie. With mess-tins they followed me out into the yard. I saw Ted and immediately went over to him.

"Come, Ted, you old rustler, get into the saddle beside me."

Ted's eyes nearly popped out. Sneezigs came up, and both stared to laugh.

"Miller, what happened? You are almost tight." Ted grinned at me.

"The tighter, the better. It's Christmas, and we are supposed to be happy, aren't we?"

"By Gosh!" Sneezigs sputtered, "something is wrong with your, Miller. It's the first time I ever saw you anxious to get tight."

"Nothing wrong at all," I laughed. "Come on. See if you guys can stay with the best of them."

Ted fell in beside me, grinning: "Well, I'll have to get tight now and stay with you to see that you don't get into trouble."

Ted helped himself to several good drinks in order to catch up with me. The boys were now filling the cook's dixies and going around from billet to billet with the refreshments. Everyone was singing and shouting hilariously. The celebration ran high!

My mind became confused. I felt myself beginning to stagger and realized that I was becoming inebriated. Yet I continued to take drinks; I was intent upon drowning my grief forever; and all the wine in France was not enough to cure my insatiable desire. Gradually I became more unsteady, and my sight became indistinct; figures wavered uncertainly before me.

I awoke next morning, feeling wretched and sick, with a sick headache and a disordered stomach. The fumes of intoxication had vanished. The inevitable grief remained. The effect was more depressing than before. To try and drown sorrow in drink was not at all pacifying, for in addition I now suffered pangs of remorse for my foolishness. Henceforth I would banish all afflicting thoughts form my mind, and allow Time to heal my wounded heart.

The owner of the brewery discovered the theft of the wine and laid a complaint at headquarters: the result was that we all had to contribute towards paying five hundred francs for the hogshead of wine. However, no one begrudged the money. We had well received its worth.

Orders came to move to the front. The weather was cold and wet, making us feel miserable. I carried my revolver and first aid kit of instruments and medicines. Allen carried two sand bangs of rations, and Ernie two sand bags of dressings.

We arrived at a dugout in the support line and prepared to establish our dressing station. After hanging the Red Cross flag at the side of the dugout and arranging everything handy as it should be, we sat around smoking and talking.

The front was very quiet. During the night, a few men reported sick with high temperatures. The M.O. thought it was trench fever and treated them with different medicines. Some got better after about twenty-four hours, but others became worse and had to be sent out to the hospital.

For heating purposes, we used a coke burner. Every evening after refilling the burner with coke, we set it outside the dugout, to allow all the gas to escape, before we brought it inside. One night one of our fellows brought the burner back and set it in the corner next to the entrance. Dropping the flap, which served as a door, we lay down to rest.

A drowsy feeling began to steal over me. My head ached, and heart palpitated rapidly. Thinking that I was getting sick, I covered myself with a blanket and tried to get some sleep. I had lain there for some time and was about to doze off, when someone in the dugout shouted: "Gas! Clear out everybody!"

There was a mad scramble for the entrance. I tried to get up, but found that I was helpless – my arms and legs were without feeling. My head was aching badly, and I could not open my eyes to see. Faintly, as if coming from a far-off distance, the doctor's voice came to me – "Take Miller up! Quick! He's badly gassed." Strong arms lifted me. I seemed to be floating on thin air. Black waves passed softly over me, and my mind lapsed into sweet oblivion.

Suddenly I was aware of the M.O. taking my pulse and could hear his voice. "I think he will be all right again. Hold this under his nose."

But I did not smell anything. A sudden intense pain shot through my head and when it had passed, I was able to open my eyes. The sun was shining brightly. I was lying on a stretcher in the trench, with the doctor, Allen and Ernie standing around me. I tried to get up, but they restrained me and told me to lie still. The doctor told Ernie to break another tube of aromatic spirits of ammonia and hold it under my nose. After inhaling several times my head cleared and I sat up.

The doctor smiled at me. "That was a close shave for you, Miller. Better keep the flaps of the entrance up next time, or we may all be gassed one of these nights."

For the next few days my lungs and my stomach were disordered. I lay around doing nothing, but feeling very miserable.

The New Year, 1918, dawned cold and wet. With helmet and gas mask, I set out for the front line, which was about two hundred yards ahead, to find Ted and see how he was getting along. I found him sitting in a funk-hole, with his feet wrapped in sand bags to keep out the mud. He was nibbling at a hard-tack, and beside him stood a newly-opened can of peaches.

"Good morning, Ted, and a Happy New Year to you," I greeted.

His eyes lit up. "The same to you Miller and many of them."

"Are you celebrating something?" I asked, indicating the can of peaches.

"No, not exactly," he grinned. "I bought those at the canteen before we came up here."

"Well, Ted, old timer, how are you getting along since the old gang split up?"

"It's awful lonesome up here," he said sadly. "These new fellows haven't got the pep we had; and furthermore, I don't make friends with them."

I saw that his face was drawn and pale, and there were dark circles around his eyes.

"You are not feeling well, Ted."

"No," he admitted. "Sometimes I wish the end would come, as I can't see how this war can ever stop. Just take a look over the top."

I got up and looked over. All I could see for hundreds of yards ahead was entangled wire, brown with rust.

"That's what they call the Hindenburg Line," Ted remarked grimly; "and we are going to have a fine time trying to cross it."

"Oh, cheer up, old fellow, you may not have to cross it," I comforted him.

We talked until it was time for me to return.

"By the way, Ted, where is Sneezigs?"

"Go to the right and you will find him."

"Well, I'll see you again soon. Cheerio, Ted."

"So long, Miller."

I went down the trench a little way and found Sneezigs sleeping in a funk-hole. Not wishing to disturb him, I turned and went back to our dressing station.

Chapter 18

Meritorious Service Medal

The Battalion finished its turn in the line without any serious loss and moved back to the village where it had spent Christmas.

On the second day out, the M.O. came into the medical office; and with outstretched hand, he strode up to me.

"Congratulations, Sergeant Miller!"

I stared at him in amazement.

"Yes, Miller, you have been awarded the Meritorious Service Medal and promoted to Sergeant for delivering a message to the front at Paaschendaele, while under heavy enemy fire. Here are three stripes: take off the one you have and sew on these."

The sudden news of this augmentation astounded me. I hardly believed myself awake. As my mind grasped the true meaning, a modest feeling of pride swept over me. The rest of the boys on the staff congratulated me in turn. I laid my stripes on the table and went outside.

Ted, Skinny and J.C., laughing and talking noisily, were coming down the street toward me. As they drew near, Skinny shouted, "Congratulations, Sergeant Miller!" and clicked his heels in a stiff salute. Sneezigs' eyes were filled with tears of laughter. J.C. was walking on his toes, his face turned sideways in a conceited manner.

Only Ted maintained a serious expression.

Ted shook hands with me and said soberly: "You three guys have been suck-holing around the captain lately, eh?"

"What do you mean?"

"Because you all got stripes and medals."

"Who got stripes and medals?" I feigned surprise.

"Now quit kidding the troops," said Skinny. "We know all about it."

"Well, I don't know what you are hinting at," I pretended.

"Come on down then, and we'll show you in black and white. It's in the orders."

"And who are the fortunate ones?"

"You, for one," said Ted; "you won the M.S.M. at Passchendaele and are now made Sergeant. Sneezigs here, our jam eater, gets the D.C.M. and is also made sergeant for throwing a couple of eggs at a machine gun post at Vimy. And our friend, J.C., is promoted to the exalted rank of full Corporal in charge of the water cars; he hasn't got a medal yet, but there may be one in the ration bag for him tonight.

"No," said Skinny, "if J.C. gets a medal, it will be the Croix de Guerre from General Foch, for supplying the troops with wine for Christmas."

"Steady there, lads!" J.C. said severely. "I will not tolerate your speaking that way about your superior officer. Attention at once!"

"You go to the devil," grinned Ted. "If you were made General tomorrow, I'd be darned before I'd ever salute you. But all kidding aside boys, we must celebrate the occasion tonight – just the five of us; and you all got paid yesterday, so there is no excuse that you are broke."

"Now you struck the right chord," I said. "Where shall we have it?"

Sneezigs knew a good place. "Let's have it at the 'Walk in and Back out'."

We agreed to meet there at eight o'clock and parted. I went back to my billet to write letters.

The first letter was to my mother, telling her not to worry about me; the rumors she had heard had been false, for I was as physically fit as ever. I also told her about my medal and promotions; and that she was not to worry now, as my duties and dangers would be lighter.

I finished the first letter and wrote another to a lady in Toronto, whose address I had found in a pair of hand-knitted socks with a note asking the wearer to acknowledge receipt of the article. I thanked her warmly and told her of the comfort and splendid service her handiwork was rendering me.

That night, at eight o'clock, the boys called for me, and we went down to the estaminet. I ordered a bottle of champagne, but the old dame shook her head. "Fini, Monsieur."

Ted looked up at her and growled. "Don't start that fini stuff again. We want the best in the house."

The poor woman was taken aback, and mumbled meekly: "Je ne sais pas, Monsieur."

Skinny, who could master the French language quite well, asked her what she had in the line of drinks.

"Vin blanc, vin rouge, beer, mulligas -"

"That's fine, old girl," Ted broke in. "Bring us five mulligas."

The old dame served us and we drank to one another's health.

"That's real stuff," said Ted, licking his moustache with great satisfaction. "I used to drink that in Paris."

"Can you still remember Paris?" J.C. asked soberly. "I heard that you got so tight there that you lost one of your putties in the middle of the street in broad daylight."

Ted stared at him for a moment, and then burst out: "Darn your soul, J.C. Where did you get that stuff?" He turned to me glowering: "Miller, you didn't tell him that, did you?"

"No, Ted," I assured him. "The only time I saw you in Paris was the day you and I were in that saloon and the French dame came up and tried to seduce you with her charms."

"What!" J.C. stammered, and then burst out laughing. "A woman trying to seduce our Ted? Oh boy, I'd give a hundred francs to have seen it. Here, Madame, another drink – that's worth a drink on me boys."

Ted lapsed into silence for a while. We kept on drinking and joking and finally restored him to good humor. Then we talked about our past experiences; but when J.C. mentioned the mine at Ypres, Ted's jaw dropped out of sight, and he would not say another word.

Our party became quite lively, and J.C. made a few incoherent vocal attempts. Ted and Sneezigs became fairly well lit. They were sitting a little apart from the rest of us, and I noticed that Ted was becoming quite sentimental, for he started to tell Sneezigs about his girl getting married to another fellow. A tear began to trickle slowly down his cheek. His affliction reminded me too much of my own experience, and I turned away, sorely touched.

J.C. moved in behind Sneezigs and leaned over with careful ear to overhear the conversation. He straightened up suddenly and began to sway back and forth in paroxysm of laughter, until I thought he would fall off his chair.

Ted turned around and looked at him, astonished. "Say, what is the matter with you? Are you going or already gone crazy?"

"Well, that beats anything I ever heard," J.C. laughed. "So Betty got married on you. I don't blame her at all: she showed good sense anyway. But remember, Ted, you can always fall back on the old school ma'am."

"Yes," said Sneezigs, wiping tears from his eyes, "it's all your own fault, Ted. I told you not to send her that funny picture, and to send her a picture of me instead. But never mind, the old school ma'am is the safest bet. By the time you marry here she will have a nice little nest egg laid away to help you along on the homestead."

Ted became sober as a judge. "Never mind, fellows. I don't wish you any hard luck; but I'd give my life to see every one of you married to some old Indian squaw. That would suite me just fine."

We tossed off a few more drinks and then left the estaminet. It was past midnight, nevertheless, Sneezigs invited us over to his billet for a bite to eat – he had bought some biscuits and peaches at the canteen. We thought it a good idea and followed him.

On arriving there, Sneezigs stuck a few candles around the walls and brought out the peaches and biscuits. We started to eat, digging out the peaches with our fingers. The supply of biscuits ran short. Ted excused himself and went out, returning about fifteen minutes later with a large round loaf, about twenty inches in diameter, of French bread.

"Where the deuce did you find that? Sneezigs gasped in surprise.

"Oh, leave it to this kid," he grinned. "I can dig up anything."

"I'll be doggoned!" said Skinny. "I tried all day yesterday to buy some French bread; but no matter where I went, they wouldn't sell me a loaf for any price. They aren't allowed to sell it and are scared to death of being caught.

After lunch, Ted favoured us with a recitation which told about a certain dog of low pedigree that was very unfortunate at every turn – being forced to lead a dog's life. I still remember the first verse, which goes something like this –

"I had a dog, and his name was Rover.

He was the cutest little pup,

He would stand up on his hind legs,

If you held the front ones up."

J.C. began to sing again; but he had scarcely started an interesting number, when the other occupants of the billet, who had gone to bed, made violent objections to this melodious entertainment, and invited us, in a wrathful and very undignified manner, to depart. So the party broke up.

The following weeks were miserably cold, with odd spells of rain. We made several trips to the front. Everything was quiet on both sides, which, notwithstanding the intense cold and damp weather, rendered front line life easier to bear.

Our dressing station was a place of great activity. Everyday men reported sick, feeling weak and faint, with high temperatures. The M.O. tried everything, and watched each experiment carefully, in hopes that he could discover some way to cure the peculiar malady which he was unable to diagnose; but his efforts produced little effect; and he grew despondent as the conditions of the sick men grew steadily worse. Those, whose conditions were beyond helpful treatment by our limited facilities, were sent back to the hospital and few of them ever returned; the less severe cases were kept in a dugout for treatment.

About the middle of March, we moved to the right into a valley below Vimy Ridge. The front here was livelier; gas shells and high explosives came over at odd intervals. During spells, it was necessary for us to wear gas masks throughout the greater part of the day.

The sickness in the trenches increased alarmingly. Some nights we sent out as many as six men with dangerously high temperatures. The doctors were baffled by the dreadful plague which was rapidly spreading throughout the army. Later it was called "Spanish Influenza" and the only beneficial treatment in the lines was quinine.

On March 21st, 1918, in the dark and small hour of early morning, we were relieved and started back. Our progress was slow and difficult, being handicapped by the many sick men. We were almost across the valley, when a heavy bombardment started on our left and grew into a steady continuing roar. On reaching the top of the ridge we were ordered to halt and stand to; word had been received that the Germans had launched a severe attack on a wide front, of which we were on the extreme right flank.

There we lay for three days, in bivouac encampment, cold and shivering; watching the smoke from the bursting shells. Many rumors drifted about; some that the Germans had broken through and were on their way to Paris; others, that the Fifth British Army Corps had been captured, and that we should be rushed in to regain the lost ground.

At last the firing eased up, and all grew quiet again. We continued back and arrived at a small village behind Lillers. Our medical office was situated in the front room of a house; but on account of the shortage of room, we on the medical staff were billeted in a barn.

The "Flu" broke out in full force, and was soon raging badly amongst our men. The cold, wet weather was a potent factor in aggravating the scouring plague to greater fury. Ambulances were busy, running night and day, going to and fro, and carrying out the sick men. Allen and I kept going from one billet to another, administering whatever medical treatment we could, and gathering up the critical cases to be shipped out to the hospitals. We hardly slept, night or day. Now and then we were able to snatch a few minutes rest, only to be roused out of our slumber by another call. Day after day, the same steady grind. I wondered how long it would last until our ranks would be depleted entirely.

One day I began to feel sick and faint. My head felt heavy and dense, and hot and cold chills alternately seized me. I went into our office and took my temperature; the thermometer registered 120 degrees. Quite worried, I sat down to wait for the M.O.

When he entered I told him how I felt.

"I'll fix you up, Sergeant." He wrote something on a slip of paper and reached into his pocket for a five-franc note. "Here, go down to the canteen and buy yourself a bottle of whisky. Drink all you can stand, then go to bed and stay there until tomorrow morning."

I went down to the canteen, purchased a bottle of whisky and returned to my billet. That night Allen and I drank the entire contents and went to bed. Next morning, I awoke feeling fine. The doctor's prescription had certainly served the purpose.

The days dragged steadily by. The weather became warmer, and soon everything was fine and dry. The terrible epidemic began to ease up; every week our sick cases diminished in number. Our battalion had sustained heavy losses, however; and many reinforcements were required to replenish the ranks again.

The German drive had been halted, and all was quiet on both sides. We heard that the Germans had the "Flu" and were unable to advance on account.

This suited us fine. We lay around, quiet and peaceful. Every week we went to a small mining town nearby for a bath and clean change of clothes. We were well fed and felt like our old selves again.

The months of May and June were spent in training and sham battles. We practiced on a large, mapped-out field, advancing under smoke screens, guided by aeroplanes overhead, or led by tanks. Day after day, the same drilling for the big drive which was rumored to come of soon. Our only discomfort was the dread that we should be picked as the chosen troops to be the first to go over the top.

July 1st arrived, and we all attended the Corps Sports. We greatly enjoyed the baseball, football, high jumping and peg-picking by members of the cavalry.

On our way back, Sneezigs spotted an orchard on the outskirts of our village, and we expressed hopes of visiting the same sometime in the near future.

After supper, Ted, Sneezigs and J.C. came to my billet. They had discovered a cherry tree in the orchard, not far from the house.

"Are the cherries ripe yet?" I asked.

"Yes, just right for a nice feast," said Ted. "Are you coming?"

"Sure, when do we start?"

"Right now," said Ted. "Take our gas mask and come along."

We started off down the road and arrived shortly at the orchard. In the back yard, behind the house, stood a lone cherry tree, its branches so laden with the luscious fruit that props were braced under to support the weight. We were about to enter when Sneezigs noticed a sign nailed to a post – "OUT OF BOUNDS FOR THE TROOPS".

Ted sized up the cherries for a moment, then turned to me. "Well, boys, that sign isn't going to stop this kid from getting a feed of cherries. I am going right in."

"Better wait until dark, then we'll be safer," I advised him.

We lay down for a smoke and discussed the new drive which was to come off soon. I told the boys how fortunate the four of us had been in remaining together; and that I had felt lonely since leaving the ranks.

Ted expressed the same feeling. "As long as our old gang was together, I didn't mind the front line so much. Everything went fine. But now, when I am at the front, everything seems so darn strange and empty. I haven't the same old feeling I used to have and can't stand it much longer.

"Oh, never mind, Ted," said Sneezigs. "If we have to go up the line again, we'll yust get Medical Seryeant Miller to excuse us from duty."

It was getting dark by this time. We waited another short while, until we were sure that the old froggie was in bed. Ted yawned and stretched his long legs.

"Boys, I am going over to see what we can find. You fellows stay here until I get back." He arose and went into the orchard.

We waited, listening carefully, expecting to hear a dog bark. All was still. In about fifteen minutes Ted returned carrying branches of the cherry tree.

"You should not have done that," I remonstrated. "We can get the cherries without breaking off the branches and thereby ruining the tree."

He grinned back at me. "What's the difference? If the Germans can do it, why can't we?"

After we had picked off the cherries, Ted made another trip into the orchard, accompanied this time by J.C. Sneezigs and I waited for a long time, but they did not return. We went in to find out what was wrong, and found J.C. under the tree, picking cherries into his cap.

"Where is Ted?" I whispered.

"He is doing a bit of reconnoitering to see what else he can fine."

Our caps were almost filled, when Ted appeared out of the surrounding darkness.

"Say, fellows," he said softly, "how about a roast chicken?"

"Where is the chicken house?" asked J.C.

"That white hut, over there." He indicated a small hennery built of cubes of white chalk, situated in the back of the yard.

"That's fine," said Sneezigs. "We'll pick all the cherries, and then I'll go and steal a chicken."

"No, I think I'd better go myself," said Ted. "I know the lay of the land; and besides, I know how to handle hens."

We continued picking cherries in silence. After filling our caps, we picked and ate the rest and left the tree stripped bare from top to bottom.

Ted handed me his cherries. "Now, fellows, open the gate, because I may have to make a hasty exit."

He slipped away into the darkness. We retired to the gate to await developments. Soon there was a sound of rusty hinges squeaking loudly, and a dark square miraculously appeared on the white background of the hennery – Ted was working fast. We waited breathlessly, wondering if perhaps, Ted would stumble into a trap. We heard a dull thud, and Ted's voice cursing savagely.

"He bumped his head," J.C. laughed.

A chicken squawked; then several more, filling the night with their loud cries. A door slammed and a white speck appeared, coming quickly toward us, accompanies by the strangles screams of a chicken and the rapid tattoo of Ted's number nines. He passed us, running as if the whole German army were in hot pursuit, with a white chicken under his arm squawking loudly in violent protest against this cruel abduction. Sneezigs handed his cherries to J.C. and dashed after Ted, to assist him in stifling the cries of the noisy chicken. At a slower pace, to avoid spilling the cherries, J.C. and I followed them in their flight, guided by the bobbing speck of white which was rapidly drawing away from us.

We caught up with them about a quarter of a mile from the house. Ted was lying on the ground, breathing heavily after his hard run; Sneezigs had already done the cruel deed and was wiping his jack-knife prior to putting it away; while the poor chicken in the throes of death agony, was throwing itself about on the ground giving its last feeble, valedictory kicks.

"What was all the rush about?" I asked.

"Oh, that nut there had to come tearing after me," Ted panted, indicating Sneezigs. "I did not know if it was the old froggie coming after me or not; and I didn't want to take any chance of being caught, so I just kept on sprinting."

J.C. laughed so hard he spilled half his cherries.

"What's the next move?" asked Ted. "We've got the chicken now – when do we eat it?"

"It's too late to roast it tonight. Let's wait until tomorrow night," I suggested.

"That's a good idea," said Sneezigs. "We'll yust sneak it back to our billet and hide it under the hay until tomorrow night."

After the chicken had ceased its struggles, Sneezigs picked it up, and we started back, quite satisfied with our nightly raid. I entered my billet stealthily and stored away my cherries. Next morning I shared them with Allen and Ernie, telling them how I had come by the cherries and they should keep it a secret.

An announcement came out in the orders; anyone caught stealing fruit from an orchard that was out of bounds for troops would be severely disciplined. I met the boys and we grinned at one another.

"Have you seen today's orders?" J.C. asked me.

"If you are referring to the cherries, yes," I laughed.

"Apparently the old froggie has been raising hell at headquarters; but he forgot to count his chickens this morning."

Ted grinned. We can't afford to breathe a word, or we'll get the dickens."

"When are we going to roast it?" I asked hungrily.

"That's yust what we came to see you about," said Sneezigs. "We'll go out tonight at eight o'clock, to the bluff where we train. I shall bring some clay to roast it in, and you bring a little water. Ted and J.C. can take care of the firewood. I'll show you fellows how we used to roast chickens when I was in a lumber camp north of Prince Albert.

"O.K. then and mum's the word until we meet tonight."

In the evening, we set out from the village for the bluff where we planned to have our picnic. J.C. carried a sand bag in which was wrapped our chicken; Sneezigs a sand bag of clay; Ted, a sandbag of firewood; and I carried my water bottle. We remained silent until we were beyond the village limits.

"What is it, a spring chicken or an old hen, Sneezigs?"

"That's a foolish question to ask, J.C." I cut in. "How can you expect a full-grown spring chicken in the month of July?"

"I might have known," he admitted. "Besides, Ted would pick an old hen anyway."

"Next time I'll let you do the picking," said Ted. "But don't worry at all: Sneezigs knows an old Swedish way of preparing it, by which – so he says – it doesn't matter how old the chicken is; it will be quite tender when done."

"I'll show you how we used to roast them in clay to make them tender," said Sneezigs. "For every year of the chicken you roast it one hour – this one will take about four hours."

Two officers, on horseback, were approaching along the road, on the other side of the little knoll.

"Steady, fellows," said J.C. "Brace yourselves for the worst. Those boys there may question us to take a look at what we are carrying."

"And one of them is a General," said I, seeing the red band around his cap. "We'll have to do some tall saluting."

"On which side shall we pass them?" asked J.C.

"On the left. I can salute better with my right hand," said Ted.

"Then don't keep that firewood under your right arm until you lift it to salute the General," J.C. warned quickly. "Hurry, switch the bags to the left."

"Shh – keep quiet, eyes left," I whispered.

The officers passed us in the cut. We maintained innocent respectful attitudes, and gave a smart No. 1 salute.

"Did you see the big, red nose on that old fellow?" said Ted, when they were out of earshot. "I'll bet that old boy doesn't run short of his rum issue."

"He is the cock of the walk," J.C. declared. "He doesn't have to march, polish buttons, line up at the field kitchen, or anything else. And when he feels like having a snort, all he has to say is – 'Another drink, Flunky!'"

"And supposing Flunky forgets the whisky?" I contended.

"Then he raises the roof and threatens to Flunky back in the ranks. And poor flunky doesn't forget the whisky a second time, because he knows as well as you and I what the ranks mean."

"I wonder if those fellows drink French beer, like we do," Sneezigs interposed musingly.

"Not a chance," J.C. affirmed; "they get Basses ale shipped to them all the way from England."

"Cheer up, fellows," Ted soothed, "when I become a general, I'll give you three guys bombproof jobs and all the liquor you can drink."

"What yob will you give me?" asked Sneezigs.

"Well," said Ted pretentiously, "since you claim to know how to roast a chicken, I'll make you my private cook."

"That's a yakaloo with me," Sneezigs grinned, immediately anticipating how this great, new increment would affect his sweet tooth; "and I'll eat pure strawberry yam instead of the mixture of carrots and turnips we are getting now."

"You bet. And every time you bring me a partridge from No Man's Land, I'll recommend you for the V.C."

We arrived at an old stone quarry near the bluff. J.C. dropped the chicken and we sat down. "Here we are. What do we do now?"

"Make the fire," Sneezigs instructed. He dumped about twenty pounds of clay on the ground and scooped it into a neat pile with a depression in the centre. Taking my bottle, he added water to the clay, a little at a time, meanwhile stirring it until he had a thick paste.

"That reminds me of the mud pies we used to make when I was a kid," I said, watching him.

Sneezigs turned around to get the chicken.

"Hold on, you nut," he reproved Ted who was plucking the feathers from the chicken; "don't pull the feathers out of that bird. I want it just as it is."

Ted looked up, surprised. "What! Do you mean to tell me that you are going to roast this thing, feathers and all?"

"Absolutely," agreed Sneezigs. "I told you so on the way coming up."

"How about the insides – are you going to leave them in too?"

"Sure thing. That's what gives it flavor."

Ted turned away with a grimace. "Well you can eat the darn thing yourself. You know, Sneezigs you remind me of the cooks on the Lapland, who served us with Australian rabbit; but those guys at least had the sense to pull off the skin."

"What's the matter with you, Ted?" Sneezigs said in a hurt tone. "A few minutes ago you yust promised me a cook's yob when you are a Yeneral –"

"You will never be my cook as long as you live," Ted rebuked him.

"And you will never be a Yeneral as long as you live, so we are quits," Sneezigs returned.

Sneezigs laid the chicken in the mud pile and applied a layer of the yellow paste all around, rolling and smoothing it until, when finished, it looked like a large rugby ball. Then he rolled it gently into the fire, which J.C. had going by this time, and covered it up with coals and burning sticks. Settling back comfortably, he produced his snuff box and took a pinch of snuff.

"Take it easy, fellows. It will yust take about four hours until it is done."

"Holy smoke!" J.C. exclaimed, that means we have to keep this fire going till midnight."

"Sure," grinned Sneezigs. "We shall be yust in time for midnight lunch."

"Then we had better find some more firewood." I said.

"That reminds we of a joke about an Englishman, who couldn't find any firewood," Ted started up –

"Never mind the yokes now," Sneezigs interrupted; "you can tell them while we are eating the chicken. Get some firewood before it all burns away."

"Yes, come on," I said, starting off. "Talking about firewood isn't going to keep the old fire burning."

Gathering firewood in the dark was a hard task, but we managed to keep the fire replenished until Sneezigs announced that the chicken was done.

"I wonder what kind of mess he made of the thing," said Ted, as Sneezigs drew the dark, cracked, steaming lump out of the fire.

"Don't worry, Ted," Sneezigs assured him; "You never tasted anything like it in your life."

"I suppose not," Ted responded with some irony. "I think you wasted a good chicken with your foolish Swedish ideas."

With the long point of his jack-knife, Sneezigs pried open the steaming lump; along with the chunks of baked clay, feathers and skin came away clean, exposing the white meat of the body of the chicken. He carved away dexterously, handing each of us an equal share, except Ted, who received but a very small portion.

"That's because I am a poor cook," said Sneezigs.

"It tastes very good, Sneezigs," I praised him. "If only we had a little salt."

"I have some," said J.C. and be produced a little box of salt. "Always carry it to put some tang in that insipid French beer."

We ate every tiny morsel of the delicious meat and afterwards licked our fingers with great satisfaction. Ted was reconciled.

"It was very good," he admitted. "Only one thing lacking and that was a little gravy."

The weeks passed quickly, and we began to feel the suspense of the coming drive. It was bound to come off soon.

One day the boys had orders to hand in their bayonets to be re-sharpened. This looked serious; and some of the new fellows winced and turned pale as they realized the bloody purpose.

While on the way to the canteen for cigarettes, I met Ted carrying his bayonet.

"Where are you going, big boy?" I asked.

"Over to the quartermaster's to get this tooth pick sharpened."

"That looks like a bad business."

"Yes, I suppose so," he said grimly. "I hear that the Canadians have been chosen as the shock troops and that we are going in at Amiens. Maybe the long-hoped-for end is coming."

I noticed that Ted was quite unhappy and knew that he hated going over the top. We had gone over the top four times together and had come out safely every time – but how long was this going to last?

"Say, Ted," I spoke confidentially, "if you have to go over the top, I'll get you a slip to excuse you from duty."

"And what if you get caught?"

"It would mean the ranks for me. But don't worry old man. I'll contrive it some way that I won't get caught." And I unfolded my scheme.

"If anyone questions you, you can say you have a pain in your back."

He gazed at me for a while. "Thanks, Miller. I knew all the time that you would. But what I want to know is; shall you be going over?"

"Yes, but not in the first wave; I shall follow in the second wave."

"That's all I want to know. If you are going over, Miller, than I am too: and if I get wounded, you'll be there to attend me."

"You can bet your life on that, Ted. But I hope you will come out safe."

I gazed after him as he went on. What a friend! As much as he dreaded going over, he would not stand back when he knew that I was going into battle. I would lay down my life for him any time, and knew he felt the same way towards me. Did ever a truer friend exist? "If you are going over, Miller, then I am too -"

A few days later, the doctor told me that we should be going to Amiens. The big drive would start from there. We received a large supply of medicines and dressings, and I realized that we were in for a long and terrible combat.

One morning, in the latter part of July, we packed up and started out. After long marches, we arrived at an open field, three miles behind the front at Amiens. We encamped in shell holes, with canvas overhead, and made preparations for the big drive. We received minute instructions for the great event which was to come off soon.

A panicky feeling swept over us as we waited, expecting every day the inevitable command to go over the top.

Chapter 19

Soldiers being treated for injuries

On the night of August 7th, 1918, we moved to the front and landed at a sunken road which was to be our jumping –off place. At daylight, we would go over the top; 4:00 A.M. was the zero hour.

We lay around in funk-holes, silent and tense, awaiting the hour of death. The night was dark and very quiet. From the distance, far behind the German line, came the faint rumble of motor lorries and limbers. Waiting, waiting – what a long word! Time dragged painfully by. It was a terrible suspense – that suspense which comes before every battle, when uncertain dread fills one with growing trepidation; and he wishes desperately for the critical moment to come, that, in the heat of action, he may lose his reason – and his fear.

I sat beside the doctor, with two sand bags of dressings, ready to follow the first wave. My old, worn-out nerves were quivering and twitching. I crouched lower against the side of the road, wishing that the earth would open up and swallow me.

"Are you nervous, Sergeant?" the doctor whispered.

"No," I replied, tremulous, yet trying to be calm, "but I wish it were all over."

The darkness slowly lightened into that murky twilight which comes before the break of day; morning was approaching; soon the inevitable hour would come!

Our officers came around with last instructions. "That ridge about a mile away is our first objective. On the other side of it is a village which is our next objective."

The new fellows grasped their rifles and whispered excitedly. This was facing real Death! The older fellows, with tightly clamped jaws, pale and trembling, crouched low, - any minute might be the last!

The sky grew lighter and lighter. Dawn was breaking. Our time had come. The hum of approaching aeroplanes came from behind our line; the airmen were coming to direct the drive. There was a long flash in the sky, like one streak of lightening, accompanied by a sudden, loud, discordant, road, as all our guns opened up as one. Like a heavy hammer the barrage struck the ground in front of us and instantly transformed it into a cataclysm of quaking and groaning.

The barrage lifted and our men sprang over the top. The doctor, Allen, Ernie and I stayed for a minute, and then followed over. The heavy barrage of fire and smoke was thundering and rolling ahead like a mighty cloud impelled by some great, unseen force, and followed closely by our men in extended order. A second wave rose from behind the sunken road and followed the first. German machine guns opened fire, doing great damage to our ranks; their retaliation lasted but a moment then was silenced.

We found many wounded, here and there a few dead. Hastily we bandaged the wounded and went on, leaving them for the field stretcher bearers who were following closely. While crossing a ripe, wheat field, I saw a dead Frenchman who evidently had fallen in the last big German offensive. The skin on the face was black and parched, shrunken tightly over protuberant cheek bones; the only natural feature remaining was the red, bristly beard.

We reached our objective and stayed in the village for about three hours. While ransacking the former German rendezvous, we found a quartermaster's store, well stocked with provisions – fresh meat (horseflesh), potatoes, canned foods, cigars, cigarettes, tobacco and someone even discovered two large glass jars of whisky, upon which discovery everyone suddenly expressed great thirst or need of vital energy. Some of the boys indulged immoderately and soon began to show effects of taking frequent, large drafts of the potent liquid. Allen proceeded to fill his water bottle; but, knowing from past experience that there were times when water was more precious than whisky, I kept mine full of water. After helping ourselves to all the supplies we could carry, we went on.

We started north-east and came to the Amiens-Albert Road which we followed until we came to a ravine. Here we held up, because our right flank has not yet reached its objective; and we secreted ourselves in some woods. The Germans began to shell us with long range guns, and we moved on again, following the road. On our right the French were fighting desperately; everywhere were rising puffs of smoke from bursting shells. We came upon a wagon lying in the middle of the road, all smashed up, with the two horses still hitched and the drive lying at the side – all dead. A shell had struck him before he had been able to get back to his transports.

A long flat lay before us now, stretching far off to the left. Some of our tanks lay there, burned out and stranded. We saw one near the road, with the bodies of its operators inside; apparently not having had time to open the steel door and get out, they had been burned to death. As far as we could see lay these derelict engines of war, all abandoned and useless. Occasionally we heard the report of a gun we had never heard before and supposed that it must be the new German anti-tank rifles.

Late in the afternoon we came to a trench and stopped to occupy it. The Germans were now coming forward by the hundred, some sad; others laughing, happy to be taken prisoner. I spoke to one, a very young fellow who seemed very frightened, and asked him if he were hungry. Yes, he hadn't eaten anything since last night. Had they expected the early morning attack? No, it had been a complete surprise. I handed him a tin of bully beef and some hard-tack.

We were ordered to move on again and landed in an old trench fourteen kilometers from where we had started that morning. The Germans had fortified themselves in some woods about two hundred yards ahead of us.

Shells began to land around us, inflicting many casualties. A Scottish division came up from behind, leapfrogged us and went on toward the woods. While they were crossing our trench a shell made a direct hit, killing two men and wounding one very badly.

I attended the wounded man on top of the trench, but saw that there was little hope for him. A splinter from the shell had ripped open his left side from the arm down to the hip, thus exposing his heart and one lung. It was useless to bandage him up, so I gave him two hypodermic injections to lessen the pain, but it did not help any. Piteously he entreated me to shoot him; and when I refused, he directed a volley of abuse and curses at me. I could not bear to see him suffer so and was tempted to pull out my forty-five and comply with his entreaty; but I did not have the heart to do it; and had to leave him to die slowly, hoping that another shell would land near him and end his acute suffering.

I walked back and forth, tying up the wounded. Some had stomach wounds; others were shot through the face, arms or legs; some were only a bundle of raw, bleeding flesh, with a thousand wounds from the scorching blast of a shell.

One of our fellows climbed out of the trench – it was his last climb on this earth. His head suddenly disappeared, severed from the trunk by a passing shell. The decapitated trunk reeled drunkenly for a few short steps in a semicircle and toppled back into the trench, the neck spouting blood like a fountain.

Shells continued to fall around us. The trench was dyed with red, the sticky blood soaking into the dry earth and oozing around our boots. I heard the wounded man on top of the trench, still moaning in extreme anguish – would the fellow never die? – However his voice was getting lower and lower.

I found Allen in the trench, eating bully beef and hard-tack.

"Have you any water for tea?" he asked.

"I have a little left but I'd like to save it," I replied.

"How about that fellow up there? He pointed. "He has no more use for his water."

I climbed out of the trench and went to get the dying man's water bottle. To my relief he was dead. I felt his body and found it warm and still twitching. Thank God his suffering was over! I felt no compunction for not having shot him; though sadly I remembered that in the five hours of his suffering, he had not prayed to god once – only curses had passed his lips. Well, God had given him enough time, anyway.

We made some tea, and had a light lunch.

In front of us, only two hundred yards ahead in the woods, was raging one of the most terrible battles fought in the history of the war. The 51st Scottish Division (as we heard the next day) was completely wiped out. We lay on top of the trench and there, in the twilight, watched the terrible battle. Some of our planes were above the woods, dropping bombs and firing their machine guns into the woods to drive out the Germans. An enemy plane came over and fought desperately with ours, only about five hundred feet above the ground. I admired the German's courage in undertaking the overwhelming odds. He dived everywhere, shooting right and left at our fellows who were all around him. Suddenly his plane took a great impact that I felt the earth tremble. There was a loud explosion, a flame shot up like a rocket, and the wrecked plane was enveloped in a cloud of black smoke.

The colonel and his staff came around and after gathering together what was left of the battalion, ordered up to move to the left. We arrived at a small orchard and halted for the night; we had gone far enough for one day. There were a number of grave-like slots dug in the ground, which apparently had been occupied by the Germans as shelters from the shrapnel. Some were large enough to hold three men, some wide enough only for one. We occupied these shelters and tried to get some sleep. The Germans, however, knew only too well the location of their previous shelters, and we were shelled and bombed all night long. We cowered low, burying our faces in the soft earth, while the intense racket continued. My body was stiff; only my nerves quivered with fear as I hoped and prayed for daylight to come.

After our first push we were taken out of the line and taken back as far as Arras, where we received more reinforcements. Another drive, surely! But what was the use of worrying? It was our daily life, and we must keep on going, through mud and water, over shell holes, wire entanglements, and dead men. We were men no longer; only automata used with mechanical precision in the bloody recourse and impelled by the higher forces above us. Ahead, ahead, keep going ahead! – These were our orders; it was all that mattered; everything else was to be secondary only and insensible to us; we must not be affected by the sight of bloody men; our ears must be deaf to the hollow moans of dying men in mortal anguish. My nerves – damn them anyway! – A man would be better off without them; they were responsible for my emaciated condition – my mental agony – my dead soul. It would be better to be killed altogether. Then one would be out of it forever; one would be able to rest in peace; but alive, and fit, it was only the same thing over again – on, on ever and anon!

The battalion went back into the line, but by some streak of good fortune, was not picked to go over the top. Another battalion cleared the way, and we followed, going toward Cambrai. We had the Germans on retreat and pushed steadily forward so as not to give them the opportunity to dig in. At night we slept in old dugouts, shell holes or open fields. The enemy planes bombed us repeatedly, but this impeded us little, and every morning we pushed on. Sometime in late August we captured Monchy and from there continued on toward Cambrai. Our transports followed closely and kept us well supplied with food. Slowly we made our way, steadily ahead. Day after day the same steady grind.

The last week in September we were held up in front of Cambrai. The Germans had fortified themselves in Bourlon Wood and a strong line of trenches to the left, and our advance was checked by their stubborn resistance. As usual, when a difficult obstacle confronted us, it was the old C.M.R.s that were picked to go over the top to break down the barrier. The same applied here; we were the chosen troops. One morning we were lined up, ready to take the line of trenches about seven hundred yards ahead. Our medical staff was headquartered in the rear, waiting for the barrage from our artillery to clear the way. Nervous and tense, we waited. This would be our hardest fight; and the least we could expect was a terrific hand-to-hand encounter with the Germans in order to overcome them in the redoubtable position.

With a heavy roar, our artillery opened up. To our great alarm, we saw that some of the shells were dropping around us; and the barrage was pouring into our own front line. This heavy deluge of death lasted but three minutes, and then lifted. There was a shout for first aid and we rushed forward. The three minutes of deadly fire from our own guns had almost wiped out the whole battalion. Wounded men lay everywhere, crying and moaning; dead men, fallen over one another, with bodies horribly mangled. To my joy, I found Ted unhurt although he looked more dead than alive. We quickly bandaged up the wounded and set to work burying the dead. In one large grave, on the outskirts of Cambrai, we buried seventy-one men – all on account of a mistake on the part of our artillery. We learned later that through an error in computing the range, they had fired seven hundred yards short. Just a trivial miscalculation – that trivial miscalculation was the cause of seventy-one men dead and hundreds more horribly maimed for life.

It was on one of these trips, while maneuvering around Cambrai that I saw a sight which gripped me at the time, and the memory of which still impresses me to this day. To the left of Orange Hill, on the bank of a sunken road, was a small cemetery, pitted and torn up by heavy shell fire. In the centre stood a statue of an angel, once beautiful, but now sadly mutilated and blasted almost beyond recognition; the head, left arm and wings of the symbolical figure were blown off entirely, the bust cracked and shivered into fragments, many of which had fallen away; but that defiant, upraised right arm, with four fingers of the hand shot off, was yet intact to the poised body, with that index finger remaining and pointing Heavenwards in mute testimony of the awful human atrocity and conveying the terrible warning that God in Heaven would not allow this unholy infraction to pass unavenged.

We marched back behind the line and were reinforced. We were also joined by the brass band of a battalion that had been split up to replenish the ranks of other battalions. Here we stayed for about a week, while the new fellows received some drilling and instruction.

I received a long letter from my mother. A terrible epidemic was sweeping throughout my home town and district. The schools had already been closed and the families that were stricken were quarantined. Many were dying from the dreadful plague which the doctors called "Influenza". Fortunately, however, no one in our family had contracted it so and all were in good health.

On reading this news of the devastating disease already having spread over to Canada, I was alarmed. Only too well did know Influenza and the many deaths it left in its wake: I earnestly hoped that my loved ones would be spared from the dreadful disease.

A few days later we were again at the front, advancing toward Valenciennes. Slowly we fought our way ahead. Now and then the Germans put up a weak resistance, but our advance was too formidable and swept steadily onward. Hundreds of prisoners were captured every day. As we went along, the shelling grew lighter and we suffered only a few casualties. The Germans had mines laid under most of the important cross roads and as a last recourse these were blown up, but impeded us very little.

Going along the highways, we passed hundreds of French civilians moving from behind the Germans lines to the towns and villages from which they had been forced to flee. It was a pitiable sight to see these indigent, half-starved victims of war moving along with their few belongings; old men pulling two-wheeled cars that were loaded with bedding and cooking utensils; women pushing wheel barrels upon which were piled bedding with small infants perched on top; others leading their little ones; all going one way – back to their homes. Their faces were lined with great anxiety and suffering – not a smile to be seen anywhere. No one knows how these poor people felt when, on arriving at their respective villages, they found their homes in utter ruin.

Valenciennes was captured and we kept on towards Mons. The weather was becoming colder; in the mornings mist hung heavily over the fields. We heard rumors of peace; but I had little hope because I had heard such rumors before. This war would not cease as long as Germany still had a few men, even though they were mere youths, ragged and half-starved; not until we drove the Germans completely out of Germany. I should be dead by that time; my mind and body were being taxed beyond endurance; my nerves were only a bunch of jumpy fibers; I could sleep only when under the influence of liquor – the pace was too much. And what matter if the war ever ceased? What future was there for me to hope for?

One day I met Ted. Poor Ted! – emaciated, haggard, worn; his uniform hanging loosely on his skeleton-line frame; his lips pale and thin; and cheek bones protruding from under hollow, sunken eyes.

I put my arms around him. "You are not feeling well, Ted?"

His voice was dull and lifeless. "I am done for Miller. Can't rest at all any more. It's getting me at last."

"Oh, forget it, Ted. I heard a rumor that peace will soon be declared."

He only shook his head hopelessly. My poor mate! His eyes were dim; the happy sparkle which I used to see there was gone. I knew the look; I had seen it on many dying men – it was the sign of a soldier's last. Ted would not last more than a few days at most.

Chapter 20

Canadians passing through the streets of Mons after liberation

Late in the evening of November 10th, 1918, after a hard push, we arrived at a small village and were billeted for the night. We were only five kilometers from Mons and would advance on that city in the morning.

The night was very quiet; now and then the solitude would be broken by the sharp report of a field piece or the momentary coughing of a machine gun. Allen, Ernie and I were billeted in a glass-enclosed kitchen. We stretched out on the tile floor and rolled into our blankets. But sleep would not come to me; my nerves tossed me about all night.

After shat seemed an age of restless tossing, I perceived, through the transparent roof of our quarters, the first signs of dawn. It was quiet misty outside and looked like rain. I arose and went out. It was getting lighter now and all was still. In the cold grey dawn, everything looked dismal, enwrapped, as it seemed, in Death. I shuddered at the aspect and turned to go back into the house. The appalling stillness was shattered by a loud, muffled boom in the distance – another cross-road blown up.

I started the Primus and made some tea. While drinking the scalding liquid, I decided to write a letter home to my mother – there was time for that now, and only God knew if I should have another opportunity. Hastily I dug into my pack and brought forth my writing pad.

"Dear Mother: I am still alive and --" I could not go on. Again and again I tried, but it was not use. What could I say? I was still alive and – what else? There was nothing else to say. Sadly I put away my pad: 'O Mother! If only I could pour out my trouble to you; only you, who understands me can pacify my troubled mind."

Suddenly I straightened up. The reflection of the long mirror which hung on the wall opposite me caught my attention. Oh Grief! What a sight! My uniform creased and covered with countless stains – the blood of many wounded – hair disheveled; face drawn and pale and twitching nervously; and bloodshot eyes staring defiantly back. It was some strange image of Death! The grim features smiled bitterly, almost frightening me. Surely it could not be that that ghastly countenance was my own! My mother – what a shock it would be for her to see me now! What a change! "Oh Mother, is this your boy? No, no – your boy is no more; he died when you clung to him and kissed him good-bye – ever so long ago."

The mist lifted, and sun rose majestically, shedding its golden rays over the landscape and dispersing the gloomy twilight.

While we were eating breakfast, a sergeant appeared with orders to be ready. "We are taking Mons in the morning."

We packed our equipment and waited for the order to fall in. Everything was quiet and placid; not one shot was fired. The golden disc grew smaller as it mounted higher in the sky. The hours passed – nine o'clock, ten o'clock, eleven o'clock – and still not orders. Something was wrong; maybe they had discovered some stratagems on the part of the enemy and changed the plans. I became restless – why did the order not come.

"I wonder what is wrong." I said to Allen.

Before he could reply there was a loud shout outside. Skinny came dashing into our kitchen as if there were ten devils after him.

"Peace, Miller! Peace is declared!" he shouted excitedly.

I gazed at him in amazement. Then a thought dawned upon me; poor Skinny! – It was getting him too!

The door opened and the doctor came in, smiling joyously. He stretched out his hand to me. "Sergeant, the war is over. They signed an armistice at eleven o'clock this morning."

I smiled at him and shook my head. "I can't believe it."

"Yes, it is true at last. We shall have our dinner and then go to Mons." He turned and skipped through the door like an excited rabbit.

Skinny and I went outside. The whole village was in an uproar; everybody was cheering and yelling in jubilant exaltation. The shouts of peace rang in my ears. It seemed like incontestable proof that peace had really been declared, yet, somehow, this wonderful truth was too good, too strange, and too immense to be grasped by my vague faculties. A persistent doubt lingered in my mind – might it not be just another false rumor? Too often I had drunk the bitter dregs of disappointment.

Our brass band started up; playing all the snappy songs we used to sing, and ended with 'O Canada'. Skinny was jumping around like a chicken with its head cut off. He tried to turn a hand spring but landed on his seat. Undismayed and laughing, he got up and continued his antics.

The last traces of doubt vanished. Peace had really been declared! The war was over, our bloody days were ended. It meant no more shells, no more wounded men, - it meant emancipation from death! I became animated with a fierce joy. Where was Ted? I must find my dear, old pal and tell him the glad tidings.

I hurried about in the milling mob of half-crazy soldiers until I found him. He stood alone, quietly watching the performances of hilarity around him. I grasped his claw-like hand and gave it a good shake. "Well, Ted, old boy, it's all over!"

He was inclined to be pessimistic. "Don't be too sure about it Miller. If the Germans don't accept our terms, we'll have to keep on going."

"Yes, but there is no danger of that."

"Maybe not, but I won't feel safe until we are on the boat, going home."

With much singing we started off for Mons. On arriving there, we found the city in an uproar. Multitudes of people, cheering loudly in acclamation of the wonderful peace, thronged the streets. Soldiers, old men, women and children – all were singing and shouting at the tops of their voices, feverish with excitement and joy; the air was filled with flying hats, caps and other articles of apparel. A staff car, loaded down with high army officials and one German officer holding up a flag of truce, sped through the streets. The clamor increased; women shouted vociferously after the moving vehicle. Everybody was gripped by the abounding elation of the long-hoped-for armistice. Bubbling over with rapture – drunk with joy!

Our battalion was billeted in a large building which the Germans had used for a hospital. After we had settled, I went up town. Everybody was still shouting. I passed a French beer wagon standing in the middle of the street, with soldiers and women crowding around and enjoying free beer; mess-tins were handed up, filled, emptied and refilled.

That night, in contrast with former times, the city was brightly illuminated. I walked slowly through the streets. The cabarets and beer shops were crowded; soldiers and women thronged at the bars, drinking and cheering. Some of the girls were so hoarse from yelling, that they could only squawk. I passed a place where they were dancing. Soldiers, drunk and boisterous, were leading women, likewise inebriated and only half dressed, around the floor. I became disgusted and turned back to my billet. It made me very sad to think that these people were so exhilarated with joy at the great liberation that their mentality was entirely depraved; and instead of thanking God for their deliverance from the horrible war, they were reveling in promiscuous drinking and immoral conduct.

On arriving at our quarters, I found Allen busy trying to connect a two burner gas stove under a bath tub. I sat down to write a letter home to my mother.

This time I was not at a loss what to write. Line after line I poured out the good news; Peace had been declared; the war was over; God had answered her prayers and had guided me safely through. In the letter I enclosed my photo which I had had taken some months before at Bruay.

Allen got the gas stove working at last, and the water in the tub soon heated. After enjoying a good, hot bath, we went to bed on some stretchers we had fixed up and for once we felt real comfortable and at ease.

The days which followed were heavenly days; we ate, slept and rested. Our rations were better now; porridge, bacon and beans for breakfast, and fresh meats and vegetables for the other meals. We on the medical staff drew our rations from the quarter master's store and did our own cooking. Allen was our cook and made up the meals in great style. We were especially fond of the hamburger steak which he made by chopping up fresh beef with an old Germans saw-bayonet that I carried as a souvenir.

Our only discomfort was the M.O.'s batman, Cecil, who was very fond of porridge. Every morning, as soon as it was cooked, he was the first one at the stove, treating himself very generously, and leaving only a little to be divided amongst the rest of us. After a few days of this, we decided that we should take some steps to cure Cecil of his voracity and thereby save our rightful shares of porridge. I thought up a scheme and propounded it to Allen and Ernie; we should crush about a dozen No. 7 calomel tablets into small granules and add them to the porridge while it was cooking; and then let Cecil help himself - to all of it, if he wished. Allen and Ernie thought it would work, so we planned to try it the next morning.

Next morning we carried out our plot as planned. Cecil came in, took a bowl and walked over to the stove. As soon as the porridge was cooked, he helped himself as usual to the greater part of it, and set to, eating heartily. Allen and I could hardly refrain from laughing out loud, and I heard Ernie trying to stifle a snicker. Cecil looked up once or twice, suspiciously, but seeing us looking very innocent, he finished the porridge and rose.

"Say fellows, that porridge tasted kind of funny. Did you get a new issue of oats this morning?"

"Aw, go on," Allen said blandly. "You must have been drinking last night and have a bad taste in your mouth."

He shook his head, saying very seriously, "No, I don't drink," and went out.

Cecil did not show up until dinner time. When all were assembled, we sat down to have dinner, as usual. Cecil got up, suddenly, looking very pale, and dashed out. We all burst out laughing.

"That ought to fix that son of a gun," laughed Allen. "He'll never eat our porridge again."

Cecil returned, looking quite sick, and sat down.

"How about a little tea?" he asked meekly, "without milk or sugar please."

"Why, of course, Cecil," Allen responded generously, "you may have anything you wish. There is still some porridge left from this morning; would you like to finish it up now?"

"No thanks, Allen," he said in a tone of distress.

"Why, what's the matter, Cecil?" Allen regarded him sympathetically. "Are you sick?"

"I don't know what's wrong. My stomach is in a terrible roar, it's been warbling and ribbing all morning. I've spent most of the time --" He turned pale suddenly and rushed outside.

We burst out roaring. Allen rolled on the floor until we thought he had taken a fit. Our trick had worked fine, and Cecil ate no more porridge after that.

After the second week at Mons, our battalion put on weekly dances. As soon as our brass band started up, everyone rushed for a partner. The soldiers had a merry time. At midnight, our cooks made a lunch of bully beef sandwiches and tea. Some of the French and Belgian woman had several helpings; and some of them even stuck sandwiches into their coat pockets to take home.

After three weeks of rest and good food, I was feeling fine. My face was losing the deathly pallor and taking on better colour. My nerves became a little calmer, only at nights was I troubled. My dreams were horrible; some nights I was under heavy shell fire or bombing again; some nights we were going over the top again; again there were dead men around me or wounded and dying screaming in death agony. I would wake up, nervous and trembling, my bedclothes wringing wet with perspiration and try to remain awake until morning.

During the second week of December, we moved further east and landed at a place called Ohain. Our medical staff was billeted in the front room of a large building, but many others had to occupy barns. The weather was quite cold and damp and I felt sorry for the less fortunate ones.

Christmas Eve came around and we were happy. The sergeants would have a special dinner that night – roast leg of pork and rum punch; the rest of the battalion would celebrate next day. Our feast was to be held in a large room above my quarters.

Happily I grinned to myself as I prepared for the great feast. This would be a real Christmas. Painfully I recalled the last Christmas and my heart suffered a pain at the bitter memory. However, I banished the thought from my mind; there was nothing to suffer for now, so why should I worry about the past? I should have a real time tonight, and tomorrow, maybe another.

I removed all the stains from my uniform and brushed it carefully. I polished my buttons until they shone like gold. I cleaned my boots until they were spotless. After shaving, washing, and brushing my hair, my toilet was complete. I stood before the mirror and surveyed myself. Immaculate and orderly, a happy sparkle in my eyes; I felt proud of myself. I was ready for the big event.

The sergeant-major called for me, and we went up together. We walked up to the large bowl containing the refreshments and each had two cups of punch. Then we sat down at the gaily-decorated table for dinner.

Our colonel was in attendance for the festal occasion and gave us a speech of commendations, lauding the sergeants highly for the good work they had performed during the war. Every one of us present felt proud at the wonderful words of praise.

We ate as much as we thought was good for us and drank a great deal more. After the diner, some members of the brass band came up and started to play. At first the men coupled up and danced together, but there was little sport in this form of entertainment, and some of our fellows went out and brought up girls and old women to dance with. Everybody had a gay time. Drink, dance and be merry. Our arms encircled about some young girl or old, toothless hag, no matter which, we whirled about on the smooth floor, stimulated by the potent liquor and captivated by the blaring music.

Next morning I awoke with a heavy head. The night's activities had been too strenuous; the music still rang in my ears and I could still feel the effects of the punch. Nevertheless, the good time had been well worth the after-effects. I smiled to myself reassuringly – this was Christmas.

The mail came in and I received a letter. Instantly I recognized the fine hand-writing of my father and a feeling of great joy surged through me. Happily, I skipped back to my billet. This was the first letter from my father since my enlistment four years ago. The war was over and my father had forgiven me! This must be a Christmas blessing.

Hastily I tore open the letter, my heart beating in happy anticipation. But only a single page and only two lines:

"Diene Mutter ist gestorben.   Ach Gott! Was soll ich mit der Kindernian?" ("Your mother is dead. O God! What shall I do with the children?)

This was strange news indeed! It must be that damned rum. I drank too much of last night! Somebody's mother was dead. Yes, very strange; I laughed queerly. But the letter is from my father! Surely it cannot be my mother who is dead! No, no, she is alive and well and I will see her soon! My father must be mad to write such things to me! A strange feeling of dread stole through my body. My knees began to tremble. I became dazed. But I cannot allow it! I must fight off this dreadful vision! "Father, you lie! My mother, dead? No, no, not if there is a God!"

But there it was, those thirteen words challenging me; their terrible meaning was inevitable. Slowly, the truth registered in my befuddled brain; a strained, parched feeling crept into my breast; my heart grew heavy, was filled with despair, anguish, grief; my soul was desolated – I thought I was dying. I must get away! These terrible words are killing me! I cannot remain to be tortured by that awful, choking truth!

On, on, - where will these steps lead me? No matter, there is no relief anywhere. My only relief, my only hope, my only peace is gone. My mother, my dear mother is dead – lifeless – cold – dead – dead – dead! The thought was unbearable. My head began to ring louder and louder, fiercer, until death seemed to float before my eyes. The earth heaved, rolled and reeled drunkenly before me. Soon I was on the brink of an abysmal death of darkness. Sweet oblivion rolled over me – my knees tottered – all was darkness.

Consciousness returned and with it despair and grief.   The haunting words tore through my stricken mind; she is dead, gone from me forever. She will not be there to embrace me and welcome me home when I return. My dear mother who fondled and caressed me, who soothed away my troubles, who cared for me when I was in distress, who loved and understood me, who prayed for me always, - she is gone; she lies cold, cold in the earth five thousand miles away, while I lie here, broken crushed in despair and grief. What deed have I done so ghastly to deserve this? Thy awful vengeance? Oh God! Take away my spirit; let me repose her in death!

Oh death! horrible and cruel to me, who I have so often encountered, escaped, cheated of my soul, then this is they sting! then thou hast spared me and taken her, my dear mother, sweet, honest, pure. Oh death! proud, mighty and dreadful, come; willingly will I now relinquish this broken spirit.

Oh earth! in whose rolling upheavals, tremors, quakes and groans, through fire, smoke, mud and blood. I have wallowed all these years – now that thou hast peace, take me from this void, cruel world to rest with thee! Earth! which holds that dear body of her, take me up in they bosom, bury me, engulf me forever!

But my anguished cries were in vain. There was no relief, no peace. I was afflicted by overwhelming grief. My body was cold and numb, my heart pained as if it were congealing into ice, while burning passions continued to rage in my head. Oh Mother! who have entreated me so often; entreat for me now, to ease me from this terrible suffering which is choking me. Oh Mother! who have prayed for my safety from shells and bullets, from disease, from staling death – thy prayers are answered; I am alive; I am unharmed; I will return safe and sound. But Mother! Mother of an unworthy son although I also prayed to God for my life, I did not pray to Him to spare your life; my selfishness is responsible for they untimely death. Oh Mother in Heaven! Forgive me, lay thy sweet hand on my throbbing temples and soothe me – as oft in dreams-

The vision of that lovely, angelic face floats before my eyes. (Maybe it was the product of an overwrought mind – I do not know. Explain it, those of you who can; I cannot.) Dear Mother! speak to me, lay your hand on my forehead, stroke me. Smile not at my sorrow Mother! When I kissed you goodbye, you were not smiling, you were sad for your boy!

The hot fit of despair softened into cold, passive misery. For many hours, I lay on the frozen ground, in a half-stupor, sorrowfully contemplating on the cruel irony of Fate, which, after allowing me to survive the war, had stolen from me the greatest gift which man has in life.

The sun was sinking slowly, reluctantly, in the west. I arose cold and shivering and looked around. I saw that I was about three kilometers from the village and dimly tried to recollect how I had come here and when.

With faltering steps, I set out for my quarters.

Chapter 21

The RMS Baltic

The days passed drearily.   No more did I enjoy the companionship of others. I held myself aloof from everyone, desiring only to be alone – alone to suffer and let sorrow eat out my torn heart. My past life unveiled itself before me, I lived over the happy days of my youth; young, innocent, carefree – life had been easy. Then had come the war, my youth turning suddenly into manhood, the desire to fight for my dear country, my enlistment against the wishes of my parents; war, cruel war; trenches, gas, bombardments, bullets and bayonets – Death over all, snatching away millions of lives, ruthlessly, without mercy. I had lived through many dangers, had many close encounters, and escaped death only by a narrow margin. Sometimes it had been a miracle. And now there was peace – but was it really peace for me? I was suffering more now then ever before. My mother, to whom I had clung so tenaciously for advice and philosophy, to whom I had looked forward to sooth away my trouble and again fill my life with redundant happiness, was dead, gone from me forever; nothing could ever fill that voice space in my heart. She had been my earthly Goddess, my polar star, my only pivot of hope in the fight against her dear Fatherland! Nobly and stoically she had kept her feeling from me – "Do your duty son..." and all the while suffering, intensely, silently. The great sorrow I had brought her had hastened her death, yet she had clung to live long enough to pray for my safety until the end of the war. There was nothing to live for now. My greatest hope was shattered, my only comfort was gone – the world was empty for me. I was lost – utterly, hopelessly lost.

Day after day I was afflicted by this perverting, mental agony. Satan, World and Sin appealed to me persistently; I was tempted to plunge myself into dissipation and vice to alleviate my distress; but my conscience warded off the vile temptations. Could I, straight and honest while she lived, drag myself into shame and disgrace her name now that she was dead? No, for the safe of her dear memory, I could not defile myself, ever. Yet I was sorely harassed. Day and day, my thoughts drifted on the gloomy sea of despondency.

My old mates called in on me repeatedly and tried to stir me out of my abstraction. Skinny and J.C. came in and tried to cheer me; they told me about the great times they were having at the estaminets – plenty of women and lost to drink – and tried to persuade me to join. Nothing was further from my desires and I refused every time with the pretense that I was feeling sick. Ted was more sympathetic. He spent a great deal of his time with me, patiently trying to rouse my spirits. Sometimes we would sit and talk quietly until he subtly suggested that we do something lively; this would dampen my spirits and I would relapse into a sullen mood. Ted would take his leave, reluctantly, looking at me sadly. I could not meet his gaze, so full of compassion and brotherly feeling.

The battalion moved east again, landing at a village near Waterloo. Some of us were billeted in a large chateau, while others occupied barns and houses.

One morning Ted, Skinny and J.C. called for me and prevailed upon me to go with them to see the monuments at Waterloo. As we approached the great historical landmarks, I was filled with admiration. The British monument was a huge, pyramidal mound, with a lion perched majestically on the flatted peak.

First we entered the museum and inspected the rifles, swords, bayonets and cannon balls that had been used in the olden days. At the side of the pyramid was a large circular building called "The

Panorama". We entered, and after going up a flight of stairs, found ourselves on a platform in the centre of a large room. The circular wall was one immense canvas painting, a panorama of the Battle of Waterloo. I was greatly impressed with the wonderful work of art. It seemed very realistic. In the rear, sat Napoleon on a white charger, surrounded by his staff, looking on anxiously while the terrible battle was raging. The British formation was making the one great stand which has been famous throughout history. The artist certainly depicted the battle vividly enough, conveying a true picture of the great event.

We went outside and climbed up the huge pyramid. The lion, cast of metal from captured guns, stood on a great, square stone base, defiantly facing the direction from which the French cavalry had charged. We walked around on top for some time and had a good view of the old battlefield. I could picture the great battle being fought and could almost fancy hearing the beat of war drums and seeing the two great forces clash. We inscribed our initials on the foundation, then descended; while descending we counted the steps – there were two hundred and ten.

After looking at the German and Polish monuments, we came to an old wall in a farmyard, wherein were buried several hundred soldiers who had died on that great day. I remained at the well for some time, while the others went on, and was lost in deep thought. Here were buried other soldiers, killed in another war. I wondered if when alive, any of them had felt the same as I; had they also suffered other sorrows, not pertaining to actual war. But they were gone, and had rested now for more than a century and were all forgotten.

We moved east once more, landing at a small village near Renaix. There we stayed until the 20th of February, 1919. Then orders came to entrain for the coast. We arrived at Le Harve and took a boat for South Hampton.

This was the first sign that we were going back home. Everyone was happy and there was much singing en route. My feelings were, strangely, of longing and indifference; being in company with so many happy soldiers had a psychological effect on me, though, for the most part, I remained by myself, alone with my thoughts.

On arriving in England, we went in camp at Branshot; where we were billeted in long huts; we stayed for a month. Our routine was practically the same every day; dental inspections and repair, medical examinations, eye test, blood tests; we had to undergo various official formalities and fill in many necessary forms.

There were several battalions in this camp. "The Flu" broke out again and raged badly; every day there were a number of funerals. The oldest man in our battalion was carried off. He had gone to France with the original unit, had fought in almost every battle and had survived them all – only to die here, at Branshot, after the war. At the last moment, Fate robbed him of his life and the glory and honor that was due him for his great, unrivalled record.

I received a long letter from my father, giving me full account of my mother's death; she had succumbed to the deadly "Flu" on November 29th. He begged me to come home as soon as possible, for he longed to see me and have me back again. As I finished reading the letter, my heart grew lighter – I knew that my father had forgiven me. Poor father! In my grief I had not thought of him; how he must have suffered, for he loved my mother dearly.

At last the orders came to be ready. We were going back to Canada! On the morning of March 12th, 1919, we left Bramshot by train, and arrived at Liverpool that evening. After a light lunch, we were ordered on board the steamer "Baltic" which was lying in the harbour.

When all were on board and quartered, the whistle blew. We were off for Canada! Slowly, with the help of two small tugs, the big ship began to move away. Gradually its momentum increased. The low setting sun cast the glow of its last rays on the beautiful city which was drawing itself away from us. Twilight descended and darkness; the coastline became blurred from our vision; only the myriads of small lights twinkling on the distant horizon remained to mark the receeding shore of Old England.

Morning dawned, clear and bright. After a fitful slumber, the ocean breeze was very bracing. The promenade deck was a scene of great activity; everyone was up and strolling about, arms locked together and smiles lighting up the happy countenances.

J.C., Ted, Sneezigs, Skinny and I stood on deck, enjoying the morning air.

"Well, boys," said Ted "here we are, the five of us still together. That's a record, eh?"

"Yes, we are still alive," J.C. grinned, "although I did not expect to see you come through it all. I figured that between Paris dames and rats, the war would finish you."

"Never mind, J.C.," Ted growled, "you aren't back in Canada yet. I may take a notion any time to feed you to the fish, just to get even with you for all the dirt you've been handing me."

"That's all right, Ted," J.C. returned soothingly. "I am glad you came through, because I shouldn't like to see the old school ma'am broken-hearted."

Ted moved as if he intended to carry out his threat and J.C. backed away, laughing.

When good humor was restored, J.C. suggested, "Well, fellows, what about a little game? I still have my old crown and anchor board."

"Fetch it up then," said Sneezigs.

J.C. went below and returned with the old board and dice. He spread it out beside a ventilation funnel and started to rattle the bones. A crowd of soldiers gathered around, placing bets, while J.C. kept calling: "Come on fellows, the old-sergeant-major wants you to try your luck. Everyone place your money on the board, so that I can get married when I get back to Canada..."

I was not in the mood to participate in the exciting pastime and leaned against the rail to look over the side. I was soon lost in somber musing. Somewhere, in the far distance, lay England; and further to the right was France. France! France! Could I ever forget that shell-torn country in which I had fought and suffered so? But I had lived through it all and was going back to where I had started three years ago. It was three years since I had come over, wondering if I should come back alive – three long years I had suffered for my King and Country – three long years I had stood and slept in mud and water, summer and winter – three long years in wet clothing and ill-fitting boots, I had walked the cobblestone roads, from one front to another – three long years I had suffered in the filthy trenches infested with rats and lice – three long years I had taken irregular meals, in trenches, shell holes, barns, amongst dead corpses – three long years I had lived from one second to the next, my life in the hands of Fate! Again I recalled the words of the General at the Somme – "You are fighting for your sweethearts, mothers...For your King and Country..." Alas for me, my sweetheart had married another, and my mother had died eighteen days after the Armistice. All this, then, I had done for my King and Country. I had given my life for my Country. True, I was going back now, and alive; yes, alive, my body was alive – but my soul was dead, buried with the shells in France! Sadly I turned from the rail.

J.C. was still playing his crown and anchor board and calling excitedly. "Come on, fellows, heap her up high. Put some on the rest of the board too, not all on the sergeant-major. All right, then, up she comes."

I heard the rattle of dice. There was a sudden exclamation of surprise, followed by shouts of glee. Above the din, I heard Ted roaring excitedly -

"Aha, J.C., I caught you that time! Three crowns! Ho! Ho! Come on, fork over, big boy."

Ted and J.C. emerged from the crowd, Ted laughing gaily. J.C. silent and glum. Ted held a large roll of money under J.C.'s nose.

"How do you like that J.C.? That's one I pulled one over on you. I had you covered that time. That almost evens you and me for all the dirt you've been slinging at me for the last three years. So, you were going to make enough money to get married, eh? It's too bad, J.C., and I'm as sorry as the dickens, but this is the kid thats going to get married. Yes, and to my school ma'am at that. How do you like that? Ha, Ha!"

J.C. said not a word. He slowly gathered up the canvas and the dice.

"Broke again! Darn the luck!" he muttered savagely, and flung the crown and anchor board over the side. "Well, boys, that's that. Now let's go below and have a game of hearts."

What lads!

Chapter 22

A train full of soldiers returning from the war

The train was crowded with soldiers discharged from active service at Brandon and returning to their respective homes. At every stop two or three alighted and were greeted by sweethearts, mothers or sisters. What a reunion! My heart ached as I watched the happy mothers and sweethearts, as they flung their arms about their soldier boys and wept tears of joy. How happy these fellows felt to be taken up by their loved ones again! If only I could happily anticipate such a meeting! But, alas for me, my loved ones were gone; there would be no such ones there to meet me.

The train pulled steadily on, and the stations began to have familiar names. Soon I should be there! At last the name of my home town was called out; and with fast beating heart, I gathered my things and prepared to alight.

The station was crowded. Not wishing to meet many people I went through to the last coach and alighted. There, before me, stood my father, happily expectant, as if he had known that I was going to alight there. Silently, we shook hands, and started for home, following a side street to avoid people to whom I should be obliged to speak. Father and I hardly spoke on the way. Poor Father! What a marked change since I had seen him last, three and a half years ago! His hair was white, his face lined with sorrow and anxiety and worry; he seemed broken in spirit and body. I felt strangely guilty; my absence, as well as Mother's death, had been the cause of his premature aging.

On reaching the house, I was embraced by my aged Grandmother who, although overjoyed at my return, broke into tears and sadly remarked that I had changed and that I looked so old and worn. My father immediately telephoned a few near relatives and friends, advising them of my arrival and inviting them to dinner.

Then the children returned from school, my brother and my four sisters; but I hardly knew them – so changed and grown since I had seen them last. My sisters were quite shy – I was, after all, practically a stranger to them; but my kid brother, attracted by my accoutrements, lost no time in getting acquainted, and we soon became fast friends.

The guests began to arrive, each one warmly congratulating me on my safe return. When all was in readiness, we sat down to the feast which had been elaborately prepared in my honor. I felt strangely out of place, the only one in uniform. I was not used to the company of civilians; and my embarrassment was increased by the relentless discourse of those present, which consisted mainly of adulatory remarks and glances of admiration at my military dress.

After the sumptuous repast, my attention was claimed by the men who were intent upon having a first-hand description of the wonderful horrors of the war. Two of my uncles acted as chief spokesmen and, much to my discomfort, plied me with innumerable questions –

"Did you see many Germans over there?

"It is true that they nailed a Canadian soldier to a barn in Belgium?"

"They cut off the breast of women, and stuck young infants on fence pickets, didn't they?"

"How many Germans did you kill?" and so on.

I became disgusted and hesitated to speak about the war. Their minds had fallen prey to the propaganda which had been circulated throughout the country to encourage hatred against the enemy. What did they know about it, anyway? It was a great relief to me when at last they all departed.

The house seemed strange to me; yet stranger still, the silent, sad influence which prevailed throughout the rooms. I felt lonely, something was lacking, and I knew only too well whose presence. However, not a word was said about Mother; everyone tried to make me as comfortable as possible; but the cheerful atmosphere, for which I hungered, was not there.

I went out for a stroll. Involuntarily, it seemed, my steps led me to the cemetery. There were many new graves, but only a few were marked. I looked over all of them in search of mother's, but in vain, it was not yet marked.

Next day I asked my sisters to accompany me to the cemetery and show me her grave. On the way, I asked if mother had received the letter containing my photo. Yes, she had received it the day before she died, but her condition had been such that she could not speak. With tears in her eyes, she had gazed long and longingly at the photo, unable to say a word.

We arrived at the cemetery and I was shown her grave.

I knelt down at the foot of the grave which held her, my dear mother. I was back now, but she was gone. My heart suffered a severe pain. "O God! For this did I prepare myself, but I am yet too weak; the cup of sorrow is yet too bitter! I can only pray for forgiveness and that I may some day rejoining her in heaven. O Mother! you are an angel now – but what a sad angel you must be to see you dear boy kneeling at your grave...!"

I felt a cold drop on my cheek. The sky was clouded; dark shrouds of sorrow it seemed, drifted overhead. It began to sprinkle lightly – fresh, pure tears from Heaven, mingling with the salt tears of a sad, broken soldier.

Conclusion

In the summer of 1919, I attended the fair at Melville, Saskatchewan. While walking down the street, I was addressed by a familiar voice behind me. "Hello, Miller!"

I turned around and received the surprise of my life. There, before me, stood Giese. I was dumbfounded and could not speak for a moment.

"Hello, Giese! How in the world did you get here? The last time I saw you, you were lying in Regina Trench, naked and dead."

He grinned at me. "Yes, I was hurt pretty bad, but not dead. When I woke up I was in a German hospital. I was laid up for over two months and then held prisoner until the war quit."

"Well, you were lucky to get out of it. How were you treated over there anyway? I heard some of the fellows were treated pretty rough."

"Well, I was treated fine," said Giese. "Everyone was treated well as only as they kept quiet and obeyed orders. There were a few cocky guys who tried to get tough, so the Germans got tough with them too, though I think some of them deserved it. If German prisoners had acted the way some of our fellows did, no doubt they would have been punished lightly also."

****

In the spring of 1924, I met one of our officers at Brandon. He had been with us at Caesar's Camp in England and had gone over to France with us, but had been blown up by a shell at Ypres and sent back shell-shocked. At first he did not recognize me. I told him who I was and that he had been our officer at Caesar's Camp.

Suddenly he remembered. "Oh, yes, Miller. I remember you. You are the man we suspected of being a German spy and kept an eye on for a long time. That's the reason you were in quarantine with a guard stationed outside your tent to watch your movements."

****

Last fall I met Skinny. We discussed our many old experiences together.

"Well, Miller," Skinny grinned. "It wasn't a bad war after all, now that it's all over and almost forgotten."

****

I have never since the war met Ted, J.C. or Sneezigs. Maybe someday in the future we will meet again – it is hard to tell. At any rate, it would give me great pleasure to see them again, especially witness a meeting of J.C. and Ted.

****

It is now fifteen years since the Great War. Many of the horrors of the great struggle have been forgotten. The growing generation is not interested in what we ex-servicemen have gone through. What do they care if an old soldier has had a few hard lines in his day? We are in a class by ourselves – a poor bunch of physical wrecks. Nobody cares – our usefulness ended with the war. But there will be more wars – and more suffering. It will be the old battle-scarred veterans of the last war who will be able to sympathize with the youths who go forth to serve their country. In the meantime, it is hard to make a living with a little tin box full of medals and a few souvenirs. Politics come first – old soldiers are not wanted…

Appendix A: Attestation Papers

ATTESTATION PAPER. No. *4 25084*

Folio. *Copy*

CANADIAN OVER-SEAS EXPEDITIONARY FORCE.

QUESTIONS TO BE PUT BEFORE ATTESTATION.

(ANSWERS).

1. What is your name? ... *Jacob Miller*
2. In what Town, Township or Parish, and in what Country were you born? ... *Lemberg Austria* *19 years in Canada*
3. What is the name of your next-of-kin? ... *Philip Miller father*
4. What is the address of your next-of-kin? ... *Neudorf Sask*
5. What is the date of your birth? ... *19th January 1891*
6. What is your Trade or Calling? ... *Farmer*
7. Are you married? ... *no*
8. Are you willing to be vaccinated or re-vaccinated? ... *Yes*
9. Do you now belong to the Active Militia? ... *no*
10. Have you ever served in any Military Force? ... *no*
    If so, state particulars of former Service.
11. Do you understand the nature and terms of your engagement? ... *Yes*
12. Are you willing to be attested to serve in the Canadian Over-Seas Expeditionary Force? ... *Yes*

Jacob Miller (Signature of Man).

H Ashford (Signature of Witness).

DECLARATION TO BE MADE BY MAN ON ATTESTATION.

I, *Jacob Miller*, do solemnly declare that the above answers made by me to the above questions are true, and that I am willing to fulfil the engagements by me now made, and I hereby engage and agree to serve in the Canadian Over-Seas Expeditionary Force, and to be attached to any arm of the service therein, for the term of one year, or during the war now existing between Great Britain and Germany should that war last longer than one year, and for six months after the termination of that war provided His Majesty should so long require my services, or until legally discharged.

Date *Dec 23rd* 1914.

Jacob Miller (Signature of Recruit)

H Ashford (Signature of Witness)

OATH TO BE TAKEN BY MAN ON ATTESTATION.

I, *Jacob Miller*, do make Oath, that I will be faithful and bear true Allegiance to His Majesty King George the Fifth, His Heirs and Successors, and that I will as in duty bound honestly and faithfully defend His Majesty, His Heirs and Successors, in Person, Crown and Dignity, against all enemies, and will observe and obey all orders of His Majesty, His Heirs and Successors, and of all the Generals and Officers set over me. So help me God.

Date *Dec 23* 1914.

Jacob Miller (Signature of Recruit)

H Ashford (Signature of Witness)

CERTIFICATE OF MAGISTRATE.

The Recruit above-named was cautioned by me that if he made any false answer to any of the above questions he would be liable to be punished as provided in the Army Act.

The above questions were then read to the Recruit in my presence.

I have taken care that he understands each question, and that his answer to each question has been duly entered as replied to, and the said Recruit has made and signed the declaration and taken the oath before me, at *Melville* this *23* day of *December* 1914.

John N Skilton (Signature of Justice)

I hereby certify that this is a true copy of the ... I certify that the above is a true copy of the Attestation of the above-named Recruit.

Louis Clark *Lieut-Col. O C 15th Overseas Battalion*

Fred Wilkinson (Approving Officer)

900 M.—8-14.
H.Q. 1771-1-14

Description of _Jacob. Miller_ on Enlistment.

Apparent Age _23_ years _11_ months.
(To be determined according to the instructions given in the Regulations for Army Medical Services.)

Distinctive marks, and marks indicating congenital peculiarities or previous disease.

(Should the Medical Officer be of opinion that the recruit has served before, he will, unless the man acknowledges to any previous service, attach a slip to that effect, for the information of the Approving Officer).

Height _5_ ft. _5_ ins.

Chest measurement. { Girth when fully expanded _38½_ ins.
Range of expansion _2½_ ins.

Complexion _Dark_

Eyes _Grey_

Hair _Black_

Religious denominations. { Church of England
Presbyterian _Yes._
Wesleyan
Baptist or Congregationalist
Other Protestants
(Denomination to be stated.)
Roman Catholic
Jewish

CERTIFICATE OF MEDICAL EXAMINATION.

I have examined the above-named Recruit and find that he does not present any of the causes of rejection specified in the Regulations for Army Medical Services.

He can see at the required distance with either eye; his heart and lungs are healthy; he has the free use of his joints and limbs, and he declares that he is not subject to fits of any description.

I consider him* _fit_ for the Canadian Over-Seas Expeditionary Force.

Date _Dec 23_ 1914.

Place _Melville_

Medical Officer.

*Insert here "fit" or "unfit."

NOTE.—Should the Medical Officer consider the Recruit unfit, he will fill in the foregoing Certificate only in the case of those who have been attested, and will briefly state below the cause of unfitness:—

CERTIFICATE OF OFFICER COMMANDING UNIT.

Jacob Miller having been finally approved and inspected by me this day, and his Name, Age, Date of Attestation, and every prescribed particular having been recorded, I certify that I am satisfied with the correctness of this Attestation.

Ges H Clarkson (Signature of Officer)

Date _Dec 23_ 1914.

Appendix B: 45th Battalion. Winnipeg, 1915.

Jacob Miller is far right on the 3rd row

Appendix C: Summary of Service

(From the Canadian War Archives)

Report.	Date.		
	From whom received		

IR.

Name **MILLER, Jacob** Reg'l No. **425084**

Rank   IIn perm. Corps; Married or Single **Single**
What Unit?

Unit **45th Battn.**

Place and Date of Enlistment **Melville, 23rd Dec, 1914.** Place of Birth **Lemberg, Austria**

Name and Address, Next-of-Kin **Philip Miller.** Relationship

Meudorf, Sask, Canada.

Assigned Pay Monthly $ Payable to   Relationship

Separation Allowance $ Payable to   Relationship

Discharge, Date and Place   Reason   Character

Record of promotions, reductions, transfers, casualties, etc., during active service. The authority to be quoted in each case.   Place   Date   REMARKES Taken from Official Documents

Arrived in England		
6.6.16	Embarked for France, Shorncliffe	6.6.16
14.6.16	Taken on strength.	
15.8.18	Awarded Meritorious Service Medal	
11.12.18	Promoted Sgt	11.12.18
	C M R PROC, TO ENGLAND	*12.2-19, D.O. ,12
11/3/19	Ret k Canada. Sail 3x Eng. V.	11/3/19

O.B. Cond.

Fill tr Only.—Unit, Number, Rank and Na~.

Casualty Form—Active Service.

Unit, Regiment or Corps. 🖅 45th Overseas Battalion. 🖅

Regimental No. 445994 Rank Pte Name Muller Jacob

Enlisted ... Terms of Service (a) ... Service reckons from 23/7/15

Date of promotion to present rank. } ... Date of appointment to lance rank } ... Numerical position on roll of N'C.Os. }

Extended ... Re-engaged ... Qualification (b) ...

Report		Record of promotions, reductions, transfers, casualties, etc., during active service, as reported on Army Form B. 213, Army Form A. 36, or in other official documents. The authority to be quoted in each case.	Place	Date	Remarks
Date	From whom received				taken from Army Form B. 213, Army Form A. 36, or other official documents.
6/6/16	B.O.O.	Transferred to 46 ...	...	...	...
		Embarked Canada ...	...	6/6/16	E. Dunel Captain Adjutant 45th Battalion, C.E.F.
3-6-16.	C.B.D.	Landed in France	C.B.D.	8-6-16	N. Roll.
9-6-16	do	Left C.B.D. for Unit	Field.	9-6-16	do
10-6-16	Unit	Joined Unit in	Field	10-6-16	B.213.
12.8.17	"	Gr'ds 10 days leave Paris	...	4.8.17	R.213
14.8.17	"	(Retard.) Unit	...	15.8.17	"
18.11.17	"	Sick & Hosp	Roll	8.11.17	"
3.2.18	"	Rejoined R.A.G.C. to Short. Durg	...	29.1.18	R.213
10.2.18	"	"	...	8.2.18	R.213
17.6.16	"	Rejoined from Command & Unit	...	30 ...	R.213
29.9.18	"	Grs'd Meritorious leave medal	...	29.6.18	...
		Grs'd 14 days' leave UK	...	23.9.18	...

(a) In the case of a man who has re-engaged for, or enlisted into Section D, Army Reserve, particulars of such re-engagement or enlistment will be entered.
(b) Signalling, Shooting Smith, etc., also special qualifications in technical Corps duties. [P.T.O.

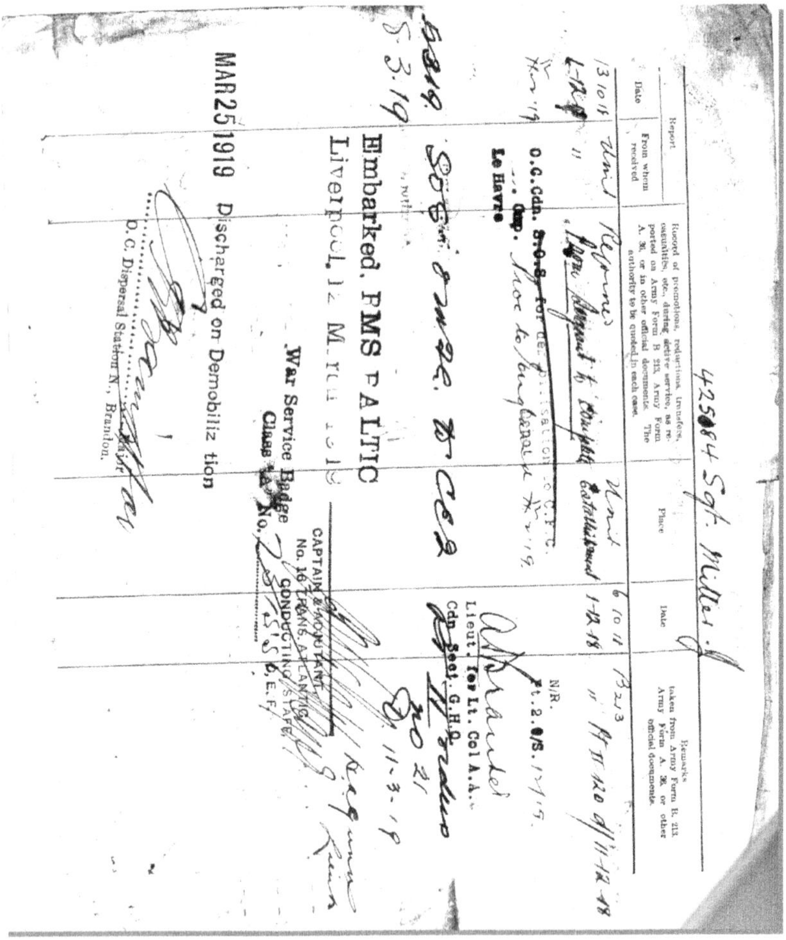

Appendix D: Vimy Ridge, War Diaries

Vimy Ridge, April 9, 1917

REPORT ON OPERATIONS CARRIED OUT BY THE

35

1st C.M.R. BATTALION on the 9th APRIL 1917.

. . . .

Frontage allotted to the Bn in which it was to attack, capture and consolidate was a sfollows:-

First; the German Front Line System of Trenches, situated approximately beyond a point running from the Twins Craters to and inclusive of B.4 Crater.

Second; the SWISCHEN STELLUNG Trench from the Sunken Road on the left and, approximately, Dump Avenue on the right.

Third; and final objective; extending from the beginning of the Sunken Road at S.29.b.6.1 to ANDROS CORNER at S.29.d.8.1/2. From there in a southerly direction to the junction of the Cross Roads S.29.d.7.2.

. . . .

Complete detailed Operation Orders were issued to each Company the day previous to the attack.

D Company at that time was holding our then Front Line. C Coy was in supports at NEUVILLE ST.VAAST; and B and A Coys had been moved up to NEUVILLE ST.VAAST, occupying cellars and dug-outs in that immediate locality.

Separate Jumping Off Trenches had been prepared for each Coy of the Battalion and, commencing at 2 a.m. on the morning of the 9th, the Coys moved from their different locations into their respective jumping off trenches; all being in position before 4 a.m.

The 2nd C.M.R.Bn. was also assembled during the night in jumping off trenches on our left and the 5th Canadian Infantry Brigade on our right.

Zero hour was fixed for 5.30 a.m. and three minutes after zero all companies were to advance. D Coy occupied the front jumping off trench and were to take the first German system of trenches. C Coy, who occupied the next jumping off trench, were to take the SWISCHEN STELLUNG. B Coy, occupying the next jumping off trench, were to go through both the others and take the final objective; while A Coy was to go through all other three companies and establish strong points a considerable distance in front of the final objective.

The advance was predeced by a three minute barrage on the first German line. And immediately the barrage lifted to the second line all four Companies of the Battalion left their jumping off trenches and followed each other across in the order above named.

As soon as we had reached a point where the German lines were discernible, flares of all descriptions could be seen along the whole German front, evidently "S.O.S." Signals; and what barrage the enemy was able to put on came very quickly. The leading Company - "D" - had to pass through it before they were in the German front line. And each Company in turn had to go through it, and in doing so sustained rather a considerable number of casualties.

D Company were not long in cleaning up the three front lines. Machine gun crews were immediately placed on the enemy's lip of the craters and as far as was necessary covered the advance of the front troops. The front lines were not strongly held but it is safe to say that not one of the enemy escaped from them..... All were either killed or taken prisoners.

The trenches and all immediate ground had been most terribly cut up by our artillery. After crossing No Man's Land the advance of the troops was very difficult owing to their having to pick their way

1st CANADIAN MOUNTED RIFLES BATTALION.

REPORT OF OPERATIONS on 9th,
10th and 11th April 1917.
. . . .

38

April 9th 1917.

5.30 a.m.	Battalion assembled in jumping off trenches according to orders.
5.30 a.m.	Barrage opened on enemy's front line system.
5.33 a.m.	Companies advanced in the following order:-

   (1) - D. Company.
   (2) - C. Company.
   (3) - B. Company.
   (4) - A. Company.
keeping close to the barrage.

6.05 a.m.	SWISCHEN STELLUNG reached and cleaned up.
6.45 a.m.	B. and A. Companies advanced behind barrage towards final objective.
7.34 a.m.	Objective reached by B. Company and two guns of Brigade Machine Gun Company. A. Company at this point could muster only forty (40) men, and these were placed under command to help B.Company consolidate this position.
8.50 a.m.	Battalion Headquarters had been established in vicinity of SPANDAU HOUSE.
11.35 a.m.	A. Company of the 5th C.M.R. was ordered forward to reinforce the front line under Major Taylor at ANDROS CORNER.
12 noon.	A. Company had patrols out to their strong points and objective and had connected with the 2nd K.O.S.Bs on the right.
12.15 p.m.	A. Company of the 5th C.M.R. had reported to Major Taylor, O.C. Front Line.
12.35 p.m.	General situation as follows:-

B.Company had reached its objective and had joined up with the
2nd C.M.R. Bn. on the left and the 25th Bn on the right and
was digging in.
Two Brigade Machine Guns were in position in strong points
on right.
About One Hundred (100) men of the 5th C.M.R. had been ordered
forward to reinforce B.Company.
Supplies of S.A.A. were very limited, and the men were too
tired to be used as carrying party.
The trenches were unrecognisable; mud beyond belief.
The whole of our Battalion frontage was alive with men of the
2nd Division, consisting of 20th and 24th Regiments, who had
swung right across our front. Situation was then being
cleared up and these men were being sent back to their own
areas. It was noted that only one Officer of the 2nd
Division was met with in our area, and that these men were
hopelessly lost and without ideas of their flanks.
No word had then been received of A.Company's position, but
D. and C. Companies were digging in in FLIRT Trench, between
PRINZ ARNOLF GRABEN and SWISCHEN STELLUNG. An attempt was
then being made to join up with the 26th Bn on our right, who
were then only in SWISCHEN STELLUNG and not one hundred yards
in front of it, as was understood.
Four Subalterns were ordered up from our rear through Brigade,
as well as Medical Officers; and Brigade were asked for
stretcher bearer parties to get further forward and that we
were badly in need of shovels.

258 BEYOND MY GRASP

-3-

40

April 10th 1917.

Up to 4.00 p.m. situation normal.

At 4 p.m. two strong patrols were sent out under command of Lieuts.Matheson and Lawson. These patrols consisted of 25 men, and succeeded in occupying the first three German lines and sent scouts out to a point about 75 yards in advance of the three lines.

No serious opposition was encountered.

This enterprise cost 1 killed and four wounded by snipers operating from VIMY. The two Brigade Machine Guns, under Lieut. Morgan, covered this party.

At about 7.45 p.m. the patrols were withdrawn on orders from Brigade, the withdraw being effected without loss.

The position entered was consolidated by our party, but its left was in the iar.

April 11th 1917.

Situation normal, except for some heavy shelling which took place at 9 a.m., lasting for an hour, and again at 1.00 p.m., lasting for four hours.

At 12.45 p.m. on the 12th inst., the Battalion was relieved in the front line by the 60th Battalion, and the supports by the 52nd Battalion.

Total Casualties for the Tour:
·365 - Killed, Wounded and Missing.

Prisoners taken estimated at - 350.

Machine Guns captured and taken out - 1.

. . . .

Made in the USA
Monee, IL
03 December 2020